*THE MAN
MENCKEN*

THE
MAN MENCKEN

A Biographical and Critical Survey

BY ISAAC GOLDBERG

ILLUSTRATED *and* DOCUMENTED

SIMON AND SCHUSTER

NEW YORK · 1925

Set up, electrotyped and printed by the Vail-Ballou Press, Binghamton,
N. Y. Bound by the Plimpton Press, Norwood, Mass. Printed on
a rag paper made especially for this edition by the Reading
Paper Mills, Reading, Penn. Illustrations printed in
aquatone process by the United States Printing
and Lithograph Co., Brooklyn, N. Y.

TO

EMANUEL HALDEMAN-JULIUS

FOR

MANY

OPPORTUNITIES

Preface

"Biographer: an unjust God." Thus Mencken, in his *Little Book in C Major*. Let me therefore hasten, fellow immoralists, to disclaim both any undue bias and all divinity. This book is the contemplation of one very human being by another. It is written, naturally, out of a fundamental sympathy,—a sympathy which is none the less an independent harmony, not a colorless unison with the subject. It is addressed to those who find in the performance of the human, as well as of the literary, comedy, an æsthetic rather than a justiciary satisfaction. I consider Mencken the man in the same light that I consider his books: rather an artistic phenomenon to be enjoyed than a text to be stretched into a sermon. Since understanding, properly subordinated, is no small part of pleasure, there is much in this book of a factual, though never of a didactic, nature. It is not the facts, however, that make the man important. Though they throw light upon his activities, they are really illuminated more by him than is he by them. For it is not they that confer significance upon him; they acquire it from him.

The present book was planned in 1923, and is based upon an acquaintance with the writings of Mencken that goes back to the earliest days of his co-editorship on *The Smart Set,* in 1914. Shortly after I had begun to write the literary department for the *Haldeman-Julius Weekly,* published at Girard, Kansas, by the firm that has made the series of Little Blue Books a national institution, I suggested to Mr. Emanuel Haldeman-Julius the inclusion in that series of a number of booklets devoted to living writers. He accepted the suggestion readily; the first of these to be published, in 1924, was No. 611, entitled *H. L. Mencken*. Previous to formal publication it appeared as the August, 1924, issue of yet another of the firm's publications: *Life and Letters*. This was, in effect, a miniature rehearsal in print of the book that you have just opened. It consisted of something under 15,000 words—the average length of the Blue Book—and did not, of course, permit expatiation. The volume now stands as originally conceived.

My aim has not been to produce the conventional biography or the conventional critique. I have not been interested in "definitive" criticism, although I reject, on the other hand, the professorial dictum that one cannot really criticise one's contemporaries. I have, in the midst of an account that is on the whole chronological, not hesitated to dance about in time and space. Here, in short, is the portrait of a living sitter, who is far more lively than sedentary. Accordingly the canvas is meant to grow, not feature by feature in a steady view, but stroke by stroke; now a daub at the chin, now a smudge at the ear, here a return to a preliminary line, heightening it by contrast with the new pigment, there a sudden completion of a surface that was previously but hinted. At the end, the picture comes to life, and only at the end. Whereupon the sitter smilingly arises, looks at the portrait, looks then at the artist, and leaves with his own thoughts.

PREFACE

For kindnesses incidental to the writing of this book I wish to thank the following:

Mr. Theodore Dreiser, the novelist; Mr. G. D. Eaton, author of *Backfurrow;* Mr. Carroll Frey, the bibliographer of Mencken; Mr. George Jean Nathan; Mr. Harrison Hale Schaff, of John W. Luce & Co., publishers of Mencken's books on Shaw and Nietzsche, as well as of some of Ibsen's plays edited by him; Howard L. Spohn, of Chicago, one of the most pertinacious of Mencken collectors; my wife, for compiling the Index. To Mr. Mencken himself I am indebted for exemplary patience under the long and continuous fire of a most impertinent curiosity.   Heaven will reward him.

For permission to reprint, in part, copyrighted matter originally written by me for various publications I am grateful to the Boston *Evening Transcript* and its musical and dramatic editor, Mr. Henry Taylor Parker ("H. T. P.")—one of the few true critics of the stage and concert-hall that the United States has produced; the Stratford Company; the Haldeman-Julius Company. For permission to reprint early Menckeniana I am likewise grateful to the Baltimore *Herald,* the *Sun* of that city, *Short Stories* and *The Red Book.*

And, finally, the dedication of the book is explained by the fact that Mr. Haldeman-Julius, of the hundreds of thousands of words that I have written for his firm during my association with it thus far, has altered not a one. In his columns I have enjoyed the utmost freedom of thought and print, and have exercised it on all subjects to the limit.   There I have had the one thing to which Mencken's life has been dedicated over all others,—

liberty. It is not, in these cramped days, a mean gift.
I shall be happy to receive in care of the publishers addenda to the Menckeniana contained in this book, for possible use in later editions.

ISAAC GOLDBERG

ROXBURY, MASSACHUSETTS.

Contents

CONTENTS

Illustrations

ILLUSTRATIONS

THE MAN
MENCKEN

CHAPTER ONE

Prejudices: 1524

I

FREDERIC. A paradox!
KING (*laughing*). A paradox.
RUTH.   A most ingenious paradox.
           We've quips and quibbles heard in flocks,
           But none to beat this paradox!
           Ha! ha! ha! ha! ho! ho! ho! ho!
           —W. S. GILBERT. *The Pirates of Penzance*. Act II.

SOME men are born legendary, others achieve the distinction, while others still have legend thrust upon
them. There is a Mencken legend. It grew inevitably
out of his personality, just as similar legends have crystallized into the dubious haloes that encircle a Cellini or a
Poe. In our own day and generation, legends have
formed about living persons. There is James Branch
Cabell, south of Mason and Dixon's line; south of the
Rio Grande we have witnessed the spectacle of Rubén
Darío—Nicaraguan by birth, pagan errant by fate and
preference—turning into a god, as it were, before our
very eyes; that same Darío, writing of Blanco-Fombona
—Venezuelan by birth, European by exile—dipped the
man into his magic ink and drew him forth from the
bottle a sixteenth-century swashbuckler, a free-verse poet

3

of life. The Mencken legend has been fashioned out of the fear and wonder of his contemporaries; out of the metaphors and similes that bestrew his pages; out of his thousand and one sarcasms, thrusts, parries, insinuations, lofty flights and low buffooneries. He is too good, too bad, to be true; *ergo,* make him a legend until the distant day arrives on which he is labeled at last and filed away.

Every legend has its core of truth. What is the truth at the core of the Mencken legend? Simply this, that the man is manifestly different. The ordinary mind, which means the popular mind, interprets difference in terms of suspicion and fear. Religions, said De Gourmont somewhere, revolve madly around questions of sex. Let a man, then, be different; let him abandon the consecrated altars, and his dissension at once assumes a sexual significance. He is different, therefore he is immoral. It is an ancient fallacy; the earth moves, as Galileo did not say, yet we have not progressed to that point where we can view with equanimity, without mental reservation, the man who looks upon the world out of other eyes than our own. A Mencken, or any true skeptic, uncomfortably cradled in his uncertainty, may view difference with philosophic, if not with verbal calm; the passionate dullard who has had every problem settled for him beforehand is alone supreme in his certainty.

Mencken, with roots that sink deep in America, is everything that the Average American is not. He is not religious; he is not "moral"; he is, by temperament, therefore by philosophy, an anarchist; he is a natural aristocrat; he is an anti-pedant. In other days he might have been hanged; today, his opponents must be content with tying a line of type around his neck. Perhaps his fellowmen could endure these anti-social qualities, were it not for the personal style in which he couches his comment upon the inhuman comedy. Yet that style is the man himself,—the body, the "soul." The personality has not been polished out of it; it wears no easily donned disguises; it is in its way, as "unbuttoned" as Beethoven's music—the verbal image of its free creator. Imperfect? Go look for perfection where you found certainty.

The Mencken legend has created an irreverent, bacchanalian buffoon; an immoral, unpatriotic smasher of ideals; a low, intriguing fellow whose place is in the court-room, awaiting sentence. And all the while, there he sits in judgment over judging America, shaping a new generation, carrying the intellectual fame of his country abroad, crystallizing ideals despite himself, breaking his lance in noble causes, wearying his hedonistic flesh with the hopeless task of perfecting mankind. He is a double paradox: he is not what simple America thinks him; he is not what he thinks himself to be. There is something in all his violent antagonism that brings him strangely close to the very creatures he opposes. He defends the present economic order, yet every battle he wins for Capitalism is a Pyrrhic victory. He calls all Socialists fools, yet Socialists read him with delight, and win strength from the tonic of his vigorous dialectic and his spirit of independent inquiry. He berates idealism, and aspiring youths from South America, who have been nurtured in the placid, eloquent nobility of Rodó, carry his books back with them to their hinterlands and put him fragmentarily into Spanish and Portuguese. He damns the professoriat and turns out studies that they might well envy. He excoriates America and erects a monument to her linguistic and cultural independence.

The buffoon legend, applied to Mencken, is as ill-founded as when applied to his spiritual ancestor, Rabelais. For all the frequent release of his soul in laughter, for all his Nietzschean dancing with arms and legs, there is in his work a surgical earnestness that denotes the care behind his carefree attitude. Such laughter rises from a deep learning that goes beyond books. Such intoxication, like Rabelais' own, reeks of a wine that is of a vintage as ancient as Adam's blood. There is much to be said about Mencken's gesture of "devil-may-care." For he is the devil, and he cares.

The Mencken legend, then, is true, as a nightmare is true; it is a fantastic distortion of facts, concealing, behind disguises weird and hectic, the essential statement of his individuality. In all this evil there is a soul of goodness, garmented in the flesh of paradox. Mencken is the Lucifer of the American paradise, leading the revolt of the angels. As a leader he is as dangerous as all true leaders should be; he dares to differ even with himself. This is the last, the most perilous freedom. It is worth all the certainties in the world. Without it, the rest is death.

II

There is a cartoon by McKee Barclay, called "The Subconscious Mencken," that presents as an "inductive synthesis" the Baltimorean of this nightmare. There

THE SUBCONSCIOUS MENCKEN

*A cartoon made by McKee Barclay in 1912. It was used
whenever Mencken's picture was printed in connection with
his Free Lance column. Most Baltimoreans accepted
it as an authentic portrait*

MUSIC-ROOM AND STAIRWAY AT 1524 HOLLINS STREET

is, as in all good caricature, truth in the distortion, which shows a Mencken utterly unlike the reality,—the Mencken, in short, imagined by the good souls that he has outraged. There was a time when the Methodists of his native city used to hold prayer-meetings in his behalf. Mothers have been known to threaten their children not with the bogeyman, but with Mencken. That he lives in brothels is assumed without question. Yet what, ladies and gentlemen, is the sober truth? While these vivid imaginings compensate dullards for the virtuous anonymity of their existence, the subject of their speculations sweats away at 1524 Hollins Street over the eternal sheets of his profession,—blank sheets to be filled, written sheets to be edited, printed sheets to be proof-read, bound books to be reviewed, and a host of books as yet unwritten, clamoring for birth. Work, to this luxurious idler of the popular mind, is a physical and psychological necessity. Sloth to him is anathema. And the city that reviles him has been hymned by him with a fervor so deep that the selfsame fervor, in cooler moments, has turned upon itself in a spirit of burlesque. Mencken, lampooner of the Babbitts and the town-boosters, himself a loyal Baltimorean? Impossible, but true. Let me quote him from an article in *The Evening Sun* of his city, under date of February 16, 1925:

Some time ago, writing in this place about the Baltimore of the eighties, I permitted myself an eloquent passage upon its charm, and let fall the doctrine that that charm had vanished. Mere rhetoric, I fear. The old charm, in fact, still survives, despite the boomers, despite the street-wideners, despite the forward-

7

lookers, despite all the other dull frauds who try to destroy it. I am never more conscious of it than when I return to the city after a week in New York. There is a great city, huge, rich and eminent, and yet it has no more charm than a circus lot or a jazzy hotel. Coming back to Baltimore is like coming out of a football crowd into quiet communion with a fair one who is also amiable, and has the gift of consolation for hard-beset and despairing men.

I have confessed to rhetoric, but here I surely do not indulge in it. For twenty-four years I have resisted almost constant temptation to move to New York, and I resist it more easily today than I did when it began. I am, perhaps, the most arduous commuter ever heard of, even in that town of commuters. My office is on Manhattan island and has been there since 1914; yet I live, vote and have my being in Baltimore, and come back here the instant my job allows. If my desk bangs at 3 P. M., I leap for the 3.25 train. Four long hours follow, but the first is the worst. My back, at all events, is toward New York! Behind lies a place fit only for the gross business of getting money; ahead is a place made for enjoying it.

.   .   .   .

I believe that this feeling for the hearth, for the immemorial lares and penates, is infinitely stronger here than in New York— that it has better survived here, indeed, than in any other large city of America—and that its persistence accounts for the superior charm of the town. There are, of course, thousands of Baltimoreans in flats—but I know of none to whom a flat seems more than a makeshift, a substitute, a necessary and temporary evil. They are all planning to get out, to find house-room in one of the new suburbs, to resume living in a home. What they see about them is too painfully not theirs. The New Yorker has simply lost that discontent. He is a vagabond. His notions of

the agreeable become those of a vaudeville actor. He takes on
the shallowness and unpleasantness of any other homeless man.
He is highly sophisticated, and inordinately trashy.

The fact explains the lack of charm that one finds in his
town; the fact that the normal Baltimorean is almost his exact
antithesis explains the charm that is here. Human relations, in
such a place as this, tend to assume a solid permanence. A man's
circle of friends becomes a sort of extension of his family circle.
His contacts are with men and women who are rooted as he is.
They are not moving all the time, and so they are not changing
their friends all the time. Thus abiding relationships tend to be
built up, and when fortune brings unexpected changes they survive those changes. The men I know and esteem in Baltimore
are, on the whole, men I have known and esteemed a long while;
even those who have come into my ken relatively lately seem likely
to last. But of the men I knew best when I first began going
to New York, twenty-five years ago, not one is a friend today.
Of those I knew best ten years ago, not six are friends today.
The rest have got lost in the riot, and the friends of today, I
sometimes fear, will get lost in the same way.

·   ·   ·   ·   ·   ·   ·   ·   ·   ·

In human relationships that are so casual there is seldom any
satisfaction. It is our fellows who make life endurable to us, and
give it a purpose and a meaning; if our contacts with them are
light and frivolous there is something lacking, and it is something
of the very first importance. What I contend is that in Baltimore, under a slow-moving and cautious social organization, such
contacts are more enduring than elsewhere, and that life in consequence is more charming. Of the external embellishments of
life we have a plenty—as great a supply, indeed, to any rational
taste, as New York itself. But we have something much better:
we have a tradition of sound and comfortable living. A Balti-

morean is not merely John Doe, an isolated individual of *Homo sapiens,* exactly like every other John Doe.   He is John Doe of a certain place—of Baltimore, of a definite *home* in Baltimore. It was not by accident that all the peoples of the Western world, very early in their history, began distinguishing their best men by adding of this or that place to their names.

The secret of this panegyric lies largely in the one English word that Mencken has italicized: *home*.   Champion of the bachelors, though scarred by twenty-eight proposals of marriage, including eleven from widows of easy means; mocker of Cupid, and therefore implicit extinguisher of the domestic fires, he yet can sing the praises of the household gods.   It is home, rather than Baltimore, of which he thinks,—the home in which he has lived for more than forty years, a paragon of brotherly and filial devotion, though he would blush to own it.   It is such a devotion, indeed, as much as any philosophy of urban disparities or of single blessedness, that has kept him from migrating to Bagdad-on-the-Subway or taking unto himself his Adam's rib.   Today it is impossible for him to do any writing in New York.   The pressure of distraction is too great, for one thing.   For another, this gentleman who has been loftily berated for his lack of scholarship cannot work without his books.

"I don't believe," he has told me, "I ever write so much as a page of typescript without stopping to look up a reference.   My memory for names and dates is very defective—but I always know where to verify them. My stuff is not allusive.   That is, I do not adorn it with the customary trite quotations from Emerson, Goethe,

Shakespeare and the Bible. I seldom quote even the men I admire most, for example, Nietzsche, Huxley, Beethoven and Carlyle. Nevertheless it is packed with allusiveness, and this allusiveness must be managed with care, for every time I make an error it is detected and denounced. Few men, I believe, work under worse pressure of that sort. The country seems to be full of pedants alert for every chance inconsistency or inaccuracy that I am guilty of. Even my newspaper stuff is apparently scrutinized with bilious and eager eye. I am proud of the fact that I am seldom detected in downright error. Sometimes my pen slips, but it is not often that I have to change my tune." [1]

In New York, Mencken is the scholar as business man; in Baltimore, the business man as scholar and as Playboy of the Western World. At 1524 he houses his host of prejudices, labors and invites his soul.

Yet in this mocker, as in all great scoffers, there is a generous dose of self-mockery. Eighteen years ago, in the Baltimore *Sun,* he was "joshing" the Old-Home-Weekers with an editorial on *The Climate of Baltimore;* re-reading it today he will, of course, detect in it a strain of that burlesque exaggeration which in him is appreciably hereditary. He may detect, too, a certain sin-

---

[1] One of these rare retractions occurred in 1914. Mencken had printed a paragraph about the shipping trade between Baltimore and Liverpool. He was called to book for an error by Ernest A. Boyd, then recently arrived from England as British Vice-Consul in Baltimore. During the first few weeks of the war Boyd was in charge of the Consulate and, in duty bound, pointed out the mistake. Mencken at once apologized. Mr. Boyd soon left the consular service, to the greater gain of letters in America, and has been a close friend of Mencken ever since.

cerity beneath the dithyramb, and, at the same time, a
comicality that provides the best antidote to all such excessively emotional allegiances.

Wrote the youthful editor of those distant days:

No doubt the fine weather of Old-Home Week has amazed
and delighted many visitors to this, our fair city, but to permanent
dwellers in good old Baltimore it has seemed nothing extraordinary.

As a matter of fact, the weather here is always good. The
breezes and blizzards of the North, the cyclones of the West, the
malarious mugginess of the Gulf Coast, the filthy fogs of Pitts-
burg, the dismal rains of Philadelphia and the sunstrokes of New
York are all unknown here.

It seldom rains in Baltimore, and when it does the rain is
soft and soothing and bears a faint odor of roses and mi-
gnonettes. When it snows the town is garbed in dazzling, spotless
white for exactly 24 hours, and then the snow suddenly and
completely disappears.

The only time the wind blows is in the summer, when it is
needed. The only time the sun shines hotly is in the winter,
when its heat is needed to take the chill off the air. It never
hails here, and not even the oldest inhabitant remembers a hurricane, cyclone, tornado, mistrail or sirocco.

No doubt the unexampled meteorological charms of Baltimore
are due in large measure to its proximity to the Eastern Shore of
Maryland. Over on the Sho' the weather, like the girls and
the applejack, is absolutely and utterly perfect. The air there
contains 99¾ per cent. of pure oxygen, and is as invigorating
as strychnine. A stranger breathing it not uncommonly jumps
into the air and cracks his heels together. People have to grow
accustomed to it before they may take it into their gills without
danger.

The skies that vault the Sho' are so pellucid and so blue that they make the famed skies of Italy look like the soiled backdrop of a one-night-stand "Uncle Tom's Cabin" company. They are always clear, and even when it rains there are no clouds in sight. No doubt this is due to the fact that rain on the Sho' is seldom composed of water. As a rule, the descending drops are spheres of molasses incased in rose petals or globules of honey, with kernels of ice-cream. Anon there comes a fall of chocolate soda water or old peach brandy or smuggled Canary wine.

When the wind blows upon the Sho' the trees give forth such beautiful music that strangers are overcome, and frequently sink into unconsciousness. When it snows the snow looks like silver and tastes like angel cake. When the sun sends down its affable rays one feels that one is awakening from a deep and restful sleep, and that a host of beautiful cherubs, smoking sweet-scented Havana cigars, are pouring champagne down one's throat.

No wonder the climate of Baltimore is pluperfect!

III

The bugaboo at 1524, then, is plainly a "character," a cauldron of bubbling idiosyncrasies that boil over every other minute and scorch his cautious contemporaries. Upon the walls of his home hang the pictures of his ancestors; in his bookcases repose their letters, their numerous works in Latin and in German; in his vaults are kept their relics; and all the time their blood is flowing in his veins, a stream of passion and paradox. Beyond these walls lies America. Within, is the man Mencken, compact of courage and contradiction. Here the hater of labels and pigeon-holes has everything of his own duly labeled and pigeon-holed, ready for refer-

ence at an instant's notice. Here the anti-Christ of the
nation makes a fad of theology, mastering it so thoroughly that he is called upon at times, by both Catholic
and Protestant clergy, to help settle difficult points.
Here the editor of *The American Mercury* peruses a very
limited number of fellow magazines, sedulously avoiding
those which most nearly approach his own in scope and
appeal. Here the critic of Shaw, Ibsen, Huneker,
Dreiser and Conrad sits reading through his horn-rimmed
glasses, affecting to be—as he insists—not a literary man
but a journalist, even as Huneker shrank into the asser-
tion that "I'm only a newspaper man." Here the books
that claim his closest attention are not fiction, not criticism, but theology, biology, economics and modern history.

For consistency in criticism, indeed, this widely-quoted
critic has small respect. "It is part of the puerile craze
for 'definitive' criticism," he has asserted, in one of his
electrical letters. (The letters of Mencken! Lines
dashed off on the edge of the typewriter-ribbon. Paragraphs concealing a passion wrapped in strips of jocular-
ity. Pages almost audible with the ring of opinion and
conjecture. Essays upon the arts. Volumes of candent
Menckeniana. Torrents of Bacchic allusion!) "I do not
pretend to know what the truth is. I can only present it
as it appears to me today. Tomorrow it may seem something else. 'Definitive' criticism, like 'constructive' criticism, is practised by asses. No 'definitive' judgment in
an æsthetic matter has ever lasted. The first aim of
criticism is to interest the reader in the work criticized—
to make him think about it, and, if it is good, to enjoy it.

DOORWAY AT 1524 HOLLINS STREET

Doors, paneling, fanlights and iron rail were designed
Edward L. Palmer. The door-frame and steps were
done by the unknown architect of the house.
The white marble trim is very charac-
teristic of Baltimore

SITTING-ROOM AT 1524 HOLLINS STREET

The second aim is to give him pleasure with a piece of writing that is itself a work of art. Æsthetic purpose nearly always turns out on examination, to be simply moral purpose in disguise."

The attitude is by no means a recent one; I find it in his very first book of prose, the rare *George Bernard Shaw: His Plays* (Boston, 1905). There, on pages xiv and xv of the introductory remarks he writes that "No two men can see the same thing in exactly the same way, and there are no fixed standards whereby we may decide whether one or the other or neither is right." Another time he has sketched the obverse of this picture. "I believe fully only in what may be demonstrated scientifically. All the rest is pure speculation—beautiful, perhaps, but not important. That Shakespeare was a great poet is not a fact; it is simply an opinion. It may be abandoned in the next century, as the doctrine that the Bible was written by God has been abandoned since 1850. But the fact that there is sodium chloride in the blood will never be abandoned. It is immutably true."

Alas, important, but not beautiful. And between the unimportant beauty and the important truth swings Mencken, finding truth often less important than its unimportant sister and even able at times to effect the union that a Keats has embodied in a famous line and an Ellis in a fecund life. There is a core of health in Mencken's suspicion of pure literature as an exclusive diet. It makes only learned idiots, he maintains, adding that no man who doesn't know the elements, at least, of all the physical sciences seems to him to be educated. I have just mentioned Keats and Ellis; by happy coincidence, both were trained in medicine at the same hospital,—St. Thomas's in London. Science hardly seems to have impoverished their artistry.

Mencken is a sophisticate who has a nostalgia for the days of barbarism. He is fond of stripping a thing to its essentials whether it be etiquette or the duel of the sexes. He thus takes pride (and, to my way of thinking, a justified pride) in the "provincial French principles" of his table manners, "with modifications suggested by the Cossacks of the Don." Yet allied to this elementary simplicity is a fussiness with food, a highly specialized interest in and acquaintance with the culinary art, that suggests both the gourmet and the gourmand. For a barbarian, he is chained to the city by a curse that has become a necessity. That curse, which he considers the worst in modern civilization, is the mechanical appliance. "Take my own case," he explains. "I'd like to have a house in the country, such as my father had all through my boyhood, but I hesitate to buy one because I fear I'd be uncomfortable in it. My house in Baltimore is highly mechanicalized. Dishes are washed by machinery, and so are clothes. The heating is done by steam generated by gas, and a thermostat regulates the temperature. It is never necessary to look at the furnace or even to go into the cellar. I fear that the lack of these comforts in the country would make me unhappy. In 1915 I bought an automobile. I sold it in 1918 as a nuisance. I never attempted to take care of it myself, but I drove it, and the business of having it greased, changing tires on the road, laying in gasoline, etc., annoyed me greatly. Moreover, it was expensive. Now I use taxicabs, as

more rational. There is a stand a block from my house.
I can get a cab at any moment of the day or night. The
cost is much less than that of keeping a car. If I
bought a country place I'd have to keep a car, and maybe
look after it myself. That would bind me to a machine
again. On the other hand, I'd miss all the machines that
I'm now a slave to."

This urge toward the past, paradoxically concomitant
with his urge toward the future, reveals itself in many
curious ways. He goes abroad and studies the tombs of
his ancestors. He makes a detailed study of the family
history. His sense of the family, indeed, leads him the
more readily to accept the theory advanced by Dr.
Herskovitz that the race is not the unit of civilization,—
that there are in reality no races, but powerful families,
clans. Incidentally, though he has been blessed with a
Pinaforean plenitude of relations,—eleven uncles and
aunts and eighteen cousins,—it is on record that he has
never quarreled with any of them. Just as it is not his
city that he loves, but his home, so it is not any race he
sponsors, but his clan. Yet clearly he stands out from
these various backgrounds, alike in eccentricities as in
accomplishments.

IV

Let us, somewhat after the manner of the apocryphal
Owen Hatteras,[1] follow a procession of those "flashing
points" which are too often overlooked or under-

[1] Consult—that is, if you can lay hands on a copy,—*Pistols For Two*,
by Owen Hatteras. A. A. Knopf, 1917. The pamphlet is now a curio
of contemporary American letters.

estimated amidst the more imposing apparatus of the conventional biography. At the same time, we must remember that Mr. Hatteras himself, for all his pretensions to a closer approach to the truth, was neither infallible nor unfailingly veracious. The fellow, in fact, had a touch of the charlatan in him,—of the hoaxer, the "kidder." I use his information warily, and do my best to save you from his snares.

Mencken, then, is five feet, eight and a half inches in height, and in maturity his weight has varied from the huge bulk of two hundred pounds to the more presentable one hundred and seventy-five. There is, however, nothing ungainly in his appearance; he is, at most, stocky, and carries his weight well.

His repertory of drinks is unlimited, but he prefers Pilsner. He not only drinks it, but his letters are full of it; there are days on which, in his enthusiasm for his native clime, he assures you that the bulbuls are singing in the Pilsner trees of Baltimore. In the absence of Pilsner, he drinks whatever malt he can get. He seldom drinks at meals and often goes three or four days with nothing stronger than water. In wine he prefers the white Moselle. He detests champagne, Scotch and rye whiskey, and gin, though he drinks them all to be polite, and has learned to drink gin since Prohibition. (Mencken, hater of etiquette, crier of "Be hard!") When there is work on hand, he avoids the glamour of the glass. Thus he drinks appreciably more in New York than in Baltimore.

He eats and enjoys all varieties of human food. There is no dish that he doesn't eat. He has eaten snails, frogs, eels, octopus, catfish, goat meat, and Norwegian cheese. He thinks that the best roasts are the English, the best table wines the Spanish, the best pastry the Danish, the best soups the German, and the best cooking the French.

He has strange, blue eyes, which fix his interlocutor. I am not so sure as is "Mr. Hatteras" that they are good; unless softened by goggles they may take on a hard, protruding stare. Yet kindness and geniality there is in them, and at rare moments a disarming softness.[1] His nose, far more than his photographs allow you to suspect, suddenly tilts upward, somehow imparting an impish expression. His mouth confirms the gentleness that is sometimes in his eyes. His ears are large. He is stoop-shouldered. His teeth, about which he is as hygienically meticulous as a cinema darling, are strong and white, if irregular. "Hatteras" is wrong when he

[1] Let me adduce unbiassed feminine testimony with reference to Mencken's expressive eyes. I quote from the report of the Scopes trial in Dayton, Tennessee, written for the *Haldeman-Julius Monthly* (September, 1925), by Mrs. Marcet Haldeman-Julius:

"E. H.-J. pointed out to me various celebrities. Among them was Mencken. I was forced to look twice, so different does that gentleman appear from the pictures and cartoons of him. He looks as if he were in his late thirties—some six or eight years younger than his avowed forty-four. He is at once stockier than I had supposed and much less ponderous in manner. He is affable and friendly. He listened to practically the entire trial standing with several other journalists and a movie man or two, on a table in a corner of the court room. He faced the pleading advocates and incidentally the audience. Mencken's most usual expression when a member of the prosecution spoke was one of delighted incredulity. He has the most amazing china-blue eyes that survey the world with a sort of 'Where-did-you-come-from-baby-dear' surprised, ingenuous look, which changes directly he begins to talk."

asserts that "one could not imagine him in the moving pictures." Were Mencken to put on his plug hat he could pass as a political district leader; (he was once, indeed, elected Boss of Baltimore, in a plebiscite conducted by the Baltimore *Post!*) a few tricks of the make-up box could transform him into a Simon Legree, a Babbitt preparing for his bath, a Temperance lecturer getting ready for his annual address at the Y. M. C. A. Two parts alone would he be forbidden to essay,—that of Romeo and that of a writer.

He affects to prefer slim lassies, not under thirty years of age, with dark eyes and a sense of wit. Yet he has been seen chiefly with comely females who decidedly do not qualify, particularly as to antiquity.

"He wears buttoned shoes because he cannot tie shoe laces.[1] Neither can he tie a dress tie; if there is no one to tie it for him he has to miss the party. In general he is almost wholly devoid of manual dexterity, though he can play the piano well enough to entertain himself and is a good sight reader." Years ago, Mr. Nathan, drawing in the *Répétition Générale* of the old *Smart Set* the Portrait of a Man, wrote thus with Mencken in mind: "He ridicules any man who is vain in the matter of personal appearance, and goes out and buys a new necktie if the ones he has with him do not match the shirt he is wearing." It must be true, for on the afternoon of May 4, 1925, on the fifth floor of the Algonquin, New York, far from the madding crowd of literati below, in

---

[1] Since 1917, when "Owen Hatteras" wrote this paragraph, Mencken has acquired, though not to perfection, the art of shoe-lacing.

the midst of a most esoteric confabulation with the hero of this epic, I was without warning informed that he wore the particular necktie of that day only in Gotham, out of courtesy to the donor.

He wears a No. 7½ hat; is bow-legged; he walks fast (hence his scorn of the New York taxis). He used to snore when asleep, but an operation removed the cause of this unwelcome music. Incidentally, Mencken has been toyed with so often by the doctors that he has come to regard himself somewhat impersonally in the light of a laboratory animal for experimental purposes.

He wears B. V. D's all the year round and takes a cold bath every day.

He is his own manicurist.

He wears Manhattan garters, No. 15½ Belmont collars, and very long-tailed overcoats.

He shaves every morning with a Gillette safety razor. In 1914, while in Paris he grew a moustache and a goatee. They turned out corn yellow, whereupon off they came before the ship docked in New York.

He has retained nothing of his boyish interest in sports. He doesn't read the sport pages of the press. He cannot play tennis or golf, and has never tried. He detests cards and finds it difficult not to transfer the feeling to card-players themselves.

He doesn't dance and can't imagine what pleasure there could be in it for him. His chief enjoyment is derived rather from reading, with music a close second. He is appreciative of architecture, but painting—despite his early attempts at drawing and water-color—holds little attraction. He doesn't bet on elections or the horses, though his interest in politics as a spectacle is consuming and his fondness for horseflesh a token of intimacy that goes back to his childhood. His chief exercise is walking and—bricklaying. Years before he began to build a wall in his own yard, he had written with admiration of the bricklaying trade.

When I was a boy bricklayers always fascinated me. No other mechanics wore such a lordly and distinguished air. Even in those days they got a great deal more money than other working-men, and showed it in their manners. At noon, when the carpenters and tinners sat down in their slops to devour stale sandwiches out of tin cans, the bricklayers took off their white overalls, went to the Dutchman's at the corner, and there dined decently on *Linsensuppe* and *Sauerbraten,* with large horns of lager to flush their esophagi. Bricklayers were the only workmen who had recognized gangs of slaves to serve them, to wit, the hod-carriers. In those far-off times, in the city where I lived, all hod-carriers were colored men—usually great, shiny fellows with immense knots of muscles in their legs and arms. The Irish had already become lawyers, city detectives, saloon-keepers, gang bosses, and *Todsäufer* for breweries. These colored men, in Summer, liked to work with their chests bare. Swarming up ladders in long files, each with his heavy hod on his shoulder, they made an exotic, Egyptian picture. One could fancy them descended in a direct line from the Nubians who carried the hod when Cheops built his pyramid. The bricklayers, forever cursing them fluently, but all the same palpably friendly to them, fitted into the fancy perfectly. The mason is the one workman who has resisted all change. He does his work today as he did it in Babylon, with deft hand and sharp eyes. Compared to him, all the other mechanics of our time are upstarts; put him alongside

22

the plumber, the structural iron worker, or the electrician!
Moreover, what he does endures. The carpenter? A blower of
soap-bubbles, maker of millinery! But the brick walls of Babylon
stand to this day.

The back yard of 1524 is his gymnasium. Here he
cuts wood, carpenters, mixes mortar, pours concrete,
lays bricks. He has been working on the brick wall for
five years and it is still incomplete. The former wine-
cellar of the home was, on the advent of Prohibition,
converted by his brawn into a secure vault; two years
later he built another vault of solid brick and mortar,
with a steel door and a secret lock invented by his
brother. The job almost broke Mencken's back.

Up at eight sharp, he is at work by nine. He is as
methodical as the proverbial German, and like that
laborious paragon insists upon thoroughness and competence. He answers all mail with an excess of con-
scientiousness and expedition. He is careful not to
write love letters and never preserves them. His papers
are in better order, perhaps, than those of any other
writer in the world. He works in his shirt-sleeves. He
entertains an almost pathological dislike of union suits.

For years, at home, he has slept on a porch that opens
from his office on the third floor of the house. In the
house there is no sleeping-place for him. On those rare
occasions when a high wind forces him indoors, he sleeps
on a couch in his office. Though he prefers the heat to
the cold, cold alone has never routed him; he has slept
in his eyrie through violent storms and zero weather.
Though of great endurance, he feels the slackening effects of loss of sleep.

He exudes prejudices and predilections of the strangest assortment, a constant commentary upon himself. His conversation, in private, is sprinkled with picturesque expletives, with serio-comic exaggeration, with Rabelaisian anecdote and conjecture, with the forbidden four-letter vocables of the chalked walls of childhood. He mistrusts his musical ear, yet on a rare occasion I have heard him sing a snatch of one of his youthful compositions, and he was true to pitch.

He is capable, for example, of believing that the largest value got for a dollar in America "comes with a Pullman ticket. The difference between a day coach and a Pullman is almost as great as the difference between a Christian and a gentleman. What a joy it is to be among *clean* people—" the Menckenian Hygeia complex!—"people who do not stink! They may have every other fault, but they do not stink!"

He dislikes cut flowers, especially those that have a perfume. He has an aversion for potted plants. On the other hand, wild growth delights him. "Wild things—plants and creatures—are always interesting and charming. If I owned any land I should let most of it grow up in jungle." And yet he prefers the city to the country. As early as his fifteenth year, indeed, he was on the affirmative side of a debate that took place in the Second English Lutheran Sunday-School, Lombard Street, Baltimore; subject, "Resolved, that city life is better than country life." Today it would be difficult to lure him upon the public platform; he has received flattering offers and promptly turned them down.

He has a vast respect for the man who keeps his appointments and who keeps out of debt.

He is against individuals or nations who engage saucily upon battles with enemies who can't hit back.

He places personal honor above the static concepts of morality.

V

Beneath these idiosyncracies dwells the individual. Mencken is the creature of innumerable inner conflicts that, like so many tones of personality, make up the resounding chord of this complex human music. That chord is an unresolved dissonance, pungent with the rare flavor of an artistic uncertainty, yet suggestive, as are most dissonances, of the satisfying resolution. He has orchestrated himself in all the keys of the circle; the main themes of his symphony appear early in life and undergo every mutation of the classic form. I say classic form, for, despite the cynicism of Mencken's outlook upon life, despite the peculiar modernity and contradictoriness of the man, despite his restlessness, his healthy anarchism, he tends toward order, clearness and serenity. These may, of course, become, among traditionalists the disguises stagnation, obviousness and dullness. It is Mencken's special function to keep them ever upon the alert, paying for their liberty the price of eternal vigilance.

At the bottom of the Menckenian philosophy lurks a feeling that life is meaningless. Art, whether in books or in the direction of one's life, lies largely in spreading over that meaninglessness a patina of meaning. This Mencken has done by allowing his personality to crystallize around the meaninglessness. Never too solidly, however; always ready to break up into the original fragments and form into new shapes. There is no certitude; it is a chimera of simple minds. There may be truths, but there is no Truth. Such an outlook seeks no common center; it flees that center; it is centrifugal. It is not content with a static world to which all phenomena are to be conformed; it is alert, kinetic, alive, nonconformist; it is a *perpetuum mobile* of the spirit. Certainty implies a standard of conformity; such a standard implies, just as surely, an ethical attitude toward the world and its problems. Uncertainty, seeking just as naturally for some illusion of unity, finds it in the æsthetic reaction. Certainty satisfies the religious mind; it becomes the true faith and the problem of life resolves itself into winning infidels away from ruin to the sole salvation. Uncertainty has nothing to which it may bring converts; it smiles wrily at propaganda with a capital P; life becomes a spectacle, a passing show, a vast Vanity Fair. This is no philosophy for the soft; it is supremely realistic; its very sense of humor, its unrelaxed grip upon sheer common sense, render it hard and cruel. It involves a certain indifferentism, a calculated coolness which, by the law of opposites, may sometimes glow into seemingly deep concern. Indeed, uncertainty itself becomes uncertain, and we have the occasional diversion of a Mencken belaboring the Puritans with a fervor that is nothing less than passionately Puritan.

How, then, does Mencken impart a meaning to the chaos called Life? Essentially, by that rebellion called self-assertion. I rebel, therefore I am. Heaven and hell are fictions spawned in weaker minds by hope and fear. Earth is real, and earth alone. The body is real, and soul, far from being the anemic, fleshless abstraction of a Dante's paradise or a Shaw's *Back to Methuselah,* is body raised to the *n*th degree. Either there are no miracles or everything is a miracle. Be on guard against all illusions, minor as well as major. The superior being is he who lives with the least number of them. The great illusions are Religion, Progress, Democracy; the superior man, then, will bow to no god, no theory, no mere multitude. He will, as part of his own superiority, recognize the true superiority of others. Out of the herd rises the individual.

What does this reduce to in familiar language?

The Mencken outlook is anarchic, æsthetic, aristocratic; these attributes are the inevitable qualities of his marked individualism. The man who is more than a member of the collectivity,—more than an indistinguishable unit of the flock,—rejects the mythology of a supreme being; rejects the standards of mere quantity. Every one of these rejections is implicit in his heightened consciousness of self. He becomes a self-ruled personality wandering through an alien world in quest of the rarer emotions we call beauty. At times his failure to find what he is seeking turns him inward and becomes harsh mockery of self; more often, that disenchantment reaches outward for its revenge, and gives back scorn and satire for beauties lost or never found; the frustrated quest may even echo in clownish laughter or behind other masks for tears.

Earth is real; the body is real. Let there be joy, then. If beauty is the faith of the faithless, let joy be the prayer of the infidel. "Thou shalt not" was uttered by Certainty; then let Uncertainty reply, not "Thou shalt," for that, too, is a commandment, but rather "Thou mayst."

Such a man is a seeker after beauty, whatever its guise. He looks upon the whirling Globe as a vastly entertaining spectacle, to be applauded when well done and hissed when it could be better. His aristocracy is not the fetish of hereditary preferment, but rather the supremacy of the best. His anarchy does not bomb buildings or empty-headed public executives whose brains aren't worth the powder; it bombs ideas.

In a word, he is free. And to Mencken, to be free, within the inevitable limitations of man's best judgment, is man's greatest glory. Rebellion is but the reverse of the coin; the obverse is freedom. For the rest, much of valid non-conformity is in reality a self-conformity. It is thus that a merely wilful negative resistance acquires a positive significance. Non-conformity clears fields for battle; conformity to the supreme sanction of self alone wins victories.

Writing in the *Nation* (New York; Dec. 5, 1923) he has expressed himself with characteristic exuberance upon this fundamental theme. "What primarily and immovably do I believe in as a Puritan believes in hell? I believe in liberty, and when I say liberty, I mean the thing in its widest imaginable sense—liberty up to the extreme limits of the feasible and tolerable. I am against forbidding anybody to do anything, or say anything, or think anything so long as it is at all possible to imagine a habitable world in which he would be free to do, say, and think it. The burden of proof, as I see it, is always upon the policeman, which is to say, upon the lawmaker, the theologian, the right-thinker. He must prove his case doubly, triply, quadruply, and then he must start all over and prove it again. The eye through which I view him is watery and jaundiced. I do not pretend to be 'just' to him—any more than a Christian pretends to be just to the devil. He is the enemy of everything I admire and respect in this world—of everything that makes it various and amusing and charming. He impedes every honest search for the truth. He stands against every sort of good-will and common decency. His ideal is that of an animal trainer, an archbishop, a major general in the army. I am against him until the last galoot's ashore."

The same article ends with a luminous paragraph which, in the course of a couple of hundred words, runs the gamut of moods from suavity to acerbity and ends with a final crashing dissonance. But this is the music of a free spirit, to which Mencken dances his Dance of Life.

What, asks Mencken, has liberty to do

with the art of literary criticism, my principal business in this vale? Nothing—or everything. It seems to me that it is perfectly possible to write profound and valuable literary criticism without entering upon the question of freedom at all, either

29

directly or indirectly. Æsthetic judgments may be isolated from all other kinds of judgments, and yet remain interesting and important. But this isolation must be performed by other hands: to me it is as sheer a psychological impossibility as believing that God condemned forty-two little children to death for poking fun at Elisha's bald head. When I encounter a new idea, whether æsthetic, political, theological, or epistemological, I ask myself, instantly and automatically, what would happen to its proponent if he should state its exact antithesis. If nothing would happen to him, then I am willing and eager to listen to him. But if he would lose anything valuable by a *volte face*—if stating his idea is profitable to him, if the act secures his roof, butters his parsnips, gets him a tip—then I hear him with one ear only. He is not a free man. Ergo, he is not a man. For Liberty, when one ascends to the levels where ideas swish by and men pursue Truth to grab her by the tail, is the first thing and the last thing. So long as it prevails the show is thrilling and stupendous; the moment it fails the show is a dull and dirty farce.

So much for the theory. It is as inconsistent, as paradoxical, as life itself. Whatever logic there is to it leads to a conception of life as struggle, liberty as eternal vigilance; it produces in Mencken an æsthetic of aggression. Take a similar intellectual background in so different a spirit as Chekhov; the aggression is absent, yet how strangely akin the inner processes! Mr. William Gerhardi, in his recent study of the Russian conteur, has stated the case in words appropriate almost without change to the American critic. "He tumbles to the ingenious idea of harnessing this artistically mortifying sense of intellectual impotence and desolation to artistic ends. The want of motive is his artistic motive. . . . There is his passion for dispassion, and a

healthy zest of living amply overtopping any gloomy
moods. If Chekhov had no axe to grind, he ground it,
none the less so, to a razor blade of perpetual discrim-
ination." [1] It all comes back to the artist; he alone,—in
all the complexity of his psychic and physical organization,—is the key to his work. He *is* his work. His
theories are interesting; usually, however, they are
merely rationalizations of his product. Does anyone,
for all Poe's ingenious explanation, believe that there
was nothing more to the writing of *The Raven* than a
cold-blooded pursuit of vowels and images?

Behind and within that organization of mind and body
lies an ancestral history, which has been potent in shaping the destiny of Mencken's illusive freedom. The
line of our progenitors may not confine us utterly, but
surely it plays an important defining rôle. Mencken the
man, the writer, the force in contemporary life and
letters, is thus partially defined by his forbears on the
one hand, and on the other, by the writings that are his
alter ego. Between stands the man who completes the
circuit.

[1] See *Anton Chehov*. Duffield & Company. New York, 1923. Page 29.

CHAPTER TWO

The Menckenii in Europe

I

THE name Mencken has long been the subject of
etymological speculation. According to the family historian, Oberjustizrat Peter Heinrich Mencke, of
Oldenburg (1809–1873), the surname Mencke was originally conferred for prowess in war. Among the variants
were Magnan, Magan, Megin, Meno, Menno, Menet,
Meino and Meine; later, the diminutive suffix *ke* was
added. As the family became learned and took to the
writing of Latin, the name likewise was Latinized by
appending the common termination for proper names,
ius; since a name ending in *e* did not usually take on the
ius directly, the consonant *n* was interposed to bridge the
hiatus, thus producing the form Menckenius. Upon
later translation back into German, the name retained
the *n.* The Oldenburg branch of the family, however,
as may be seen from the name of the family historian,
have never used it; on the other hand, the learned Leipzig branch have clung to the final consonant.

Dr. Conrad Müller, in his work upon the Mother of
Bismarck and Her Ancestors,[1] suggests a different

---

[1] *Bismarcks Mutter und ihre Ahnen.* Von Dr. Conrad Müller. I. Die
Ahnen und die Jugendzeit. Berlin, 1909. Pp. 24–25.

derivation. Though he has drawn freely upon Peter Heinrich in his researches, he makes no mention of the variants just given, nor of the martial connotation they are supposed to carry.[1] He refers the name rather to a couple of verbs, *menkeln* and *menken*. *Menkeln*, originally, signified to sell at retail, to haggle or chaffer; then, to delay, linger, hesitate. *Menken*, on the other hand, referred specifically to leisureliness in eating. Wherefore Müller is tempted to relate the family motto, "Wartet und eilet" (Make haste slowly), to a certain cautiousness both in business and at table. It is, of course, possible. The Latin motto from which the German is derived may readily be applied to the table: *Festina lente*. The earliest Mencke of whom we have record was, in fact, a trader.

As to the different spellings of the name Dr. Müller likewise has his own explanation. Old spellings oscillated between Menke and Menkke. With the outbranching of the family from business into learning came the Latinization of the name and intercalation of the *n*. Thus Lüder (Lothar) Mencke became Luderus Menckenius, while Gottfried and Johann Burkhard became, respectively, Godofredus Ludovicus Menkenius and Johannes Burchardus Menckenius. This is not, by the way, the regular history in Latin for German names ending in *ke*. Henke, for example, gives normally Henkius, not Henkenius. Müller's solution of the difficulty reads plausibly. Low-German pronunciation tended toward nasalization of vocalic endings; the *n* may be taken to

---

[1] Mencke wrote down his etymological researches in a separate study that does not form part of the *Familien Chronik*. He gives no authorities.

represent, in the Latinized forms, the orthographic evidence of that tendency.

A third derivation I give for what it may be worth: *Männchen,* a little man, origin of our "manikin." In Low German this is *Männeke* or *Männeken.*

In the form Mencke the name has been familiar for centuries along the west Baltic coast. It is conjectured that the family originated in the territory of the Frisians; for many years its headquarters have been at Oldenburg, the capital of an ancient grand duchy which, in Roman times, was inhabited by the Chauci, who later united with the Frisians. Oldenburg itself has had a historical career. First referred to in a document of 1108, it seems to have owed its name to the fortress of which it may have been the site. Of old, the cheery Saxons settled upon its barren hills, while the moody but independent Frisians occupied the marshlands. When the Reformation came, indeed, it was to find a ready welcome among these liberty-loving lowlanders. Seized, in the pristine days of the German kingdom, by the Dukes of Saxony, Oldenburg was ruled by members of their house as Counts of Oldenburg and Delmenhorst. In 1448 one of these counts became king of Denmark, and afterward, of Norway and Sweden; thus, for more than three centuries Oldenburg was Danish. Despite the wars that shook the territory, down to the days of Napoleon, the town prospered and became the seat of wealthy, enterprising traders. It was made independent by the Congress of Vienna. In 1864 it took sides with Prussia against Denmark; in 1870 it joined the German empire.

Were it not for the conflagration that, on July 27, 1676, all but wiped out the town, we should in all likelihood possess far more information than is now at our disposal concerning the early Menckes. As it is, the fairly unbroken account that reaches from the middle of the sixteenth century down to the present day attests, on the part of the Menckens, old and new, an ardent sense of family unity.

Helmrich Mencke, the patriarch of what was to become the Leipzig branch of the family, was a rich merchant and died in Oldenburg in 1570. He seems to have established the family trait of antinomianism, for when the Reformation hit his town, he abandoned Holy Church. He had two sons, Gerd (?–1614) and Otto (1573–1617). To the only son of Gerd that lived to maturity, Eilard (d. 1657), is due the family Stipendium, which still exists.[1] This is a fund, originally left by Eilard upon his death, to be administered by trustees for the education of Menckens *in perpetuo*. Eilard, moving to Prussia, rose to be Archpresbyter of the

[1] More than thirty Menckens, since 1637, have gone through German universities with the aid of the Stipendium. The trustees of it are the heads of the various Mencken families, so that H. L. Mencken of Baltimore is technically one. On October 17, 1866, a meeting was called at Oldenburg and a family statute was adopted barring out his grandfather and his heirs on the ground that he had left Germany. By German law, such a family statute, when recorded in court, has full legal effect. It is likely that grandfather Mencken, had he lived to the time when H. L. was ready for college, would have raised a ruction and had his grandson restored to the benefits of the fund. Any chance of a fight by Mencken's father was frustrated by H. L.'s refusal to go to college.

Cathedral at Marienwerder, where his very elaborate tomb is still to be seen. Johannes, son of Otto, lived from 1607 to 1688. Like his father a merchant, he traveled widely; during the Thirty Years' War he ran the blockade of Kiel with a cargo of linen and got rich on the venture. He became a highly respected Rathsherr of the ancestral town.

Johannes and his brother Helmrich married the two daughters of Oldenburg's Bürgermeister, Lüder Spiessmacher. It is to Johannes' son Otto (1644–1707) that the family owes a sudden divergence from business to learning. At twenty, after taking his laurels at the University of Leipzig, he is found lecturing with sensational success at Jena, on moral philosophy; at twenty-five, after returning to Leipzig for theology and jurisprudence and traveling through Holland in a blaze of scholastic glory, he is named professor of morals and politics. Joining two of the three literary societies of the University, Otto infuses new life into the discussions, attracts new members, and hits on the idea of Germany's first learned review,—the *Acta Eruditorum.* To this remote ancestor of *The American Mercury,* Mencke soon drew some of the foremost scholars of Europe. In 1680 he set out upon a tour of England and Holland, with the express purpose of establishing personal contacts that should prove beneficial to his projected publication. He thus met Sande in Amsterdam, Grævius in Utrecht, Leeuwenhock in Delft, Heinsius in Vianen, Melder, Paul Voet and Jacob Gronovius in Leiden, the Jesuits Henschenius and Papebroch (editors of the *Acta Sanctorum*) in Antwerp, Fell, Bernard and Wallis in Ox-

DR. OTTO MENCKEN (1644–1707)

*Professor of ethics at Leipzig and founder of the ACTA
ERUDITORUM, the first learned review in
Germany*

A REPRODUCTION OF A STEEL ENGRAVING OF
DR. JOHANN BURCHARD MENCKEN (1674–1732)

ford, and Vossius, Gale and Robert Boyle in London. From its first appearance in 1682, the *Acta* assumed a leading position in its field. For almost ten years it confined itself chiefly to the sciences; here, for example, Leibnitz published, in 1684, his first paper on the differential calculus. Otto's son and grandson succeeded in turn to the editorship, issuing it without interruption until 1754. Upon the grandson's death the work was continued in the name and at the expense of the Menckes; its last editor was Professor Andreas Bal. At his death in 1782 the review ceased to be. At first printed exclusively in Latin, it later admitted articles in German and other modern languages. There were also German imitations (1712–1739). Otto's part was chiefly that of editor and organizing spirit.

Otto married Magdalena Sybilla, the daughter of Hof- und Justizrat Burchard Berlichius; his home became a center for learned visitors. Much taken up with teaching, editorial work and administrative duties as rector of the University for five terms, he wrote relatively little; his literary remains include a history of the Hohenzollerns. He seems to have been a shrewd fellow, keenly interested in literature and politics, and adept at the hair-splitting of the scholastic philosophy. On his return to Leipzig from Jena, however, he was one of the leaders in the revolt against this leaden logomachy. Fond of music, he played the zither; hardheaded, like so many of the Mencken tribe, ancient and modern, he refused as a student to take the regulation oath to obey the University statutes. He won out, too, for he was released from the oath. Dying at the age of 63 from apoplexy, he left an honored name in the history of European scholarship.

In accomplishment and in renown he is exceeded by his son, Johann Burchard (1674–1732). By the time he has reached the year of his majority Johann is a Leipzig Ph.D. Traveling, a few years later, through England and Europe, he comes into contact with the finest minds of his time,—with Beyle, Gronovius, Grævius and Burnam in Holla.; with Bentley, Locke, Cave, Dodwell and Woodw in England. It was through Woodward that he s elected at the age of twenty-four as a member of t' British Royal Society. A year later found him a f professor of history at Leipzig, at the beginning of career of astounding fertility. Upon his father's d th in 1707 he succeeded to the editorship of the *Ac Eruditorum,* prefixing to its title the adjective *Nov.* In England he had conceived a vast work upon all the known ancient historical manuscripts, in all tongues, and actually published three huge tomes (1728– 30) under the title *Scriptores Rerum Germanicarum.*[1] His works include a biography of Leopold I, Holy Roman Emperor (1658–1705), and a method, written in French, for the study of history. He was several times rector of the University. In 1715, during his second term, he demanded that the soldiers of the Saxon Army, when he encountered them on the streets, should present arms. What is more, he fought a vigorous case to victory. His library, partly inherited from his fa-

---

[1] Quoted by Carlyle in his history of Frederick the Great (Book II, Chapter VI).

ther, was so superior to that of the University that he threw it open to the students.

From his father, too, he must have inherited a hatred of pedantry. Otto had led the attack upon the hairsplitters; Johann descended upon the whole army of frauds. At Leipzig, in 1715, he published in Latin his famous satire, *De Charlataneria Eruditorum*. Its effect was immediate; indeed, it created a storm, and soon was translated into German, French, Dutch and Italian. In the original it passed through edition after edition, acquiring gradually a formidable array of notes, most of which were added by volunteer commentators.

Reading *De Charlataneria* [1] today is hardly as exciting as it must have been to its contemporaries. It interests us, in fact, chiefly as one of the numerous forecasts of the Baltimore scion. As the *Acta Eruditorum* prefigures editor Mencken of *The American Mercury*, so does *De Charlataneria Eruditorum* point, from the rationalistic eighteenth century, to the twentieth century foe of sham and fraud. *Mundus vult decipi* is the leit-motif of Johann Burkhard's dia-

---

[1] I have read *De Charlataneria Eruditorum* in three forms. First, the original: Jo. Burch. Menckenii. *De Charlataneria Eruditorum*. Declamationes Duæ, cum notis variorum. Accesit epistola Sebastiani Stadelii ad Janum Philomusum de Circumforanea Literatorum vanitate. Editio tertia emendatior. Amstelodami (Amsterdam). M DCC XVI. Second, in a German translation: *Zwei Reden von der Charlatanerie oder Marckshreyerey der Gelehrten* gehalten von J. B. Mencken und ins Teutsche übersetzt auch mit verschiedenen Anmerkungen vermehrt von H. Z. I. Cosmopolis auf unkosten der gelehrten Societät. 1719. Third, an unpublished version in a language that is a cross between Latin and English, though intended to be the latter.

tribe: The world wishes to be deceived. Whereupon
in two addresses he catalogues, through lines that evidence a vast and patient erudition, the humbuggery and
follies of the learned: their worship of the past and
denigration of the present; their chicanery in the law,
their quackery in medicine, their log-rolling in criticism,
their pedantry in study, their meticulous quibbling in
logic, their wordy fatuities in metaphysics. His animad-
versions upon what we have come to know latterly as
Ph. Demonism strike one as peculiarly contemporaneous.
The latest of the literary Menckens seems, indeed, to
have taken more than one leaf out of this notebook.
Tanto vero, Auditores, writes Johann Burkhard, *vis est
impudentiæ, etiam in re seria.* "So great, O listeners,
is the power of impudence, even in serious matters."

As a poet, Johann Burkhard printed four volumes of
eighteenth century verse, chiefly of occasional nature,
under the pseudonym Philander von der Linde. These
were verses, not for the Muses, but for the Dresden
Court. He was a favorite orator for the University
festivities. In 1708 he had been appointed electoral
Saxon historiographer by August the Strong, who, as
King of Poland, named him in the same year a Privy
Councillor; in 1723 he was made Court Councillor. It
is not surprising that he was an ardent monarchist; like
most of the Menckens, too, he seems to have married
well and to have laid up a good store of money. His
wife was Catherine Margarethe, daughter of the celebrated Leipzig publisher, Johann Friedrich Gleditsch.

To Johann Burkhard were born three daughters and
two sons. Only the sons concern us here; they were

Friedrich Otto (1708–1754) and Carl Otto (1711–1759). Friedrich continued the tradition of scholarship; Carl's profession has not been established, although he founded a military branch of the family.[1]

Friedrich was given a formidable private education and proceeded then to the Nicolaischule, Leipzig, where his courses included Greek, Hebrew, mathematics, philosophy and belles lettres. His precocity—he took his A.M. at the University of Leipzig, at the age of 17—did not maintain its initial impetus; he received his Ph.D. at twenty-two, not from Leipzig, but from Wittenberg, in jurisprudence. He was eminently fitted to carry on the editorship of the family magazine, the *Acta Eruditorum,* and founded a learned periodical of his own, the *Nova Miscellanea Lisiepsnia.* He, too, was rich in academic distinctions. His library consisted of no less than 23,000 volumes. His only son died at the age of 17 while a student at Leipzig, so that his line came to an end.

II

We have followed, thus far, the fortunes of the descendants of Johannes, one of the two sons born to Otto Mencken (1573–1617). It is from the other son,

[1] Two of the daughters died in childhood. The third, Christiane Sybille (1706–1752) married Baron Peter von Hohenthal, so becoming the maternal ancestor of a long line. The father of Baron Peter was Peter Hohmann, a wealthy merchant often called the Leipzig Fugger. He was ennobled by the Emperor Karl VI in 1717. To Christiane were born six sons. In 1736 the entire clan were made free lords of the empire, and in 1790, Counts. The Hohenthals today are among the rich and influential families of Germany. At the time they were made counts they owned so much land that its inhabitants numbered 25,000.

Helmrich (1609–1669), that the American writer is descended. To Helmrich were born five sons and five daughters, one of the sons dying in infancy. The eldest of the surviving sons, Otto (1654–1703), was educated at the expense of the family Stipendium; he won preferment in the Danish service, married well, was raised to the nobility and put a *von* before his name. His brother Johann (1662–?) may have attended a university, but became a merchant. Another brother, Anton Günther, likewise went into business.

The fourth son, however, restored the balance; Lüder Mencken (1658–1726) decided for a life of learning. Born at Oldenburg, he entered Leipzig in 1676. His cousin, now Professor Otto Mencken, took him in and tutored him. After additional courses at Jena, he returned to Leipzig for his A.M. in 1680 and his Ph.D. in 1682. This was the prelude to forty-four years of teaching, writing and public lecturing, during which Lüder rose to the position of dominant spirit in the law-school of the University. A new professorship, in Saxon Law, was created for him; he became chief judge of what would correspond to the Court of the King's Bench, and a Royal Councillor, and served for two terms as rector of the University. So great was his renown as an author and expounder of legal subjects that he was known as *Viva Lex* (The Living Law-Book) and *Das Orakel des Rechtes* (The Oracle of the Law). He is now generally credited with a poem in hymn-style; it reveals a deeply pious nature in quest of heavenly peace.

Lüder married three times. His first wife bore him a

son, Gottfried Ludwig; his second, a son and three daughters; there was no issue from his third marriage. His younger son, Heinrich Otto (b. 1690) died at 26, just as he was to join the University faculty after a trip through Germany, Holland and England, and a doctorate in jurisprudence. Gottfried Ludwig (1683–1744), educated at first under paternal direction, became in 1707 a Ph.D. in law, and five years later was made full professor in the law faculty of Leipzig. In 1714 he received a call to Wittenberg, where he remained for the rest of his life. He served as rector of the University and as judge in most of the local courts. When he married Christiane Maria Zoller, he united the Mencken strain to one of great antiquity; the Zollers boasted a line of officials and professors that reached well back into the eleventh century.

Gottfried Ludwig Mencken left three sons: Leonhard Ludwig (1710–1762); Gottfried Ludwig II (1712–1762); and Christian Heinrich (1718–1758), all of whom carried on the academic tradition. Doctorates had become part of the family heritage. Leonhard took his, in law, in 1737, and became an associate professor in the law faculty of Wittenberg; later he retired in favor of his law practice. Christian, educated at Leipzig under the provisions of the family Stipendium, became a Doctor of Law, and died at forty without issue. Gottfried Ludwig II was, together with Leonhard, instructed at home and later tutored by some of their father's colleagues at Wittenberg. Of Gottfried, more anon.

Two sons were left by Leonhard Ludwig: Johann Caspar Ludwig (1752–1795) and Johann August Ludwig (1754–1833). The first wrote nothing of any importance and died unmarried, after the expected professorial and legal career. The second, after taking his doctorate in 1782, went at once into the practise of law and continued at it until his death. In his student days he seems to have been known as a duellist and a dancer; he fought, too, in the Napoleonic wars. He had an only son, Johann Christian August Mencken, born at Wittenberg on December 3, 1797 and destined to be the great-grandfather of Henry Louis Mencken. Johann Christian's profession, if he had any, is unknown. At any rate, he signals the recession of the Menckens to commercial activity. Too young to bear arms in the wars that his father witnessed, he was by 1825 a member of the Landwehr of the Saxon army. On November 5, 1842, according to a contract at present in the possession of the Baltimore writer, he indentured his son (the grandfather of H. L. Mencken) to Heinrich Berger, a merchant of Oschatz. In consideration of the sum of 100 Thalers, half down and the remainder in three and five years, Berger was to take the boy of fourteen and a half into his household for the ensuing five years and teach him the secrets of business. The episode is of vital importance to this narrative, as shall in due course appear; for Berger seems to have dealt principally in tobacco, the trade which our own Mencken's grandfather and father were subsequently to follow in America.

III

Returning to Gottfried Ludwig II (1712–1762), we find him receiving his doctorate in 1737 at the hands of his father. Entering the practise of law in Leipzig, he pursued it for more than ten years before he was called to a professorship. He was much in demand by several universities, made many enemies and triumphed over them. The ordeal of the Seven Years' War, however, was wiping out the family. He had married in 1751; in the autumn of 1760, during a skirmish in the town of Helmstedt, whither he had gone to teach upon the university faculty, his wife was nearly killed by a shot in the neck. The shock impaired his own ill health. Two years later, when, as a result of abuses by the Prussian soldiery, his brother Leonhard Ludwig died, Gottfried went to Wittenberg for the funeral and, shortly thereafter, died himself. The family had come upon evil days. His library consisted of only 2,078 books, and his widow, with two sons and two daughters on her hands, had been left so poor that she was compelled to sell it.

Combining business with the scholastic pursuits of the family, she soon opened a boarding house for professors. She must have done well, for her two sons, Anastasius and Johann Carl Philipp, were sent to school in preparation for the university; eventually, with the assistance of the Stipendium, they entered. Johann died at the age of 19, before he could take his doctorate. Anastasius, taking his degree in jurisprudence, roused professorial ambitions in his mother's bosom. He was not an eager

45

student, however, preferring novels and plays to the more sober books of his curriculum. He had, moreover, an innate gift for light verse in the satiric vein,[1] and was fond—like more than one of the succeeding Menckens—of a good practical joke. It was natural that a young blade of his peculiar endowments should yearn for the capital and the Court; and, to be sure, on one fine day he decamped, reaching the Berlin of his dreams almost penniless. Through family friends he made headway, missing only through intrigue a position as tutor to the heir apparent of the Prince of Orange. Count Herzberg, who had managed to get the place for one of his protégés, had young Mencken appointed, by way of compensation, to the staff of the training-school for the diplomatic corps of Prussia, which was modeled after the French *Académie des Nobles*.

Anastasius was cut out for the Court. His French was as good as his German and his presence was sightly. He must have had a winning way with the ladies, for, after being appointed secretary of legation and sent to Stockholm, he managed to make friends with the Swedish Queen-Mother, Luise Ulricke, sister of Frederick and, like all the other relatives, on bad terms with the Frenchified potentate. Mencken, despite the fact that many Prussian diplomats had failed before him, actually brought about a satisfactory reconciliation, and thus won Frederick's favor. On March 28, after having been summoned from Stockholm, Mencken was named private secretary to the king, in place of the recently deceased

---

[1] See Müller, *op. cit.*, pp. 114–116, for specimens of his satiric and gallant verse, in German and French respectively.

Koeper. Four years later, however, the death of Frederick put an end to Mencken's preferment. He served under Frederick's successors at Court and in the field, but his diplomatic fortunes were on the decline. He retired from the service in 1792 and died eight years later at Potsdam.

Mencken, on September 9, 1785, had married the widow of the wealthy tobacco monopolist, Pierre Shock. To them were born on August 21, 1787, a son named Samuel Karl Ludwig, and on February 24, 1789, a daughter, Luise Wilhelmine. Of Samuel, little has come down. Luise Wilhelmine, however, inherited her mother's beauty and became the belle of Potsdam. In her childhood she played with the three sons of Friedrich Wilhelm II, and as she grew up, her personal fascination dwelt in the added glamour of a large inheritance. She could not long remain unmarried, and at the age of nineteen, seven years after she had lost her parents, she was wedded to Captain Karl Wilhelm Ferdinand von Bismarck, a brave soldier dwelling at the time in the displeasure of the king. Nine years later she gave birth to a son, who was christened Karl Otto Eduard Leopold, destined to become the Iron Chancelor. He was twenty-four when she died, serving his time in the army and known rather for an iron stomach which no amount of beer could corrode, than for the iron will that later made history.

Queerly enough, the descendants of Helmrich Mencke, like those of his brother Johannes, lead through devious paths of scholarship and soldiery to the tobacco trade. There were Menckens in Northwest Germany, too, who engaged chiefly in business, although among them were numerous lawyers and public officials. To these belonged Peter Heinrich Mencke, historian of the family and head of the clan up to the time of his death in 1873. Of his two daughters, one, Anna (b. 1858), still occupies the house built by him in Oldenburg. The other married the sugar merchant Carl Lagemann of London, who came to New York in 1915; here his wife died in 1922. Of four sons, but one survives; he is a merchant in Holland.

IV

The Mencken arms are: Azure, a linden tree between two roebucks rampant, all proper; crest: a demi-roebuck on a helmet affrontée; wreath and mantling of the colors. These arms belong to the Leipzig branch. They are to be found on various engraved portraits, as well as in a stained-glass memorial window in the Thomaskirche, Leipzig, directly under Johann Sebastian Bach's choir-gallery, to the greater joy of the music-loving Baltimorean. The Mencken arms have varied, however, even as has the name. The original Oldenberg coat-of-arms showed squirrels instead of roebucks,—one on each side of the linden tree and another squatting upon the helmet that capped the tree. Many reproductions, especially those of smaller scale and on seal-rings, lack the helmet, and the third squirrel sits upon the edge of the shield, flanked by flowery garlands. Dr. Conrad Müller,[1] for the allegorical significance of the shield, goes back, as in

[1] *Op. cit.* page 23.

CHART OF VARIATIONS IN THE MENCKEN COAT-OF-ARMS

Prepared by Dr. Stephen von Stradonitz of Berlin, expert in heraldry. The primitive form seems to have been abandoned at a very early date for the Oldenburg form, which appears upon all the graves at Oldenburg. The animal is a squirrel; the tree is a linden. The Leipzig arms first appear toward the end of the 17th century. The animal is a roebuck. This form appears upon the Mencken memorial window in the Thomaskirche at Leipzig, and upon all surviving documents of the Leipzig Menckens, including engraved portraits. Why the change was made is unknown. In a few cases the Leipzig arms show does instead of bucks. The form in the lower right-hand corner is rare. The animal there, also, is supposed to be a deer. The motto used with all forms of the arms has always been "Wartet und Eylet"—i. e. "Make haste slowly."

Luderus Menckenius,
ICtus, Consiliarius Regis Polon. et Electoris Sax.
Suprem. Cur. Provinc. Asesor Primar. Canonicus Martisburg.
Decretal. Professor Publ. Facult. Jurid. Ordinarius et reliqua.
Nat. Oldenburgi d. 14 Decembr. 1658. Denat. Lipsia d. 29 Junij 1726.

DR. LUDER MENCKEN (1658-1726)

Professor at Leipzig and Rector of the University.
Great-great-great-great-great-great grandfather of H. L. M.

the case of the name, to the family motto. This is found as early as 1683, on the memorial tablet to Eilard:

𝔚artet un𝔡 eylet.
𝔈hren 𝔊e𝔡ächtnis
𝔥errn M. Eilhardi Menckeni,
𝔈rt𝔷 𝔓riester 𝔷u 𝔐arienw.
un𝔡 𝔯iesen𝔟.

♦   ♦   ♦   ♦   ♦   ♦

𝔳on ao 1641 𝔟iss 1657
aufgerichtet
ao 1683

"Make haste slowly." The rooted tree indicates the slowness and sureness, as does the seated squirrel; the rampant squirrels symbolize the liveliness and haste. Variations of the Leipzig branch carry out the same idea with different animals. Deer replace the squirrels, as do also does later, and later still, antlered roebucks. It is these golden, graceful roebucks that shine out from the azure background and beside the green linden of the Leipzig arms in the Thomaskirche.

The latest commentator upon the arms of the Mencken family points out that dogs, too, appear in some of the variants.[1]

---

[1] See *Bibliothek familiengeschichtlicher Arbeiten.* Heft 1. *Beiträge zur Ahnentafel des Fürsten Bismarck.* 1. Stephan Kekule von Stradonitz. *Über das Wappen der Mencken.* Leipzig, 1925.

CHAPTER THREE

The Menckens in America

I

BURKHARDT LUDWIG MENCKEN, grandfather of the Baltimore writer, was born, June 7, 1828, at Laas, in Saxony, between Dresden and Leipzig, on the small paternal estate. As we have seen, he was early given into the hands of one Berger, from whom eventually he received a certificate of proficiency in business. When, on November 1, 1848, he landed upon the shores of these United States, he came, not like the immigrant of legend and of later days, poor and unbefriended. On the contrary, he had with him Berger's diploma and something more substantial in the shape of 500 Thalers. Our Baltimore Mencken, perhaps reading into the immigrant some of the notions that have made H. L. anathema to so many of his countrymen, would have it that his grandfather could foresee for Germany a long siege of political mountebankery and turmoil; that, lacking all taint of democratic notions and being filled with an adventurous spirit that informed many of the younger Germans of his day, he sought in America a haven of comfort and an amusing spectacle. If the view is suspiciously Menckenian, it is true at any rate that Burkhardt Ludwig took no part in the political events of 1848 in Saxony and that to the end he united to his intense racial pride an uppishness toward the proletariat.

Landing at Baltimore, where there was the nucleus of a German colony, Burkhardt, with his knowledge of the tobacco business, was soon seated at a cigar-bench. Learning the language as he rolled cigars, he very soon opened up a general store of his own, where he sold groceries, with a few barrels of whisky in the inevitable back room. In those days Baltimore was as much the city of cows as Brooklyn was of goats; in Burkhardt Mencken's section the bovine was such a frequent spectacle that the quarter was named the *Kuhviertel*. The man prospered, for he early gave up his general store and went back, this time as a wholesaler, to tobacco.

Under his personal supervision the business grew. He would go himself to York and Lancaster counties in Pennsylvania, from which most of his cigar tobacco came, and buy the crops of the Dutch farmers in the field. Then, after the yield had been harvested and cured, he would bring it to Baltimore, there disposing of it in the local market or exporting it. With the rise of Key West as a cigar town, he found a new market for his Pennsylvania leaf. The manufacturers of Florida were chiefly Cuban and the cigars, like the place itself, were considered Cuban as well, therefore imported and therefore superior to the domestic brand. Yet not a little of the tobacco in the supposedly superior product came, thanks to old Mencken, from the unromantic fields of the Pennsylvania Dutch.

As our own Mencken was a precocious child of twelve

at the time of his grandfather's death, and as Burkhardt
Ludwig withdrew from active participation in his business
long before his death in 1891, we have from the grandson some rather vivid reminiscences of the crotchety
fellow. With a spacious home in West Fayette Street,
he rejoiced in the possession of some twenty grandchildren. He shared the frolicsome, even tricksy predilections of earlier and later Menckens. With his one-seated
carriage, which he always drove himself, he would set
out upon a round-up of the children, squeezing one into
the space on either side of him, setting another on the
hassock at his feet, and stowing as many as three or four
upright in the space behind the seat. Off he would drive
at break-neck pace over the cobblestoned streets of the
city, and then, the ride over, he would dump his cargo
into his vasty rooms for games and pillow fights and
forays upon the larder.

He had first married in 1851; his wife, Harriet Mc-
Lelland, was sixteen at the time and had come to Baltimore from Kingston, Jamaica. Her family derived
from the North of Ireland, and into the Mencken strain
she brought Scotch and English blood. After bearing
five children, she died of tuberculosis. Burkhardt Ludwig then married a German widow, Caroline Gerhardt
(Belz) and they had one child. Of these six children,
all but Mencken's father are still living.

The old man was, with himself and others, a disciplinarian, presiding over the American Menckens with the
dignity and the wilfulness of a Biblical patriarch. He
affected a long-tailed black coat and archaic collars; when
these disappeared from the shelves of the stores they

had to be made for him by one of his daughters. Every day, punctually at three, he would arrive at his home, hang up his hat and stick in the hall and proceed at once to the table. He must have his soup at just such and such a temperature, neither more nor less. Dinner over, he must have his nap, and then farewell to business for that day.

When one of his grandchildren fell ill, he must be notified; indeed, with his plentiful personal notions as to the origin, nature and treatment of infantile ailments, he all but cured them. He had chosen their names for them; he would superintend their education. As the eldest son of the eldest son, little Henry Louis was of special interest to his grandfather. Once, displeased with the barber's work, the old man seized young Mencken and proceeded to do the job himself.

As with his grandchildren, so was he with his own offspring. At the family councils he ruled his sons with an iron hand; there was murmuring, but no open mutiny. The man had a family pride which, in his grandson, has taken the form of an intense genealogical curiosity. He belonged to none of the German organizations of the city. The wealthier Germans, who formed a close social corporation, he regarded with scorn—despite his own origin—as Low Germans. The poorer element he looked down upon as helots. Between his dislikes he steered, then, a lonely middle course.

His political affiliations seem to have been lukewarm. Although lameness, due to a broken leg, prevented him from serving in the Civil War, his sympathies went toward the South; for a time after the war he was thus a Democrat. Under the influence of his sons he later swerved to high tariff Republicanism, but in neither case was anything deeper than expediency involved. His agnosticism he transmitted to at least one of his sons and to the eldest son of that son. The American Menckens, indeed, on the masculine side, fall distinctly away from the religious preoccupations of the Oldenburg and Leipzig forbears. Burkhardt Ludwig, on this score, was amiably disputatious, especially when the beer was freely flowing. He had a number of clerical intimates, including an Episcopal rector and a couple of Catholic brothers, and despite his marked convictions, maintained very friendly relations with the men of the cloth. He was, moreover, one of the founders of the Loudon Park Crematory in Baltimore, though, by amusing irony, objections from the distaff side prevented the cremation of his own body.

II

August Mencken, father of Henry Louis, was born at Baltimore on June 16, 1854, and died there on January 13, 1899. His mother, first wife of Burkhardt Ludwig, died when her child was yet a youngster; between this date and the coming of the second wife intervened a period of domestic readjustment that seems to have brought out the harsher elements in the men of the household. From the very beginning, the first-born showed interest in and aptitude for his studies. At Walker's, an old time private school, he did particularly well in mathematics. For this he must have had a natural predilection, since, although he left school in his early

54

'teens and never had any further formal training, he retained his fondness for figures throughout life. Years later, when his own first-born was being initiated into the mysteries of quadratics and the binomial theorem, Mencken père would challenge the boy, offering to perform by simple arithmetic any problem set him in algebra. Usually, too, he would succeed, by some method of his own which he called "averages."

As a youth, August Mencken does not appear to have participated in any adventures more exciting than his occasional trips, *via* the Conestaga wagons, to York and Lancaster counties, Pennsylvania. These were not made, as one might imagine, in company of his father to the tobacco fields, but with a dealer who collected eggs and butter on the way. The round trip, which took a week, was always a path of pleasure for the youngster, who gloried in the life along the road and in the good cheer of the country inns at which they stopped.

Reaching his middle 'teens, August naturally gravitated into the paternal tobacco business. A couple of years' service at the bench, learning the trade from the ground up, was interrupted by a journeyman's tour, with a short stay at Parkersburg, West Virginia. Returning to Baltimore he considered the establishment of a place of his own and, accordingly, in 1875, we find him at the age of twenty-one boldly setting up together with his eighteen-year old brother as "August Mencken & Bro." The cash capital of the new concern was exactly $35. Just why they should not have applied for paternal aid in the venture is conjectural; perhaps the explanation is to be sought in one of the domestic disputes of those unsettled days. The younger brother, who, as a child, in defiance of his father had chosen his own times for going to school, now assumed the sales management; August Mencken ran the factory, and the business was successful from the start. The firm, luckily, had run into the Baltimore boom. The South, beginning to recover from the war, needed goods; it was without factories of its own and there were few wholesalers. For the next twenty years Baltimore enjoyed a virtual monopoly of the trade, and August Mencken & Bro. came in for their share. By the middle '80's the original capital of $35 had grown, in Bradstreet's, into "more than $100,000 first credit." The firm now put up a factory in Baltimore, established several tobacco warehouses at strategic points, and assumed a foremost position in the Southern trade.

In November, 1879, August Mencken married Anna Margaret Abhau, of Baltimore, the daughter of Carl Heinrich Abhau, who had emigrated from Hesse-Cassel in 1848. She was born in Baltimore, in 1858, of Eva Gegner. The Gegners, up to the time of the first railroads in lower Bavaria, had operated coach lines there; the new invention ruining their business, they came over to the United States *en masse* and settled near Baltimore. With business growing steadily, Mencken, in 1883, bought a newly built house in Hollins Street. In less than seven years he added to his real estate a summer house near Mt. Washington, some five miles from the city, where the family lived from May to September. His interests were by no means confined to tobacco and commerce. Like his father before him, he was fond of driving his own carriage; his own boys acquired their father's love of horses and early had a Shetland pony with a cart and a buggy for it. Thus from his boyhood, Henry Louis has learned to love and take care of horses, to drive them and to know them. Perhaps somewhere in these childish hours is rooted his aversion for the automobile, which, however, he explains on far more rational grounds.

Mencken père and his brother were moreover fond of sports. For a short time, indeed, they were part owners of the Washington Baseball Club. Thus, as a boy, Henry enjoyed the privilege of close contact with such palestral magnificos as the pitcher, Kilroy, and Sam Trott, the veteran catcher. Combining business with pleasure, August Mencken named a cigar after the popular pitcher and got the popular catcher to sell it. So great was the success of this stroke that Trott, up to the time of his death in June of 1925, was in the cigar business. One can imagine the envy with which the kids of Baltimore regarded their so much more fortunate companion, Henry. On Sundays, when his father would receive the ball-players and the magnates, there would be a crowd of juvenile hero-worshippers at the back gate to get a peep at the celebrities. Henry and his brother, by opening the gate sufficiently wide for the throng to catch a glimpse of these gods, won immense popularity in the neighborhood.

The American Menckens, a practical, hard-headed lot, made first-rate business-men. Both August Mencken "and brother" were shrewd, hard traders, with a strong sense of personal honor to offset the occasional harshness of their methods. They paid cash; they avoided debts. August, moreover, was by nature a manager of men. He knew cigars and cigar-makers. Simply by smoking a cigar he could tell exactly what varieties of leaf had gone into the blend. Like his father before him, he bought his tobacco in the field,—in Wisconsin, Ohio, Pennsylvania, Connecticut, Florida and Cuba. When he was at home, he inspected every cigar that left his place. This was before the days of machine-made products or girl laborers. At the height of his prosperity, when his men, in answer to the agitation of the Knights of Labor, went out on strike, he retaliated by operating a closed shop. Although he paid union wages, he refused to deal, inside or outside, with any walking delegates. Here, as in a number of other important instances, he seems to have prefigured the attitude of his son, although in each case the Mencken of *Men Vs. the Man* has set his prejudices upon a pedestal of reasoned opposition.

The panic of 1893, which prostrated the South, came near wiping out the firm of August Mencken & Bro. A fire that burned down their factory all but completed the annihilation. Yet, though badly crippled, the concern went on, and was still active and again prosperous at the time of August's death in 1899. It has survived, indeed, to this day, despite young Henry's employment in it for a time. Though the old firm name is retained, the property, at the time the senior member passed away, was acquired by his partner.

III

To his father Mencken owes so many traits that we are well repaid by a glance at the paternal idiosyncracies and inconsistencies.

Thus, the man who had inherited from his own father a strong sense of family pride could none the less register the family coat-of-arms as a trade mark and use it as a label upon every box of cigars that left his factory.[1] No more than the somewhat testy Burkhardt Ludwig could he brook the too social type of German; he had an aversion for clubs and associations, yet he belonged to the Freemasons and marched in Shriners' parades. With his swarthy complexion and medium height, somewhat thick-set, he looked more the Celt than the Teuton. Indeed, his mother had known only English; in his father's house English was, even after the death of the first wife, the household tongue. So that he did not speak German, any more than do his children. A pronounced agnostic, he yet went occasionally to church under mild compulsion and all his four children, including the Baltimore Anti-Christ, were duly baptized. Ludwig Burkhardt could differ most amicably with the clergy over a bottle of beer that mollified if it did not drown all theological ire. August Mencken's dislike of the reverend gentlemen was contempt as well.

He loved a good German meal, German beer, and a good tune. A bad player himself on the fiddle, he must

---

[1] The armorial bearings have been restored to something like their former splendor. They now are embossed upon the covers of the series of *Prejudices*.

nevertheless have had something to do with his son Henry's early musical proclivities. He loved, too, a good joke, particularly if it were of the practical variety, with a touch of cruelty to it; both the cruelty and the humor he passed on to the cruel humorist of Hollins Street. When, for example, August Mencken bought the summer home at Mt. Washington, and was asked by curious folk what he intended to name the house on the crest, he replied "Pig Hill." And for a time it was really believed by the community that he was planning to cover the slope with sties and raise blooded hogs. One can hardly blame his fellow citizens, for he actually had an architect draw up plans for a piggery *de luxe,* with a steeple, and made application at the county town to build it. He even went to the extent of inventing a mythical brother, Fred, who was supposed to have scandalized his father by taking to the pulpit. As the hoax aged the brother rose in dignity, until he became a bishop, and there are still persons in Baltimore who ask occasionally after the eminent prelate. H. L., however, has ended Fred's career. "He was slain in Abyssinia" is his answer to the latest inquiries.

Cards Mencken père detested; checkers he liked so well that he had a special table made for the game. Jewelry he affected to abhor, yet he wore a seal ring, a diamond stud and a massive Masonic watch-charm. Henry Louis himself, for twenty years, carried his father's huge split-second Swiss watch, with a miniature bell that struck the quarter hours in response to pressure upon a button.

Yet underneath this gaiety, this eccentricity and this

sharpness at trade, lay a more sober personality. In him, after all, flowed the blood of the European Menckenii. He early started to accumulate a library, in which Shakespeare figured chiefly upon the shelf and Mark Twain deeply in his heart. More, in his early days he had cherished a strong ambition to be an engineer; his habits of mind, his adeptness at figures, seemed to point to such a career. Later, when circumstances shunted him off this track, he brought his abilities to bear upon his tobacco business. Becoming his own efficiency expert long before graphs and schedules were inaugurated, he prepared elaborate statistical analyses of his production and costs and methods.

Henry Louis, at the time of his father's death, was going on nineteen. The three other children were sixteen, thirteen and ten, respectively, and still at school. The eldest son was much older than his years; the father, at forty-five, was in his prime, with much of boyish buoyancy. Thus the bridge between them was not too wide, and the boy's knowledge of his father was far more intimate than the usual picture, half unreasoning hatred and half unreasoning idolization, that the normal youngster achieves.

CHAPTER FOUR

*Henry Louis Mencken—Childhood—School-
ing — Creative Gropings — Business —
Death of Father*

I

HENRY LOUIS MENCKEN was born in Baltimore on September 12, 1880. His birthplace, in
West Lexington Street, near Fremont, is still standing.
At that time the neighborhood was predominantly German and somewhat heavily respectable; today it is composed chiefly of cheap lodging houses. When little
Henry was three years old his father bought the house
at 1524 Hollins Street, fronting Union Square, where
the writer, his mother, sister and younger brother
reside to this day. Forty-two years ago it had just been
completed, as part of a row,—a typical Baltimore house
of red brick, with marble front steps and trimming.

At the time of Henry's birth, August Mencken was
26 and his wife, 22. Mrs. Mencken, a slight, very youthful looking mother, was the marvel of the neighborhood;
how could this slip of a girl have been blessed with so
husky a baby, and a normal case at that? At 14 months,
the talkative tot was walking; a chubby child he was and
grew apace. His early clinical history presents no ab-

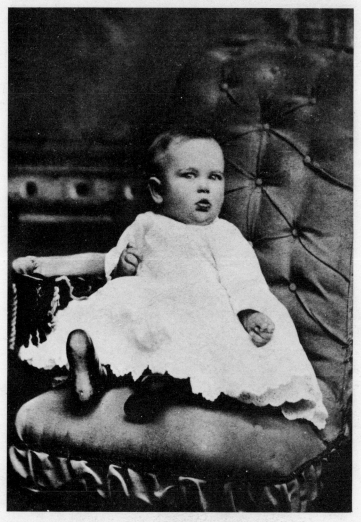

FIRST PORTRAIT
FEBRUARY, 1881, AET. 6 MONTHS

HOUSE AT 1524 HOLLINS STREET, BALTIMORE,
OPPOSITE UNION SQUARE

normalities; he had the measles and the chickenpox, yet managed to escape such childhood banes as whooping cough, scarlet fever and diphtheria, which were then almost epidemic in the city. Later he was to be troubled time and again with respiratory ailments especially, and it is possible that the environmental origin of these is to be found in the marshes that used to be situated just outside of Baltimore. Certain winds blew in mosquitoes that carried malaria; Mencken acquired the affliction in boyhood, suffered acutely for more than a year, and cured it only after heroic doses of quinine sulphate in dilute sulphuric acid. A sour beginning for a loyal disciple of the Oracle of the Bottle! "A dreadful drink," as he still remembers, "but I managed to get it down."

Mencken's first playground was the back yard of 1524. Next door was a house in the same row, which had been bought by his uncle, who had a son slightly younger than Henry. Then there was Henry's brother Charles, twenty months his junior. Together they romped among the peach trees, the pear and the plum, or played with the Negroes who lived in the houses huddled down the block, in the alley behind the garden. Here the brothers shared their pony, which rejoiced in a little stable all its own; here mama Mencken raised strawberries, flowers and vegetables, while Mencken père planted grape vines, two of which are still in bearing. Here, too, young Henry, whose interest in gardening never developed, confined his horticultural activities to spading the ground in spring. He did, one time, attempt to become a tobacco-planter; he even succeeded in raising a crop, but it proved savorless.

To the first-born the yard was the scene of far more interesting adventures. He laid railroads down from end to end; he manufactured telephones of tin-cans and cotton thread; he sailed boats on miniature lakes. With his brother he went a-hunting birds in the trees, but never brought one down with his air-rifle. Live-stock was added in the shape of rabbits, guinea-pigs, frogs, lizards, turtles, a goat. Even now there is a family of land tortoises in the yard, with whom H. L. spends playful moments while the less imaginative oldsters of his scorn drive gutta-percha spheres over the hills and dales of the golf-course.

In 1888, Mencken's father and uncle had rented jointly, for the summer, a double-house on an estate called The Vineyard, at Ellicott City, ten miles from Baltimore. The delightful place left a lasting impression upon the boy. With his younger brother, his cousins, and the little sons of the Reuss widow, to whom the estate belonged, Mencken would play upon the slopes of the high hill that commanded a beautiful view over the gorge of the Patapsco River. There was a ruined mill to thrill the explorers; there was the varied life of farm and countryside, where wild things were to be caught and trees and flowers studied in their native surroundings. Here were berries to be picked and gargantuan belly-aches to be had. Here, too, Mencken felt in him the first urge to become a journalist. The Ellicott City *Times*, still run off on a hand-press, so captivated the boy that for next Christmas he demanded a printing outfit and straightway began to issue a paper of his own. By coincidence, the foreman then in charge of the *Times*,

Josh Lynch, later served as assistant foreman on the Baltimore *Herald,* after Mencken had risen to the managing editorship of that daily.

The simple beauty of the Patapsco River must have thrilled the imagination of the boy quite as much as had the sight of a newspaper being run off the press, for among his earliest drawings is one made of a scene on that stream. The copy book that he took with him on these excursions reveals an intense activity in his eleventh and twelfth years, just before he was visited by the first of his musical inspirations. There are carefully-drawn replicas of the models provided; there is a still-life representing fruit in a dish, quite in the manner, as he now avers, of the early Cézanne; another water-color, most uncertain as to hue, is intended to depict Sunset, although a pencil version has been labeled "Gwynn's Falls." Best of the pencil drawings preserved, however, is the "Scene On The Upper Patapsco"; here the line, especially for a child, is firm and economical; the construction is simple and effective; the total impression, in a word, is that of something truly seen.

In 1890, as we have seen, August Mencken bought a summer house at Mt. Washington. This, too, was on a high hill, and overlooked the Jones Falls Valley. From the veranda there was an unimpeded view up-country for ten or twelve miles, while on summer nights the lightning could be seen as far as Pennsylvania. The nearest of the three other houses on the hill was occupied by an old friend of Mencken *père,* C. C. Lürssen, who had come from Bremen and owned a cigar-box factory. His four sons at once became so close with the younger

Mencken as to be considered brothers rather than neighbors. They played ball on a hayfield rented from the owner at $15 per year (today the field is part of the Baltimore Country Club golf course). They fell heir to the uniforms of an unsuccessful baseball team organized by Mencken's father and Mr. Mattfeldt, who lived just beyond the Lürssens. This made baseball fanatics of the kids, and when the Baltimore Orioles, with John J. McGraw as one of their stars, captured the pennant, the rest of the city went wild as well. In these games, Mencken, who was a fast runner and therefore good on bases, played short-stop; at times he pitched. He was a poor hitter, however, and never learned to throw the ball. School seemed to weaken him; at any rate, his endurance became low, and as a pugilist his record sank almost to zero. There were compensations. Though today Mencken can remember only that she wore a red jersey, it must have been sweet to feel the tender ministrations of his first girl, after the heat and blood of his childhood battles. "She assuaged my wounds. I recall nothing else about her." Nietzschean reward for Nietzschean function!

There was fishing in the stream called Jones' Falls, and in Lake Roland, two miles away. There were bicycling, pony-riding, and hiking. On one eventful day they covered twenty-eight miles. There was kodaking; Mencken became enthusiastic over the art of photography. He subscribed for all the photographic magazines of the day.

In the city there were fire-engines to follow, and gangs to fight. Mencken's loyalties were pledged to Engine

PORTRAIT TAKEN IN 1883, AET. 3

Taken in October, 1888, aet. 8

14, with headquarters three blocks up Hollins Street hill.
The gang that followed Engine 10 was composed mainly
of boys whose fathers worked at the Mt. Clare shops of
the Baltimore & Ohio Railroad. A tough bunch they
were; young Mencken, wandering alone into their
jealously guarded territory, never failed to arm himself
with a club. The No. 8 boys, though not so bad, required watching none the less. On election nights it
was the bounden duty of the various gangs to light a
bonfire and guard its flames with vestal vigilance from
the pollution of their rivals. At these vigils Mencken
won his spurs. To be sure, the hoodlums of No. 10, at
one eventful blaze, might descend upon the 14's with an
Assyrian rush and make off with every box and barrel that had been accumulated for the celebration; nay,
they would even ransack the pyre and carry off flam-
ing trophies. At the next election, however, the 14's
would be heavily armed, ready to repel the wildest assault.

On cobblestoned streets unscarred by trolley or automobile, and offering stout resistance to impatient wag-
goners, the boys played ball, leap-frog (called *par* in
Baltimore), catty, run-a-mile and the other games of
childhood. They spun tops on the cement walks, clat-
tered on roller skates and, later, rode bicycles. They
walked the tops of the backyard fences, jumped out of
stable hay-lofts, and stole potatoes off the stands of the
neighborhood grocers. Then down to the romantic
alleys, where they would roast their potatoes and go
delving for treasure in the exciting possibilities of the
ash-cans. They would hang about the livery-stables,

getting to know the colored hostlers and finding pleasure in helping them at their work.

Stretching westward for a mile toward the town of Calverton was Steuart's Hill, where the youngsters played real baseball, not the "one-two-three" of Hollins Street. Here, on a lonely walk, young Mencken was once held up by three amateur thugs and relieved of his handkerchief and his pocket-knife. The three cents found on Henry they returned; taking the money, as they explained with a sanctimoniousness that Mencken has often riddled in his later career, would be stealing. It was in vain that he reached home, collected his gang, and set out for the Hill to apprehend the highwaymen. They were not to be found; besides, Mencken, as he recalls the episode, felt a distinct, if unboyish, sympathy for the robbers.

The town of Calverton thrived on its stockyards and slaughter-houses. At its hotel the Baltimore youngsters could catch glimpses of "romantic cattlemen in three-gallon hats"; then there was the gully behind the ab-batoirs, running with waste and blood. The place was christened The Canyon, and in this gulch, invested by the kids with a rare glamour of romance, Mencken smoked his first cigarette. If you had the price, you could buy them at two for a cent; if you hadn't, there were dried grape-leaves with which you could "roll your own." Fecund vine, that bred both the revels of Bacchus and the allurements of Lady Nicotine! But, as Mencken avers, he was no smoker in his nonage, "save for a brief period of daring. When I began to smoke at last, at 16, it was at the suggestion of my father. He said that, since I was to spend my life in the tobacco business, I had better learn something about tobacco. My first smokes I made myself, in his factory. They were made of the best Havana leaf. A curious beginning! My father, of course, assumed that I was using far less expensive material." To these days, too, goes back the boy's initiation into Spanish, which his father thought would be useful in the cigar business.

For holidays, which meant for the most part, Sundays, there were visits, in company of his father and his uncle, to the Western Schützen Park, or to the old-fashioned German beer-gardens in West Baltimore. The children would be given sarsaparilla and pretzels, and Mencken has computed that before he had reached his tenth year he must have consumed at least 5,000 of the salty knots. In the shooting-park, besides the clay-pigeons, was a dancing pavilion where, at times, the German music teachers would show off their prodigies. Mencken still retains the memory of an afternoon on which an old fellow sat beside a timorous little girl in pig-tails, tapping her knuckles with a long lead-pencil every time she struck a false note.

II

The schooling of Henry Louis had begun in his sixth year. Just before his birthday in September of 1886 he had been enrolled in the private school of Friedrich Knapp, known as Knapp's Institute and situated in the center of the city, directly opposite the City Hall. It was a good two miles from Hollins Street; yet, after being taken there the first day together with his cousin, Pauline

Mencken, by his father and uncle, the children were allowed thereafter to make the journey by themselves on the horse-car. On the first eventful day of their lone trip they got off at the right street, but made a wrong turn and were soon lost, until a policeman showed them the way. Two years later the Institute was moved to Hollins Street, six blocks away from 1524.

Knapp was an old-fashioned pedagogue, stern but not cruel. He had valid ideas of his own. The day was begun with songs, usually German Volks-lieder, which he would lead with his violin. In this way Mencken acquired a full repertory that still remains with him. The fellow was a strict disciplinarian. Every morning he passed his pupils in review. They would be lined up and their hands and shoes carefully scrutinized. Dirty hand? Then it was clouted into cleanliness. Dirty shoes? A tattoo upon the backside. The atmosphere was military. At the command *Eins!* up flew all hands into the air. At *Zwei!*, arms thrust forward from the shoulder. *Drei!* Fingers touch ankles. Then came the fun. There were times when three or four offenders were ranged in a row and fanned in concert with a single swoop of the long rattan.

Knapp had, among his impedimenta, a room full of imposing physical appliances that were exhibited to visiting parents. The pupils, however, never got an opportunity to know what the machines were about. There were stuffed birds and other such scenery, to make the place look like a cave of learning. Yet it was old Knapp who first introduced into this country the system of lip-reading for deaf mutes. Under him, as his staff, were his son,

Willie; his daughter, Bertha; and his niece, Elvira. There were also a Pennsylvania fellow named Fox, who commanded the admiration of his pupils despite frequent evidence of too generous imbibing; Boynton, and Paul, a teacher after Knapp's own heart—and head—who soaked his handkerchief in cologne and delivered Socialistic harangues to his charges. Rods were not spared here, nor children spoiled. Hour after hour the youngsters were drilled in penmanship, upon which Knapp laid great stress, until Mencken acquired an excellent hand in both English and German.

Fortunately, early reports upon Mencken's progress have been preserved, and we are thus able to follow the child's scholarship from the beginning. The very first report covered the term from September 6, 1886, to December 24 of the same year. It reads:

DEPORTMENT: *Excellent*
INDUSTRY: *Praiseworthy*
ADVANCEMENT: *Very satisfactory*
CLEANLINESS: *Very neat*
ATTENDANCE: *9 days absent*
LATENESS: *Excusable when late*

Ist recht fleissig und macht gute Fortschritte, added Knapp. Leave out the excellency of the deportment, and you have a fair picture of the man Mencken forty years after.

Henry's reports thereafter attested the same exceptional abilities. To that for the next semester (January 1, 1887, to June 30) we find Knapp's son Willie adding, "A good boy and scholar." To that for the third semester (September 5, 1887, to December 23) the old man appends this panegyric in his native tongue: *Henry's Fleiss und gutes Betragen machen den Lehrern Freude. Macht tüchtige Fortschritte.* Henry, in fact, was among the stars of the Institute. He led in English and in drawing; though he wrote German excellently, his lack of proficiency in the language placed him near the bottom in that subject. This worried and disappointed the old head of the school and he must have felt happy, on one of his final reports, to assure the boy's parents that Henry at long last was making good progress in the language.

At home, Mencken was being educated in music; he began the piano, indeed, at the same time that he was put to school. He still remembers his first instructor, Charles Maass, as an excellent musician; his health was bad, however, and he soon died. For the neighborhood teachers, who followed upon Maass,—all women,—the boy could not entertain this same respect; they knew no music, he felt, and by the time he had been studying four or five years he rebelled against the disagreeable task, whereupon his music lessons came to an abrupt end. There was soon to be a revival of his musical interests, however. His early adventures with books were similarly sporadic. In this he seems to have been precocious, for he was making earnest efforts, by Christmas of 1886, to read the books that had been presented to him. Next year he was actually plowing through a serial, *The Moose Hunters,* appearing in the current issue of *Chatterbox.* Very soon thereafter he hit upon a work that was destined to influence his entire career.

Mencken père, as we have seen, was one of Twain's earliest admirers. In 1884 he had bought, upon publication, *Huckleberry Finn*. Deciphering it two years later, young Mencken naturally encountered vast areas of unintelligible matter, but there were the pictures and an eager imagination to help; Henry managed to get through it before he reached his eighth birthday. In June of 1888 he received *Grimm's Fairy Tales* as a prize at school. When the paternal library failed to stir the youthful reader, who was fast becoming omnivorous in his tastes, he drew upon the resources of the Second English Lutheran Sunday School, or upon those of the branch of the Enoch Pratt Free Library in Hollins Street. It did not take long for Henry to weary of the Sunday-School fare served up on the shelves of the church library. He came one day, however, upon a series of travel books and went through them voraciously. He read every Young Folks' history he could lay hands upon, scorning the so-called boys' books of his years. Getting hold, in 1889, of a volume called *Boys' Useful Pastimes,* by one Professor Robert Griffith, he immediately put his newly acquired technical knowledge to practical use, setting up a carpenter shop in the cellar for the manufacture of all the things that Griffith's book had taught him how to make. For at least two years he pored over its pages, learning the secrets of boat building, furniture construction, steam-engines and what not else.

His journeyings commenced in his tenth year. Early in February of 1891 he was taken, by his grandfather Abhau, on a journey to Ottawa County, Ohio. There was also a side trip to remoter relatives who lived in

Cleveland. For two weeks the impressionable child reveled in the winter work of the farm and gazed, at night, upon the countrymen who came from miles around to see his grandfather and listen to him climb his way up and down the trunk of the family tree. This was Mencken's initiation into the dubious comforts of the sleeping-car; at Pittsburgh, too, between trains, he tasted his first quick-lunch.

Arriving in Washington on the way home, on February 26, they were greeted by a telegram from Baltimore, announcing the death of Mencken's other grandfather. He still remembers coming through Union Square with Grandpa Abhau and seeing a black crepe on the door of 1524. Of the funeral all recollection has evaporated. Not so the memory of a childishly agreeable thought inspired by the token of death. For the next few days there would be no school.

By the time he had left Knapp's Institute, in 1892, Mencken had got through a mass of miscellaneous reading. His mother was one of the original subscribers to the *Ladies' Home Journal,* and took in other magazines; his father brought home the Baltimore *News* and *Sunpaper.* These the child devoured. He struggled valiantly through Dickens; through the complete works of Will Carleton; through Chambers' Encyclopædia; through Lossing's *Our Country;* through the three folio volumes of the Reverend J. G. Wood's *Our Living World;* through a history of Freemasonry; through *Ben Hur;* through all of his father's Mark Twains; through Bellamy's *Looking Backward, Peck's Bad Boy,* Ignatius Donnelly's book on Atlantis. Shakespeare was hardily

tackled; Dante, in the edition illustrated by Doré, re-
pelled the boy,—"naturally," he avers. He has never
been able to read it since. There was no system to the
child's reading, which was chiefly determined by the presence of the books upon his father's shelves. One
cannot help noticing, thus early, a predilection for prac-
ticality, for fact, for humor. In part, of course, this
was outwardly conditioned by the tastes of Mencken's
father, which were reflected in his library. The rest,
however, must have been rooted in the budding personality of the child.

. . . .

From Knapp's Institute Mencken proceeded to the
Baltimore Polytechnic. Why the change from a private
to a public school? Perhaps the municipal institutions
had gained prestige during the six years of the boy's
private tuition. Certainly they had enjoyed no high position in Knapp's esteem; he could think of nothing worse
with which to brand his pupils than the accusation that
they were as stupid and dissolute as a public school student. There were the Lürssen boys, too—they were
already at the Polytechnic, and their influence may have
operated in the choice; it is quite likely that the paternal
leanings toward engineering played no small part in the
selection. Besides, the Polytechnic was then a new
place, recently developed out of the Baltimore Manual
Training School, and was for a time in the public eye.

Thither, then, rode Henry and later his younger
brother Charles, dodging fares whenever possible, or
walking home at times from school, thus saving three

cents each. Charles was two years behind Henry at
the Polytechnic; later he lost a year and dropped back to
three. The youngest of the boys, named after his father, did not finish his course at the same institution; a
spell of ill health forced him to suspend, and he never
returned. Eventually he followed the same profession
that Charles had adopted upon his graduation in 1899:
engineering. Strangely enough, Charles, who had been
rather wayward as a youngster, and seemingly cut out
for anything but the discipline of mathematics, spontaneously chose the career which stood for the frustrated
ambitions of his father. Not until years later did he
learn from Henry of their father's boyhood dream.
Charles Mencken is now a member of the Engineering
Corps of the Pennsylvania Railroad. August Mencken
is engineer for a contracting firm in Baltimore and a
stockholder in it. He has built many miles of state
roads in Maryland.

The principal of the Polytechnic, John W. Saville, a
retired naval officer, was far more devoted to the ladies
than to the technicalities of steam engineering, and soon
paid for his weakness with his position. Yet the boys
thought none the less of him for his all-too-humanness,
and Mencken believes that his influence on the whole was
for the good. The boys must have exaggerated his doings; yet every time he shut his office door the word was
spread that the master was up to his tricks. "It filled
the school with pride in him, and atoned for his morning
Bible reading, which was prescribed by law. All but a
few of the boys regarded this Bible reading as an affront
to their dignity."

Thanks to the intensive, disciplined training at Knapp's, Mencken was a year in advance of the public school boys of his own age at the Polytechnic. Already his critical faculties had been awakened, and he was judging these youngsters harshly against his own measurements. At Knapp's, he recalls, the so-called pure American children were the dunces. It was a German Jew who led a cosmopolitan roster composed of Irishmen, Germans, and a few Frenchmen, Jews and even Cubans. At the Polytechnic, despite his scholastic virtuosity, Mencken was placed in the lowest class because of his deficiency in algebra,—a deficiency which, with the unsolicited aid of one of his teachers, Richard H. Uhrbrock, he was able to make up after hours. Within three weeks, thus kindly tutored, the eager youth went through the year's work and was at once advanced to proper standing.[1] Thereafter, all was plain sailing. The classes were in anatomy, physiology, history, chemistry, German, mathematics and physics; there were also declamation and shop work. For his teachers, however, Mencken could not feel the same respect which that benevolent old tyrant, Knapp, had won. This one talked his charges to death; that one was an eccentric who finally went insane in his classroom, "greatly to the delight of his pupils"; the other, derided by his class of

[1] Mencken has never forgotten this kindness. It was publicly acknowledged in *Prejudices,* Series III, 1922. See article on *Education,* which is built up on the observations and experiences of Mencken's years with Knapp and the Polytechnic pedagogues. Years later when Uhrbrock was still a teacher and the former pupil was a City Editor, Mencken was able to give him assistance in a fight he was waging against the School Board.

hoodlums for raising a bush of black whiskers, wreaked vengeance upon them by turning his room into a shambles; a couple of the men were drunkards; still another Mencken even scorned as knowing less of the subject over which he presided than did this particular pupil. Yet from his Bacchic English teachers Mencken learned two of his most cherished arts,—those of chewing tobacco and savoring English prose.

The high average of Mencken's work is again attested by reports that have been preserved. For the four years of his attendance they ran as follows:

Monthly average for the first year:

ARITHMETIC	95
ALGEBRA	94
ENGLISH	99
PENMANSHIP	82

For the second:

ARITHMETIC	81.4
ALGEBRA	90
GEOMETRY	93
ENGLISH	89.8
HISTORY	92.3
GERMAN	86.6
PHYSIOLOGY	100
PHYSICS	97.1
DECLAMATION	66.8

The marks in physiology and declamation may be significant. To this day Mencken displays a veritably hypochondriacal interest in the body and its functions;

he is, as was his grandfather Abhau, almost as ready to prescribe for physical as for theological ailments. As to public speaking, he has, as I have mentioned, refused golden offers to appear upon the lecture platform. There was shop work in the Polytechnic curriculum, at which young Mencken does not seem to have shone. He carpentered above 80 in sloyd; as a blacksmith, however, he could not strike the anvil for higher than 73.3. The metals did not attract him.

For the third year the marks run pretty much the same as in the second, with the addition of 89.6 in trigonometry and 98.6 in chemistry. German, as of old, was his weak point, with but 73; physiology redeemed him with another perfect mark. The final year maintained the excellence in mathematics; such practical studies as electricity and steam engineering suffered a marked lapse. Yet at the final examinations Mencken attained an average above 96; it broke all records for the Polytechnic. At the Mencken household excitement was at fever pitch. Henry and two other fellows, in the general examination that extended over a fortnight, were running neck and neck for first place, whereat Mencken père, throwing his purse into the ring, promised his son a prize of one hundred dollars if he carried off highest honors. Spurred on by this pot of gold, Henry began a desperate eleventh-hour cram in subjects that were anything but his forte. Thus, the night before the examination in electricity he pored for some seven hours over the text book and amassed such a store of information that next day, to the amazement of the teacher, he passed with a grade of 100. By this *coup*

Mencken clinched not only the hundred, but a gold medal as well. To be sure, much to the indignation of the family, the rules were hurriedly revised so as to retrieve the medal from Henry L. The boy himself, with his accustomed objectivity, found the action just. To cap the climax, who delivered the honorary address at the Polytechnic commencement on June 23, 1896, if not Henry Louis Mencken, today the hater of declamation, condemner of oratory, and mocker of all such as ply the tongue!

So much for secular training. It should be remembered, however, that for all the Laodicean attitude of the Mencken household, Henry Louis had been baptized in infancy. As a boy he was sent to Sunday-School, not so much for religious edification as to provide the family with a few hours' respite from his presence. The first Sunday-School was, as irony would have it, a Methodist one, presided over by a hatter of French extraction named Garrigues, an acquaintance of Mencken père. The music appealed to the boy; he enjoyed it so deeply that he has a long repertory of Methodist hymns to this day, finding pleasure in them still and regarding them as the true folk-music of America. (The estimate is worth more than passing attention, if only because it suggests a corrective to the Indian and Negro theories.) Later in childhood Mencken was transferred to a Lutheran Sunday-School, a Low Church establishment where hymns also rang in the rafters. Strangest of all, the boy followed these lessons in sacred lore until his fifteenth year, and on Palm Sunday of 1895, sporting his first pair of long breeches, he was publicly confirmed.

Far from raising objections, August Mencken attended the ceremony in which his son was inducted into holy living; he was none the less relieved, however, when Henry abandoned the Sunday-School together with his short trousers.

III

The years at the Polytechnic were taken up with other subjects than those rehearsed at school. While such studies as physics, electricity and steam engineering bored the youngster insufferably, the creative fervor of adolescence was in his blood. During his first term he made his first attempt at newspaper reporting, describing by plays a professional game between the New Yorks and the Baltimore Orioles. The early printing-press had given way to the fascinations of the camera, which in turn guided the inquisitive youngster into an enthusiasm for chemistry. He set up a laboratory at home and made good use of it. Too good, in fact, for comfort at the Polytechnic; for, when he enrolled in the chemistry class in 1894, it quickly became evident, to both teacher and pupil, that the student knew more about the science than did the instructor. In this home laboratory, indeed, he had shortly before discovered a new method for toning silver prints with platinum. Carefully he set it down in the guise of a formal article—the first he ever wrote—only to be overcome with shyness when ready to submit the formula to the photographic journals. For Mencken once was shy. Chemistry and journalism were struggling for supremacy in the adolescent's breast; in the article for a moment he united the antagonists. Chemically, however, he had written himself out in this early piece; interest in the practicalities of the science gradually subsided, yet the laboratory was part of the Hollins Street household until as late as 1910. Luckily the article itself was filed away with the carefulness that has distinguished Mencken since childhood. It is thus possible to present, for the first time, the very first formal article written by Henry Louis Mencken. It is entitled

A NEW PLATINUM TONING BATH, FOR SILVER PRINTS

Ever since the introduction of platinum paper, various toning baths have been described in the photographic magazines for giving silver prints the color of the platinotype. The basis of all these has been potassic chloroplatinite—a salt, by the way, which is difficult to prepare—combined with sodic chloride and a weak acid.

But the potassic chloroplatinite is a rather expensive compound, and furthermore, most of the processes are too elaborate to be used by the ordinary amateur, while in one formula, at least, I have seen auric chloride a constituent, which of course makes the bath an ordinary gold toning solution.

Nearly every one knows that gold and platinum are identical metals as far as their chemical properties are concerned, and therefore there is no reason why platinic chloride should not be used instead of the more expensive auric chloride.

Some time ago an article appeared in "Photography," written by Mr. W. D. Welford, describing a gold toning bath containing auric chloride and sodic bi-carbonate, the special feature of which was the comparitively large quantity of the latter salt employed.

ANOTHER PENCIL SKETCH DONE IN 1892

After using this formula and obtaining good results, I determined to try platinic chloride instead of gold.

The chloride of platinum is made by dissolving scrap or sponge platinum or platinum wire or foil in a mixture of hydrochloric acid, 4 parts, and nitric acid, 1 part. Evaporate the solution thus obtained to dryness, then dissolve the brown powder obtained in the smallest possible quantity of water. Evaporate again, and to every ten grams of platinic chloride add $\frac{1}{4}$ oz. water. This is the platinum solution.

The following solution I have found to work best on aristotype paper, particularly Solio.

Take of

Platinum solution	1 dr.
Sodic bi-carbonate	85 gr.
Water	8 oz.

To tone, immerse prints in the foregoing until they are a few shades darker than desired when finished, because hypo bleaches them considerably. They should be printed darker than ordinarily, and require a good washing before and a slight rinsing after toning.

The colors obtained are red, red-brown, brown, brown-black, grey and platinum black, according to the time of toning. A small quantity of aluminum chloride or alum can be added to this bath in warm weather, to prevent the film from melting. Biborate of sodium (borax) can be used instead of the bi-carbonate, but the exact tones cannot be obtained. Fixing should be done with a weak hypo solution (1 to 8, for instance), for if it be too strong, yellowness will result.

Though I have not tried them, I think the chlorides of uranium, iridium, palladium and osmium could be used, since these metals are analogous to gold and platinum.

Like his drawings and his music, this first article is

notable for a simple directness. There is not a superfluous word. There is no attempt at showy adornment. Already the clearness and succinctness of the mature author are present.

Then came the first real sweetheart. At 15 Mencken fell in love with the daughter of a German neighbor,—a fetching little *backfisch,* very blonde as to tresses, very striking as to lineaments. To the three or four years that the tender passion lasted may be attributed not only the reams of poetry that ran from Mencken's pen, but his renewed interest in music. A chaste and virtuous affair it was, yet at this same time, in less glamorous surroundings, the boy was being initiated into the cruder biological realities of sex.

He wrote in school and out of it,—planned comic operas, sonatas, short stories, debates and essays. He had been trying seriously to write since his twelfth year. To these days belong his earliest poems; his first short story, *Idyl,* does not come till his fifteenth year. In the meantime he has received his baptism of print in the Baltimore *American,*—a poem. The comic opera libretto of which notes remain is entitled, perhaps symbolically, *Bluebeard.* The *dramatis personae* and program read as follows:

ALMIRA, *a widow*
FATIMA, *her only daughter*
SALOME, *an orphan, adopted by Almira*
ABDUL HASSAM, *Fatima's lover*
ABDUL SEBA, *Fatima's brother and Salome's lover*
ZADOK, *a slave, attendant upon Fatima and Salome*

BLUEBEARD, *a rich widower*
DANCING GIRLS, SLAVES, SOLDIERS, *etc.*

SCENE: Bagdad

ACT I: A room in Almira's house
ACT II: A hall in Bluebeard's palace
(Between Acts I and II, three days are supposed to have elapsed.)

That word "elapsed"! How dear to the juvenile playwrights; we could never have written without it! And what a thrill it always brought upon a playhouse program! Bluebeard, slayer of wives,—have we not here the progenitor of Mencken's unholy Heliogabalus, who found his mates more to his taste alive in bed than dead in a closet?

In 1895, at the Polytechnic, Mencken wrote the words for a show that was staged by the students. Some of the music intended for *Bluebeard* may have gone into the concoction. At any rate, he played piano in the orchestra and felt the thrill of the librettist leaping across the footlights into the pit. To the projected comic opera of Mencken's youth belong some of the first stanzas that he penned. Here is a fair sample of them; it prefigures some of the hollower vaudevillianism of *Ventures Into Verse:*

> Two tom-cats on a backyard fence
>   Debated, quarreled and sang;
> A window far above their heads
>   Flew open with a bang;
> A bootjack hurtled through the air
>   And by the pair did pass;

A green-house roof below their perch
Lost thirty panes of glass.

Between this sort of stuff and a sonnet that belongs to
1898 is all the difference that stretches between the refined savagery of childhood and the purged passion of
eighteen. Mencken, as we shall see in greater detail,
was falling under the spell of Kipling; yet in the poem
that follows, the clutch of Kipling does not quite succeed
in throttling the song of Shelley. The metrical masculinity of the later Englishman is in these lines; it was
the year of the Spanish-American War. There is, however, a virginal passion that is rarely to reappear in the
author:

SONNET

Like a belated reveller astray,
Laying the ghost of care with ribald song,
The gray old world jolts noisily along,
Waking the night with tumults of the day;
Kings are afield and loyal brasses bray,
Cannon proclaim the lordship of the strong;
Faint in the shouting dies the wail of wrong,
Careless, the clamors of the conflict play;
Loud and insistent, drunken, shrill, profane,
The anguish of eternal sorrow cries;
And yet, to one, the morrow's dawn is fair
And all the road a rose-embowered lane:
I only see the starlight of your eyes,
I only feel the sunlight of your hair.

Were you, today, to point out the intensely poetical
quality of that last line, Mencken as likely as not would

reply, "Yes? A rather interesting example of synæs-thesia."

Music had been Mencken's earliest love in the arts. It is long, for example, since he tore away from the tempting tresses of Erato. In him, poetry as creation, as will appear when we consider his printed collection of verse, has been many years dead. So, despite his juvenile interest in drawing and water-color, is it with the pictorial arts. A fondness for good drawing he still retains, perhaps because it has formed an element of his unceasing activities in journalism. Painting itself, however, attracts him little or not at all, and he is inclined to attribute this blind spot to a deficiency in his response to color. Music, then, alone of his childhood enthusiasms has remained to blend into the harmonies and dissonances of his later career.

The yellowing sheets of his puberal musical manuscripts date back as far as the year 1892. At first there are the marches and waltzes that so fascinate the stumbling beginner in composition. Is not Sousa rising to fame in the United States? And over the water, in the ancestral home, is not Johann Strauss the King of the Waltz,—king, indeed, to this very day and hymned in Mencken's latest writings? The pieces are written in a steady, almost professional hand. A *Two-Step,* belonging to 1892, is firm, if thick, in progress. The *Easy Waltz,* of 1893, is but seven staves in length, trio and all, distinctly German in sway and interval, with a pretty sense of melody. A *March* and some *Waltzes* of the same year reveal the same qualities of simplicity and melodiousness. During the next ten years, in his sporadic ventures into musical composition, Mencken is to suggest the potentialities of a genuine gift. I have two pieces specially in mind: first, the setting to William Watson's poem, *April,* for the lacy words of which Mencken provided a sweet, chirping, girlish melody that seems to wander off somewhere about the middle, to find its way back safe at last. Then there is the uncompleted setting (1903) of his own words from *Ventures Into Verse:* "Ah, what were all the joys that bide in the meadow, mood and down, To me if I were at your side within the joyless town?" Here is a fine, robustious, masculine tune.

These ditties have remained with Mencken. They have followed him into his later musical recreations. In an expansive moment, recalling childhood days, he will hum the tunes in headtones, while his face takes on a genial glow that is not suggested by any of his numerous photographs. Music is at the very fountainhead of Mencken's being. It will haunt him to the end.

Graduation from the Polytechnic brought with it the problem of a career. Was it to be business or college?

Mencken himself had formed a definite ambition: Journalism. Early in his days at the Polytechnic he had become the closest of friends with Arthur W. Hawks, son of a well-known lecturer. Hawks' elder brother, Wells, was at that time a reporter upon the Baltimore *Morning Herald.* With this example to spur them on, the inseparables, upon being graduated from school, made plans to lay siege to the City Editor of the *Herald.* Arthur went straight ahead and was soon at work.

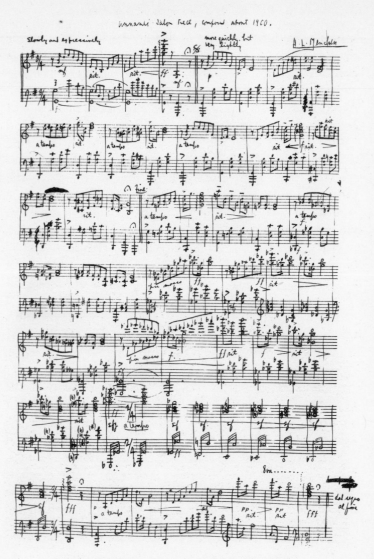

UNNAMED SÄLON PIECE COMPOSED ABOUT 1900

Taken September 12, 1898, on his 18th birthday

As for Henry, he hit against the wall of paternal objection.

Several courses were open. In the first place, the Mencken tradition was legalistic and professorial. Suppose, then, Mencken—only sixteen at time of graduation, and the youngest in his class, which ran to an average of about eighteen years—were to matriculate in the University of Maryland Law School? He needn't practise law; the knowledge would be useful in any business. Or else, there was the Johns Hopkins undergraduate school, which could prepare him for study in Germany. The recent graduate must have been hard to manage. One thing, however, he was determined upon: if he were to go into business, he would have no truck with colleges. His experience at the Polytechnic had not raised teachers very high in his estimation. He had already begun to forget most of what he had studied there. He had learned, moreover, one thing that was not in the courses: that he could acquire more information by his own efforts than he could from instructors. To this day he believes that teaching, once the elemental data have been inculcated, is largely useless. "A boy learns, not from teachers who are adept pedagogues, but from teachers whom he likes and respects and whose subjects interest him. In other words, successful teaching is still done on the master and apprentice plan."

The truth is that Mencken's father did not quite understand him; the alternative proposals made to counter Henry's rejections came but half-heartedly. The upshot of it all was that Mencken stepped, just before his sixteenth birthday, off the platform on which he delivered

the graduation address into the cigar factory of August
Mencken & Bro. The three years in this firm were to
be Mencken's university. Here, he is wont to consider,
began his real education. Here he met the men who
knew the things worth knowing and the books that held
the things worth feeling.

The days at the Polytechnic had already marked the
development of a real system in Mencken's reading.
The discovery of Thackeray completely re-organized his
view of literature. "Here was richness indeed and I
wallowed in the feast. I read the whole of Thackeray
in one winter and then proceeded backward to Addison,
Steele, Pope, Swift, Johnson and the other magnificos of
the eighteenth century." It was one of the disreputables
at the Polytechnic who had awakened Mencken's interest
in Shakespeare, and, with accustomed gusto and thoroughness, the boy went through the whole canon, and
thence to Ben Jonson and the other Elizabethans. At
school Chaucer was appealing only as he fed the porno-
graphic palate; Milton was a bore; Spenser was impossible. But Herrick—there was a likeable fellow, and
when Mencken made his first ventures into verse he
frankly imitated him. Then there was Byron, who sat
complete on the paternal shelves and was soon devoured
by the boy as compensation for dull hours at electricity
and steam. And Macaulay, Fielding, Smollett, Sterne.
George Eliot, Jane Austen and Charlotte Brontë were
passed over contemptuously in favor of Keats and Shelley, Swinburne and Tennyson. Carlyle was abandoned
as soon as met; years after he was to become one of
Mencken's favorites. For the present, however, the

new god was Kipling,—Kipling of *Plain Tales From The Hills,* issued in paper covers by *Once-a-Week,* forerunner of *Collier's Weekly,* to which Mencken père was a subscriber; Kipling of the *Barrack Room Ballads,* which are written all over the *Ventures Into Verse.* Nor was this all. Howells, Stockton, the rising Richard Harding Davis, Stephen Crane and Henry James were added to the list. Huneker was discovered in *The Criterion.* The greatest literary influence of all, however, was late in coming. It was Thomas Henry Huxley.

What the music of Brahms and Beethoven has ever been to the poetry that is hidden deep in Mencken's life, Huxley has been to the more clamorous prose. Huxley co-ordinated in Mencken the vague, disordered unbelief that had come down to him through his amiably irreligious grandfather and his contemptuously, unscientifically atheistic father. With the clearness and beauty of his English, Huxley captivated the youth; with his cogency, the "bulldog of Darwin" transformed Mencken into a violent agnostic. Writing of the great Englishman in *The Evening Sun,* Baltimore, on the centennial of his birth, May 4, 1925, Mencken evokes the youthful ardors of a quarter-century ago in a panegyric that reveals the durable qualities of that influence.

Huxley, I believe, was the greatest Englishman of the Nineteenth Century—perhaps the greatest Englishman of all time. When one thinks of him, one thinks of him inevitably in terms of such men as Goethe and Aristotle. For in him there was that rich, incomparable blend of intelligence and character, of colossal knowledge and high adventurousness, of instinctive honesty and indomitable courage which appears in mankind only once in a blue moon. There have been far greater scientists, even in England, but there has never been a scientist who was a greater man. A touch of the poet was in him, and another of the romantic, gallant knight. He was, in almost every way, the perfected flower of *Homo sapiens,* the superlatively admirable all-around man.

．　．　．　．　．　．　．　．　．　．

All of us owe a vast debt to Huxley, especially all of us of English speech, for it was he, more than any other man, who worked that great change in human thought which marked the Nineteenth Century. All his life long he flung himself upon authority—when it was stupid, ignorant and tyrannical. He attacked it with every weapon in his rich arsenal—wit, scorn, and above all, superior knowledge. To it he opposed a single thing: the truth as it could be discovered and established—the plain truth that sets men free.

．　．　．　．　．　．　．　．　．　．

For Huxley was not only an intellectual colossus; he was also a great artist; he knew how to be charming. No man has ever written more nearly perfect English prose. There is a magnificent clarity in it; its meaning is never obscure for an instant. And it is adorned with a various and never-failing grace. It never struts like the prose of Macaulay; it never simpers like Pater's. It is simple, precise, unpretentious—and yet there is fine music in every line of it. The effects it achieves are truly overwhelming. One cannot read it without succumbing to it.

There were not only books to be read, however. There were cigars to be rolled, and sold. Alternately, then, as he smoldered with resentment at having been balked in his journalistic aspirations, Mencken turned the leaves of his Spencer and Buckle and Froude, and sniffed the more odorous leaves of Havana. The tobacco business was not in itself disagreeable to him. It was bathed, in fact, in an aroma of romantic suggestion that haunts the man even now; the heavy smells of the tobacco warehouse are still ingratiating to his nostrils. The leaf came from distant countries; it was a precious article, to be handled with care. Blending it into cigars had the delicate possibilities that enter into the mixing of drinks. As long as Henry sat at the bench, then, he was happy. The trouble started when he was promoted to the office. At once the glamour and the glee were gone. The young man had not been cut out for figures; keeping the books was drudgery. He made mistakes when he was sent to the bank with checks to deposit; he could not make out his bills correctly. From bookkeeping to salesmanship spelled from bad to worse. Mencken malingered; he detested merely approaching a customer. After a short while as an outside man, he was restored to the office; discontent, however, was in his bones. By the summer of 1898 he had fully made up his mind to escape amicably if possible, but if necessary by open rebellion. He went to his father with the story; Mencken père was so plainly distressed that for the moment Henry dropped the matter.

Not to abandon his hopes entirely, however, he had, early in 1898, enrolled in the Cosmopolitan University, so named from the *Cosmopolitan,* which was edited by John Brisben Walker, founder of the "university." This was one of the earliest correspondence schools in the country. Here, as correctors of his papers, Mencken had Arthur M. Chase and Edward Tyler; as text-book, Genung's *Rhetoric.* Despite his latter-day attitude

93

toward such institutions, Mencken believes that he derived some good out of these lessons. Chase's early advice against the use of "long and pompous words" and in favor of "simple and direct language" was at once adopted by the boy and has ever since been adhered to. Tyler, writing to him on November 28, 1898, showed a seeming prescience in his criticism:

> Your lessons 5 and 6 are very good—indeed, they are as excellent work as we often receive here. Your use of conversational style and of colloquial expressions that prevail in the purlieus of a large city is very skillful.

The reference was to a short story, *An Alley Case*. Before long, Mencken was to be writing and selling a ruck of such tales. For the present, there were his father's wishes to consider.

Mencken's mother, in the silent way that mothers have, saw what was going on. Her unspoken sympathy was with the boy; all along, indeed, it had been, and he feels deeply, if unloquaciously, the part that was played by the observing, taciturn woman. It is possible that, had August Mencken lived, he would have freed his ambitious son from the fetters of office routine. As it happened, he was taken suddenly ill a few days after Christmas of 1898. On January 13, 1899, he died. Mencken, at the age of nineteen, was thus left as the masculine head of the household. The tobacco business, under one of the terms of the partnership, was at once disposed of to the surviving owner. Mencken was free for journalism.

CHAPTER FIVE

*Journalism—Illness and Travel—Printers'
Ink and Scribblers' Beer—Arts on the
Side—Books, Read and Written—A
Leader and a Judge of Men—Profit and
Loss*

I

TWO weeks after the death of his father, Mencken
went to the old *Herald* office and applied for a
job. The Hawks brothers were ready with recom-
mendations, and the late Max Ways, then City Editor,
received him very politely. After a second visit, in
February of 1899, Mencken was accepted for a number
of tentative assignments, Ways adding the practical advice that the boy stick for the present to the tobacco
factory, now owned by uncle Mencken. Henry eagerly
accepted and plunged at once into a hectic career that
quickly undermined his none too certain health. At the
time when his father had been seized with his last illness,
Henry himself lay sick at home. There were few telephones in those days, and the boy was forced to leave his
sick bed and rush out into the winter night on a hunt for
doctors. As a result he caught bronchitis which, under the stress of his combined commercial and journalistic activities, became chronic.

The first assignment was to the suburbs. Reporting

at eight A. M. for work at the factory, Henry remained until five-thirty. Then home for dinner and to change his clothes, and a dash to make the *Herald* office by seven. Again a run for the street-cars, fares paid out of his own pocket; what with the seven dollars weekly that he was drawing at the tobacco factory, this suburban scurrying fast depleted his exchequer. His health, too, for it was often midnight before he reached home. The strain continued for a month or two, seven days a week, and Ways, who was a kind-hearted fellow, felt obliged to suggest the need of Sundays off for a little sleep.

What was all this, however, compared with the thrill that Mencken must have felt to behold his first report in sober type! To be sure, it wasn't much, yet, such as it was in its tiny type, it wrote the date of February 24, 1899, red on the young man's calendar!

At Otterheim Memorial, United Brethren Church, Roland and Fifth Avenues, Hampden, Charles H. Stanley and J. Albert Loose entertained a large audience last night with an exhibition of war scenes by a cineograph.

Curious that his first newspaper item should have been about an evangelical church. Fifteen years later, it is possible, he was prayed for in that very edifice!

By the end of June, pleased with Henry's work on the more important evening assignments, Ways offered the boy a regular job at $8 a week. Mencken, in delight, seized the position and went to work on July 2, 1899.

Stronger than the imagination of the new owner, Wesley M. Oler, the ice king of the city, was the spirit of good fellowship and unanimous belief in the paper that characterized the staff. Oler might burden the columns with his own ideas of news, usually intended to advance his business interests or flatter his friends, whereat the stuff would be marked "ICE" and take precedence over all other matter. The chief editor, Colonel A. B. Cunningham, who had worked with Pulitzer, McCullagh and Cockerill in St. Louis, might be all but reverenced by the rest of the staff for his imposing appearance, his white vests, his swallow-tail coats, his plug hat and hellfire style in editorials, but Mencken seemed to see through this manner into the little matter that it masked.

The man taught his staff more about drink than about their craft. He could give generous parties and get gloriously drunk himself. At such times he would lock himself into his office for a couple of days; his office boy would be forced to climb a chair and pass in sandwiches over the partition.

Of far higher calibre, in Mencken's eyes, was the man who joined the staff later and eventually succeeded Cunningham,—Robert I. Carter, formerly of the New York *Herald*. Here was a cultured, civilized fellow who loved the arts, who knew them intimately, who could keep a cub up half the night listening to talk of music and plays. From him and from the Englishman, W. G. Owst, also of the *Herald* staff when Mencken joined it, the youth caught the contagion of good music; from that time on he haunted the concert halls whenever possible. For a few months, too, his interest in composition must have been revived, for an unnamed Salon Piece was written in 1899 or 1900, much in the style of the classic German waltz, but with an obvious attempt to dazzle the bourgeoisie by its shifting tonalities.

Down to January 20, 1900, Mencken worked for eight dollars a week. Then his market value began its slow but steady rise. Offered a better job by a rival paper, he was raised by the *Herald*. On August 8th, 1900, the salary was, under similar circumstances, raised again; by December it rose another notch; by February 1st of the following year it was $18.

Not content with the heavy work on the *Herald*, Mencken's waxing energies had been seeking new outlets. In the first place, he was reading omnivorously. Nietzsche and Ibsen were swimming into his ken. Just around the corner were Dreiser and Conrad. Stray verse was tripping off his typewriter and being sold as fast as written; later these stanzas were to be garnered from the pages of the *Bookman,* the *New England Magazine,* the *National Magazine* and chiefly from the columns of the Baltimore *Herald,* to make up the slender book of *Ventures Into Verse.*

Outside money was coming in by devious routes. Upon the opening of the New Baltimore Court-House in January, 1900, Mencken was commissioned to write the text of the souvenir book, for which service he received $25. Later in the year Lew Dockstader came to town and had the young reporter prepare for interpolation in his minstrel show some local stanzas for his comic songs. The audience at Ford's Opera House rocked with merriment at the allusions and Mencken, hidden in the throng, gave himself up to a huge authorial delight.

Then, more in line with the chosen profession of the youth, there was corresponding for out-of-town papers. By the rules of the newspaper game a periodical will pay for telegrams from a reputable journalist suggesting a story and giving an outline of the facts. Mencken, with a ready nose for news, kept the wires busy with his telegrams. His very first customer was the Philadelphia *Inquirer,* in 1899. Before long it appeared that there was too much work and not enough money in the telegram business, and Mencken turned therefore to Sunday feature articles. These would be set up in the *Herald* office, presented to that paper in return for supplying the proofs, and then sent out to prospective purchasers. In this way seven or eight dollars would be added to the weekly income. There was less profit in corresponding for such Far East newspapers as the Colombo *Observer,* the Kobe *Chronicle* and the Hong Kong *Free Press.* For this service the only payment was a subscription to the periodicals; now and then a news item in them was sold by Mencken to the American press, but the income from this was never considerable. In those days, for the youth, there was romance in things that came from far-off places. This had been true of his interest in the tobacco industry; it lay behind his foreign correspondence, too.

He was nothing if not versatile. He sold jokes to syndicates; he did odd jobs for advertisers; he composed a pamphlet setting forth with undying eloquence the advantages of an eternity spent in the commodious quarters of the Loudon Park Cemetery; he put together the pamphlets of a piano-manufacturer, of a milk-dealer, of the United Fruit Company.

An ambitious novel was on the hooks, with none other than Shakespeare as the principal character. In it Mencken planned to show the playwright as a young man at large in London; after he had typewritten a couple of chapters he gave it up because he knew too little about London of that period. Then there were occasional articles for out-of-town newspapers. The first of these, inspired by Jerome K. Jerome's *Stageland*, was one on *The Stage-Reporter*, and was printed in the New York *Telegraph* of February 14, 1900. When L. J. DeBekker, then a reporter on the Baltimore *American*, organized a syndicate to supply material for Sunday newspapers, Mencken was taken in as its star writer; his first syndicate article, dealing with celebrated escapes from prison, thus appeared in all the subscribing newspapers on March 4, 1900. During all this time he was doing features for the Sunday edition of the *Herald*. It is hardly surprising, then, that the strain should begin to tell on him.

In the spring of 1900 he was losing weight rapidly, and his bronchitis had developed into a nasty cough. The doctor feared that he might contract tuberculosis and advised a trip to the Bahamas or the West Indies. This, together with a reading of Lafcadio Hearn's *Two Years in the French West Indies*, determined him. He started for the Bahamas, missed the boat, and, discovering that he could manage the projected voyage in no more convenient fashion, he shipped on a British banana-boat bound for Jamaica. With the connivance of the captain, he deserted at Port Antonio. For a month or more he remained on the island, spending part of the time in bed and when he returned on a Danish tramp he was still ill. Making up his mind that he was doomed to an early death he resolved that his stay should be as merry as short. He plunged into newspaper work more arduously than ever, smoked to great excess, and took to drinking beer. Pursued by paradox, from the moment he gave himself up as lost, he began to improve.

There was the Stevedore's Club, which had been meeting nightly since 1899 in a saloon opposite the City Hall, and had been so named because its members were engaged in the business of unloading schooners. It could not have been a very harmful den, for at most the reporters and musicians who foregathered there at midnight would stow away a lunch and a few glasses of beer. It was enough, however, to make the first proprietor, Frank Junker, a hotel owner; and when he left, his successor, Funk, easily came to terms with the police through the influence of the newspaper men. In return for procuring him immunity from the rigors of a law that forbade the selling of booze after midnight, the men demanded special rates—and got them. Only a nickel for a devilled crab, sir, and not a cent more for a glass of beer, or ale, or porter, with every third glass on the house.

Mencken, who had come home to die, found new life in the newspaper game. Ways worked him hard, but taught him much. He didn't bawl out his reporters; he sent for them, lectured them on their errors and left them wiser than when they came. However heavy the drinking might have been the night before, Mencken turned up sober,—a virtue which at least half of the *Herald* staff could not command. As a result the less inebriate of the faculty were kept on the jump, Mencken with them; there were days when he would total more than 4,000 words in type. Assigned at first to the Southern police district, he made up for his lack of the journalistic snout with such a gift of turning out readable copy that he was soon transferred to the Central, which at that time included Police Headquarters itself. In a few months he was covering the pick of all the assignments, City Hall. Here he remained until he was made Sunday Editor in 1901.

To these days, beyond a doubt, go back his epigrams upon the law and politics and even religion. His shortest lines have thus been born of a rich and varied vital experience. When he writes [1] that "A Sunday-school is a prison in which children do penance for the evil consciences of their parents," he pens the salutary truth out of a childhood background of many years. When he asseverates that "A jury is a group of twelve men, who, having lied to the judge about their hearing, health and business engagements, have failed to fool him," he speaks from an intimate acquaintance with court-house corridors. So, too, he is on equally familiar ground when he steps from corridor into court-room and pronounces the following verdicts:

[1] See—again assuming that you can procure a copy—*A Little Book In C Major,* John Lane, 1916, from which these epigrams are taken. Much of this material was later carried over into *A Book of Burlesques,* A. A. Knopf, 1920.

A judge is a law student who marks his own examination papers.

A lawyer is one who protects you against robbers by taking away the temptation.

Courtroom; a place where Jesus Christ and Judas Iscariot would be equals, with the odds in favor of Judas.

The penalty for laughing in a court-room is six months in jail. If it were not for this penalty the jury would never hear the evidence.

To these days of the Stevedore's Club must hark back such a sad observation as this:

What a world, alas, it is! So many drinking, and so little in a keg!

And when, with the picture of the amateur musician, he illustrates Oscar Wilde's line that "Each man kills the thing he loves" he is as surely aiming at himself as when he adduces hay fever (from which he has suffered for years) in proof of the fact that the Creator is a humorist.

The relevancy of these observations to Mencken's actual experiences is no greater than that of his later books to the life out of which they came. His writings, from the very beginning, take on the quality of what Italians have called *la vita vissuta,*—life truly lived.

Sick as he was, Mencken had kept his eyes open to the main chance, even on the island of Jamaica, and had returned with articles and photographs. The series advanced no further than the third article, for Cunningham objected to the expense of the cuts.

Just prior to his sailing, while still covering the City Hall he had started what would now be known as a column. Interrupted by his sojourn, it resumed its

weekly course on November 4, 1900, under its original
caption: "Rhyme and Reason." In that same issue
appeared a short paragraph which was to prove the first
of many tributes to Mark Twain; this miniature critique,
from a boy of twenty, antedated by a decade the essay in
which William Lyon Phelps, with a generous if wavering
stroke, conferred upon Mr. Clemens the academic ac-
colade. Wrote the juvenile "colyumist":

> Some day the critics will awaken to the fact that
> his "Huckleberry Finn" is the greatest novel yet
> produced by an American writer. At present it
> seems to be regarded as a cross between the Elsie
> books and the Fables in Slang.

First announcement of a theme that is to sound loud
and often in the Menckenian music! [1]

[1] Mencken's boyish prevision of the high place to be held in American letters by *Huckleberry Finn* is best attested by two such recent books
as John Macy's *The Spirit of American Literature* (Boni & Liveright's
Modern Library) and Van Wyck Brooks's *The Ordeal of Mark Twain*
(E. P. Dutton, New York, 1920). "It is one of the unaccountable triumphs of creative power," writes Macy, ". . . and the surrounding intellectual territory has not its comrade." (Page 259.) And Mr. Brooks:
". . . we can understand the supremacy among all Mark Twain's writings of *Huckleberry Finn.*" (Page 194.) Macy emphasizes the social
and economic import of the tale; Brooks dwells upon its vast significance
in the repressed career of the humorist.

Let me, *en passant*, indicate a number of interesting coincidences in
the miniature epic of Huck Finn and the life of Mr. "Huck" L. Mencken
himself: Huck takes "no stock in mathematics, anyway"; Huck is a
hoaxer with a dislike of poetry and a fondness for good cooking; Huck
talks the "American" language; he has a mania for freedom; his
passion for music is so great that it enables him even to endure the
hocus-pocus of religious rites. "Music," he avers, *"is* a good thing;
and after all that soul-butter and hogwash I never see it freshen up
things so, and sound so honest and bully." Of course he chews to-

The column underwent several changes of name and character. On November 18 it suddenly was re-christened "Knocks and Jollies"; in this atavar it contained a great deal of verse. By December 3 it acquired an alternating alter ego called "Terse and Terrible Texts," all in prose. On February 24, 1901, there appeared, in this twin column the first of the *Untold Tales,* all of them laid in ancient Rome and dealing, in the spirit of broad farce, with local politics. Thirty-three of them, with their frequent climax of hanging, were run before they disappeared from the page on November 2, 1902. Soon the twin columns were merged under a new name: "Baltimore and the Rest of the World." Buffoonery gave way to the airing of personal opinions; already the atmosphere of the "Free Lance" column and of the *Prejudices* that grew out of it was making itself felt. This, too, was the natural transition to Mencken's duties as regular editorial-writer. Thus, during the election excitement of November, 1900, when he was still ten months short of voting-age, he wrote the chief election matter for the *Herald,* including a series of articles in-

bacco; and he "don't give a dead rat what the authorities" think about anything, "nuther." And consider Huck's ruminations upon Conscience: ". . . it don't make no difference whether you do right or wrong, a person's conscience ain't got no sense and just goes for him *anyway.* If I had a yaller dog that didn't know no more than a person's conscience does I would pison him. It takes up more room than all the rest of a person's insides, and yet ain't no good, nohow." The climax of these coincidences comes in the motto that Tom Sawyer, in the episode of Black Jim's liberation, chooses for this romantic prisoner-*malgré-lui: Maggiore fretta, minore atto,* which, as Tom translates from the Italian, having met it in his tales of chivalry, means "The more haste, the less speed." What is this but the motto of the Mencken clan? *Wartet und eylet:* Make haste slowly?

structing voters in the marking of their ballots. In the meantime, one day late in 1900, George Bronson Howard, member of the same Baltimore dining club to which Mencken belonged, and somewhat younger than the newspaper man, had handed him a copy of the first edition of *Sister Carrie*. It was an eventful day, for the book made a colossal impression upon the budding writer and turned him at once into a Dreiserista. The novels of Conrad, too, were being devoured as fast as they appeared.

Toward the end of 1901 Mencken was promoted to the Sunday editorship of the *Herald*. Coming after a year and a half of arduous reporting, the job seemed a veritable sinecure. Among his duties were the managing of the theatrical page, the planning of the colored comic supplement (still a novelty in the land), the supervision of the artists, and the preparation of the plates. There was time and to spare, however, for outside writing. There was the pick of special assignments, such as the Jacksonville fire in 1902; Mencken, too, after having himself strung up an army of imaginary Romans, was usually told off to report public executions, and in two years had the opportunity to witness what nine real hangings looked like. It must have affected the hardened newspaper man, for he became an opponent of capital punishment. Of late he has undergone a change of heart, or of head, and today believes that it still is necessary.

The magazines, which had opened their columns to him in 1899 with the acceptance, by the *Bookman*, of his poem to Rudyard Kipling, were tempting him sorely.

In February of 1900, *Short Stories* had printed his first attempt at a tale, *The Woman and The Girl*. The same magazine accepted a number of other stories. The very next year came near to luring Mencken away from the newspapers altogether. Ellery Sedgwick, then editor of *Leslie's,* had bought a story called *The Flight of The Victor,* and had been so highly pleased with it that he then and there offered Mencken the post of associate editor of *Leslie's.* The promise of $40 per week, and a free pass to Baltimore every month must have looked big to a raw youth in his twenty-first year, a-throb with literary ambitions and getting less than half of that salary on the *Herald.* But there was Mencken's mother to consider and his responsibility as the head of a house but recently bereaved. The temptation, though great, was resisted. Thus early, as so often in later years, Baltimore, in the eyes of her noted writer, saved him from the fate that New York might have held in store.

Story-writing was not without its drawbacks. How was an incipient fire-eater like Henry L. to deal, for example, with the *Youth's Companion,* which had invited him to contribute tales as early as 1900? What was one to do with a magazine that objected to a narrative depicting the death of a cat? Mencken, to tell the truth, despite his early success at short-story writing, wrote his fiction against a growing judgment that he had not been cut out for it. It was soon to follow poetry into the discard. The publication of *Ventures Into Verse,* in 1903, though seeming to mark his début as a poet, betokened the death of that ambition. It was an epitaph, not an epithalamium. Two years later Mencken was to come to the conclusion that he was equally futile as a fictioneer. It was Sedgwick who had opened his eyes, diverting him from fiction to the field of serious articles.

In 1903, Carter resigned the chief editorship and was replaced by Lynn Roby Meekins. Meekins, a native of the Maryland "Free" State, had been the chief editorial writer on the Baltimore *American* and, later, the first Managing Editor of the *Saturday Evening Post* under Curtis. He entered upon his duties under the necessity of a complete reorganization. Ways had resigned and entered politics. The staff was demoralized. Meekins, making a calm survey of the place, came to the conclusion that Mencken was about the most competent and industrious fellow in it, and accordingly appointed him City Editor. The fact that the twenty-three year old youth had just issued a book of verse did not stand in the way of this promotion. Nor did the accession to this new dignity intimidate Mr. Henry Louis Mencken, as his name still read on the title-page of his firstling. Instead, he celebrated the event by a grand clean-up, discharging some eight or ten of the worst offenders and assuming the active direction of the none too efficient remainder. He read copy, wrote it, and often had to re-write a third of what was turned in by the half-drunken underlings. The work was a terrific grind, but gradually Mencken was weeding out men and replacing them with efficient successors. Within a year he had retrieved the reputation of the *Herald's* local pages and, under the guidance of the New York *Sun,* which provided his model, he infused humor and order into his section of the paper.

Meekins proved to be an influence of the most important nature. Ways and Carter had been aids and inspirations; Meekins, however, was the real "discoverer" of Mencken. From the first he singled the young man out and advanced him as fast as the thing could be managed. Like Carter, Meekins was a man of culture; he could write and he knew good writing. The other men had been passive encouragements; Meekins was an active spur.

Mencken was now working so hard that he saw few people not directly connected with the staff. A municipal catastrophe was soon to bring him into closer cooperation than ever with Meekins, and to test his mettle as a man for emergencies.

On the Sunday morning of February 4, 1904, Mencken was pulled out of bed at eleven o'clock and summoned to the office to get out an extra. A Baltimore block was ablaze; by afternoon, it was calculated, the conflagration would be under control. By nine o'clock that night, however, after the *Herald* had run off two extras, one of them illustrated with views of the fire, word suddenly came to Mencken that the building would have to be dynamited; it must be abandoned at once. He stuffed his overcoat pockets full of copy and seized a package of cuts in each hand. Meekins suggested that the next morning's paper be brought out, if possible, on the presses of the Washington *Post*. He made a dash for the earliest train, leaving Mencken an hour in which to round up a scratch staff. On the next train Mencken arrived with three reporters and the foreman of the

Herald composing room; Meekins had already come to an arrangement with Scott C. Bone, then managing editor of the *Post,* and everything was in readiness. That night they ran off a four-page paper in Washington; early next morning it was on sale in Baltimore. Tuesday's paper was likewise printed in Washington. The *Post's* plant, however, could not stand the strain and the *Herald* refugees were forced to look for other facilities.

There was the Catholic *Mirror* of Baltimore, a weekly, with a couple of linotypes; they were pressed into service for the Wednesday morning *Herald.* The linotypes broke down; the greater part of the paper had to be set by hand. This couldn't do. Meekins, undaunted, made this time for Philadelphia. That very night Mencken, with four or five copyreaders and reporters, and some twenty-five to thirty printers, took charge of the Philadelphia *Evening Bulletin* and got out the Baltimore *Herald* for Thursday. It was a sixteen-page affair,—the best that Baltimore had seen since the outbreak of the fire. For the next five weeks, while a new plant was being rigged up in an abandoned street-railway power house of the home town, the *Herald* was printed in Philadelphia. A special train, provided by the Baltimore & Ohio railroad, made the run to Baltimore at a mad speed that violated all the rules of the company.

The first four days were, for Mencken, a waking nightmare of toil. For more than sixty-six hours on end, in the excitement of blasted editorial offices, wandering newspaper plants, overwhelming technical problems and managerial direction, he knew no sleep. There was no respite until four o'clock of Wednesday morning.

The experience, after twenty-one years, remains vivid.
At Washington, the work was, allowing for the stress
of the occasion, a pleasure. Bone, who later became
governor of Alaska, was a gentleman of great competence. At Philadelphia conditions, meteorological, financial and social, were all but unbearable. The weather
was intensely disagreeable. Rumor had it that there
was no money for salaries in the *Herald* coffers. The
Philadelphia newspaper men "were inconceivably inhospitable. During the five weeks that I was there," relates Mencken, "I don't recall any of them so much as
speaking to me—save one who came to the *Evening
Telegraph* office and tried to graft some news from me.
Philadelphia then had an early closing law, and it was
impossible to get even as much as a glass of beer after
11 P.M. A local telegraph operator employed to take
our stuff from Baltimore got cards for the whole *Herald*
staff on the Pen and Pencil Club, a Philadelphia newspaper club. Half-a-dozen of them went there every
night to eat after we had put the paper to bed. No one
ever spoke to us, save one drunken man, and he turned
out to be an Englishman. I have disliked Philadelphia
from that day to this. Try to imagine this happening
in any other American city! In Washington, when we
reached the *Post* office on the night of the fire, every
member of the *Post* staff came up and volunteered
to help us. We were engaged in solving a technical
problem of great difficulty and curiosity alone sufficed to
make every newspaper man interested in what we were
doing. But in Philadelphia no one seemed to care. At
the Pen and Pencil Club, some of the local journalists

stared at us, but I don't recall any of them volunteering to speak to us. In this Philadelphia gloom there was a ray of light. Barclay H. Warburton, then publisher of the Philadelphia Evening Telegraph, proved by exception a most amiable and helpful gentleman."

Back in Baltimore, settled in its improvised plant, the *Herald* quickly retrieved its fortunes. Like all such catastrophes, the Baltimore fire had produced a flood of transient advertising. The *Herald,* alone of all the periodicals, was issuing a sixteen-page paper and thus gathered in most of the patronage. With the resumption of normal conditions, however, this revenue fell off, and by the end of 1904 the *Herald* was in bad straits. Mencken had been appointed Managing Editor, and had hardly become accustomed to his new duties when the General Manager, Frank F. Peard, hit upon the idea of adding to the receipts with an evening edition. Whereupon Mencken found himself doing day duty and night duty, managing two papers and grinding away from eight A. M. to midnight. A couple of weeks of this almost finished him. More, it nearly finished the rest of the organization. The morning paper was abandoned. Meekins was made General Manager in place of Peard and Mencken continued as Managing Editor until 1905. Within a short while, at the astonishing age of twenty-five, Mencken was appointed Editor-in-Chief of the Baltimore *Herald.* He was, at the time, the youngest man in the country occupying so responsible a position on a big city daily.

A man of consequence, a man of the world, resourceful, still feeling his way, gaining confidence in himself and losing a too great respect for mankind. Behind him lay a year of unwonted strenuousness. Year of the great fire; year of Hergesheimer's *The Lay Anthony,* and of Mencken's first literary contact with the rotund Pennsylvanian; year, too, of one of the most laughable episodes in the Baltimorean's half-hidden life. The twentieth century, some one has written, is the century of the child. In 1904 a vast interest had suddenly developed in medical articles; that was before each daily had its syndicate physician. Sedgwick, as editor of *Leslie's* had turned to Mencken for the name of a responsible man who would write such a series for the magazine, and Mencken was not long in discovering Dr. Leonard K. Hirshberg. Hirshberg, a very intelligent gentleman with an excellent medical education, could supply all the facts in the case; handling the pen, however, was not as simple to him as wielding the scalpel. Whereupon a partnership agreement was arrived at, according to which Mencken (perhaps with fond memories of his 100% in physiology) should put into literary shape the data supplied by the physician. The combination proved so successful that the writers were sought by other magazines. Theodore Dreiser, at that time by one of life's little ironies the editor of the Butterick publications, and more specifically of *The Delineator,* ordered an entire series of articles upon the care and feeding of children. And out of such a circumstance as this, several years later, was to be born Mencken's entrance, not into infanticulture, but into the profession of literary criticism!

Just what happened at the time is uncertain. Dreiser

seems more sure than Mencken as to what took place. According to him, a fat, rosy-cheeked, but not embarrassed [1] youngster appeared in the office of *The Delineator* one day in 1904, with a medical article in his uncertain fingers. The article proved satisfactory and was the forerunner of many in similar vein. Eventually, it may be well to know, this series was published as a book under the signature of Hirshberg; until the present year, Mencken's connection with it was entirely unknown.

Far more important than the income from these articles, were the results of Mencken's strange first meeting with the novelist of his early admiration. Dreiser thought him a capable youngster; he had him on file, so to speak, in the back of his head. When, in 1908, he was approached by Fred Splint of the *Smart Set* and asked to recommend some capable fellow for the post of literary critic, he at once thought of Mencken, suggested his name, and the die was cast. But of this, more in the proper place.

For the present, the twenty-five-year-old editor-in-chief of the Baltimore *Herald* was working like a Trojan with Meekins to rehabilitate the staff. Almost all the editorials were coming from his typewriter. He was running a new literary and dramatic column, "Notes in the Margin," which had been inaugurated on October 9, 1904, and appeared weekly until the 5th of February, 1905. Upon its cessation, he continued to write independent reviews, incidentally developing an interest in Shaw that was soon to result in his first prose book, and

[1] See Mr. Dreiser's important account of this meeting, on page 378.

As Managing Editor of the
Baltimore *Morning Herald*, summer of 1904

THE OLD SALOON BEHIND THE BALTIMORE *Sun* OFFICE

Left to right, Mencken, McKee Barclay, then the paper's cartoonist; Folger McKinsey (the Bentztown Bard), the staff poet; and the late Tom Barclay, a comic artist treating of Hunekers' *Iconoclasts* in such a manner as to bring about his first personal contact with this wholesome and inspiriting influence. It was an eventful day when the proofs of *George Bernard Shaw: His Plays* arrived in the *Herald* office. Meekins, himself the author of a number of books, happened to step in, and seeing the sheets on Mencken's desk, he said: "Don't forget this day; you will never see a happier." He was not wrong. The book of poems had not counted. This, to Mencken, was his first real book. "It gave me a tremendous thrill. It is one of the tragedies of life that such a thrill cannot be repeated. When the proofs of a new book come in to-day I am conscious only of the nuisance of having to read them."

On November 26th, 1905, appeared yet another column, labeled "Mere Opinion." *The Herald,* however, was headed for failure. In July of 1906 it suspended publication.

II

Mencken had no reason to worry about a position. He had become well known in the journalistic circles of the major cities and was at once offered his pick of a half-dozen places. The Managing Editor of the New York *Times,* C. V. Van Anda, invited him to join the staff of that paper, but Mencken, out of his long-standing aversion for the city, refused the post as he had before rejected *Leslie's.* Of the Baltimore offers,—and every newspaper in the city extended a proposal—Mencken finally selected the job of news editor on the *Evening News.* The *News,* after a long and shaky career, was now, under the direction of its publisher, Charles H. Grasty, a huge success. It was even outdistancing the *Sun,* which for two generations had been the first paper of the State. Mencken's term of service, however, expired within less than five weeks. Under Editor Dr. Franklin Fabian, he wrote editorials and made up the paper. Grasty he found to be a charming fellow and an excellent newspaper man, if somewhat in the Cunningham tradition when it came to paying his men. When, therefore, the *Sun* held out the prospect of a considerable increase in salary and the relative sinecure of supervising the newly instituted Sunday edition, he promptly accepted.

There were disadvantages and compensations. A Sunday edition of only twelve pages was hardly Mencken's idea of a field in which to disport himself. He was allowed but $100 weekly for the purchase of feature material. Yet the work was easy, the associations were pleasant, and the owners of the paper, the Abells, were amiable enough. Best of all, the Sunday editor was untrameled by restrictions. It was not long before his free hand was making itself felt. On the old *Herald* he had seconded Carter as a reviewer of the drama; later, as Sunday editor, he had edited the theatre page. Returning to the playhouse, he began a sledge-hammer assault upon what he considered the frauds of the day. When the New Theatre was planned in New York, he poked fun at the colossus. He denounced Richard Mansfield. He entered the lists for Shaw.

The office began to receive complaints, by letter and in person. The managers of the local theatres called upon Walter W. Abell and made representations to him. Abell gallantly stood by his editor; it was the editor himself who, eventually, came to the conclusion that the managers had just cause for offense. Their patrons were not interested in dramatic excellence. The managers themselves had to take what the theatrical syndicate sent on the road. When, four years later, Mencken gave up the post of dramatic critic, he abandoned the ranks for good.

Work on the *Sun* alternated with new ventures into authorship. Nietzsche, Ibsen and Socialism were in the air. Brentano's, the publishers of Shaw in this country, had issued the Englishman's *Quintessence of Ibsenism,* and it had occurred to Mencken, while on the *Herald* that a quintessence of Shaw would be in order. Brentano's were the logical publishers for such a book, and, with accustomed zeal, Henry Louis fell to the work. The idea, however, failed to win the New York house, and was soon being considered by Mr. Harrison Hale Schaff, the editorial director of John W. Luce & Company of Boston. Schaff, who is still at this post, and fills it with a nonchalant leisureliness that scarcely betrays the fine taste behind the careless manner, thus occupies with relation to Mencken the author the same position that Meekins does with relation to Mencken the journalist. He "discovered" the critic.[1] He suggested in 1907, the next book, *The Philosophy of Friedrich Nietzsche,* as well as later works of an editorial nature

[1] See page 371 for an important letter from Mr. Schaff, bearing on this stage of Mencken's career.

and a series of translations from Ibsen. The Nietzsche suggestion fitted in admirably with the observations that Mencken, from his newspaper desks, was making on men and things. With his inherited bias against the rabble, with the added prejudice against the commoner that he had acquired in his father's factory, he eyed his inferiors with suspicion. The incompetents only intensified his convictions. Not that they were to be blamed; not that some of them hadn't been victimized by untoward circumstance. Yet, viewing the spectacle from the standpoint of an ingrained individualism, untempered by the recognition of class conflict, Mencken thought then, as he thinks now, that it is cowardly to bawl against luck. "Every man has both kinds. It was good luck, in large part, that made me a city editor at 23—but it was bad luck that I was not owner of the paper. It was bad luck that kept some of those reporters in jobs at $15 a week—but it was good luck that enabled them to escape driving ice-wagons. What ailed them was that they did not utilize properly the share of good luck that came to them—that they forgot it in thinking eternally of their bad luck." The statement, however debatable on the sociological side, has a hard core of individualistic truth. It was this individualism that wrote itself into the Nietzsche book. At the time, the German was new to Mencken. Characteristically, having tackled the job, he plowed through the man complete in the original, read the Biography by his sister, as well as everything available on the man in English. It was formidable work, all the more so because Mencken's German was not of the best. The book was a year in the making, and appeared in 1908.

Now, greatly to Mencken's surprise, came the invitation to be the literary critic of the *Smart Set*. The editor, in 1908, was Fred Splint; his assistant was Norman Boyer, a former Baltimore reporter; Channing Pollock, an old friend of Mencken's, and a fellow dramatic critic, was doing the monthly article on the theatre. It was natural for Mencken, at the time, to assume that either Boyer or Pollock had got him the post. Indeed, not until a year or two ago did he have the slightest inkling that Dreiser had been responsible for the appointment. Book-reviewing, up to that time, had been the least of Mencken's worriments; by November of 1908, however, he was in full blast, practising in the field of letters the same methods and manners that were to make "The Free Lance" a column to be feared.

Into this department he poured his originary zeal against fraud and in defense of freedom. His old enemies appeared in new guises: the "stuffed shirts" of the academicians, the "mountebanks" of Greenwich Village, the Comstockian "smuthounds." To the task he brought, not the rarefied atmosphere of the class-room and the campus, but the fresh winds of a freely functioning vitality. He was versed not only in the traditional lore of the schools, not only in the prescribed literary courses of the curricula. He knew politics as it can be known only to a newspaper man with clear eyes, sharp ears and mind superlatively alert. He had a wide training in the physical sciences. He had watched what was going on at home and abroad. He could handle the deadliest weapon in the arena of literary polemics: ridicule. He had no *isms* to keep him falsely true. Shortly he was rallying around the pennon that waved from his free lance a band of kindred spirits. The old urge to magazine work was growing stronger.

The resignation of Channing Pollock from the dramatic editorship of the *Smart Set,* which fairly coincided with Mencken's entrance upon his duties, was indirectly responsible for a new partnership that was to color his life for the next sixteen years. In the old office of that magazine, at Fifth Avenue and Fortieth Street, in May of 1909 he was introduced by Norman Boyer to Mr. George Jean Nathan, successor to Channing Pollock. "Fifteen minutes after our meeting," Nathan has told me, "we were seated at a beer table two blocks away. We found that we had many attitudes in common, including a common liking for the same kind of alcoholic refreshments." They drank *Brüderschaft* and the friendship and association was begun.

What with his new connections, with trips to Europe in 1908 and in 1910, with his newspaper activities, with his writing for Dreiser's *Bohemian,* and his work upon the new edition of Ibsen's plays that Schaff had suggested, Mencken was a busy man. Collaborating with Holger A. Koppel, the Danish Consul at Baltimore, Mencken labored away over the texts of *A Doll's House, Little Eyolf* and *Hedda Gabler.* The first appeared early in 1909, and was soon followed by the second. This is as far as the series went in print.

Meantime, he was becoming involved in discussions of

the Socialist question. Articles that had appeared in the *Sun* in 1909 early attracted the attention of Robert Rives La Monte, who, to his duties on the *News* of the same city, added an editorial connection with *The International Socialist Review*. A controversial correspondence began between the widely traveled investigator, who had written a number of books on Socialism, and the saucy superyouth who already had behind him a disowned booklet of verse, a pert little book on Shaw that had offended the pert and offending subject, and a vigorous exposition of the vigorous weakling of Naumburg. La Monte, having suggested that the letters be polished up and brought out in the form of an epistolary debate, was given full charge of the matter and won over the first publisher he approached. The book appeared in 1910 over the imprint of Henry Holt, and was entitled *Men Vs. The Man.*

There is irony in the account of the meeting between Mencken and La Monte that had been called for the purpose of putting the final touches to the book. La Monte had moved from Baltimore to New Canaan, Connecticut; for meeting-place his father's house at Bound Brook, N. J., had been settled upon. To Bound Brook accordingly came Mencken, defender of Capitalism, in a proletarian day-coach, uncradled in those Pullman privileges that he has hymned as one of the greatest of American inventions. To meet him at the station came Robert Rives La Monte, champion of the underdog, son of a wealthy father, accompanied by a coachman in an imposing livery seated on the box of an elegant carriage. In state they drove to the paternal mansion, where the controversialists were entertained so lavishly that little time was left for the chief business of the day.

The ups and downs of the newspaper game were soon to land Mencken back in the lap of Grasty. While the Abells were getting into difficulties, Grasty had been making a success of the *News*. He had sold it to Frank A. Munsey and for a few years devoted himself to other fields. The presses still held their old allurements, however. Returning to Baltimore in 1910, and bent upon making another fortune, Grasty bought the declining *Sun* for his syndicate, taking Mencken along in the purchase. In April he started an evening edition, and transferred Mencken to it as an editor without a title and with no definite duties, under the responsiblity of J. H. Adams. It was a busy and an enjoyable job. There were two editorials to be written daily; there was a special column article to be featured every evening on the editorial page; there were odds and ends to see to about the office. It was not long before the editorials attracted the attention of the new stockholders, and, as a result, Harry C. Black, late of Princeton, and son of the principal stockholder, H. Crawford Black, was soon suggesting to Grasty the advisability of letting Mencken run loose in a signed column of his own. The result was the inauguration, in 1910, of that palladium of pugnacity known as "The Free Lance."

Its success was instantaneous. Journalistically, this was in a double sense something new under the *Sun*. Mencken, attacking the work in ribald glee, loosed the flood-gates of his mockery and sat back to watch the fun.

Into this column he flung every grudge and prejudice and opinion that it pleased him to air. The type trembled upon the verge of sin and slander. The free lance thrust right and left. The revelry threatened to whirl into a *danse macabre*. Mr. Grasty grew nervous. Very early he approached Mencken and got him to promise, by their ancient friendship, that at least one institution should be exempt from his contumacy: the Church and its reverend gentlemen. Luck, however, was with Mencken in releasing him from this pledge. The Baltimore anti-Christ had roiled the Methodists,— the Methodists, in the bosom of whose Sunday-Schools this serpent had been nurtured! The ministers of that stern denomination, determined to do for Baltimore what St. Patrick had done for Ireland, called a public meeting and attacked the apostate. That settled it. Grasty, finding that Mencken was the party who had been attacked, instantly released his editor from the promise and agreed that Mencken had a right to reply. Reply he did in such a relentless, rollicking, ribald Five Years' War that by the time the smoke had cleared away his opponents had suffered a sad diminution in ranks and a marked fall in the public esteem. God Himself was on the side of the infidel. In the midst of the carnage, one of the Methodist leaders was caught in the Y. M. C. A. practising upon an innocent youth an ancient evil to which even sexologists refrain from referring, unless behind the mask of Latinity. He fled the town.

One by one the favorite targets of the man were receiving their baptism of bullets. One by one the frauds of the day and generation, such as they appeared to be in the eyes of this relation of Johann Burkhard, were deluged in a flood of printers' ink. Here appeared in the rôle of social defendants, the Anti-Saloon League and the Vice Crusaders and the Town Boomers and the Anti-Vivisectionists and a multitude of others who have since found their antonomastic incarnation in Mencken's famous figure of the Y. M. C. A. Secretary. Local politics, as might have been expected, played a prominent part. Thus, when the *Sun* came out in opposition to James H. Preston, then Mayor of the city, Mencken sailed into him with a passion that must have had far more to do with his love of controversy than with the particular issues at stake. He belabored the man for years, yet at this late date is excellent friends with him. For that matter, during the height of the war with the Anti-Saloon League, he was on the best of terms with its superintendent, William H. Anderson. It is the man in the ranks who must mortally hate his enemy; the generals may fraternize.

These were not, however, one-sided fights with a newspaper that refused to retract. Companioning Mencken's hatred of fraud is his abstract passion for freedom. During the days of the Free Lance column it was the rule of the paper that Mencken might be denounced as violently as it soothed his opponents to abuse him, and on his own page, too, right beside the lines where he rioted. Against his column were two others, edited likewise by him, in which the worst of the attacks were set forth unchastened. Today Mencken, with a half-earnest wish to make out as bad a case for himself as possible, insists that this, in a measure, was bombast and braggadocio on his part.   More likely it was a love of fair play combined with the love of a good row.

New York, like a siren, kept beckoning to Mencken; like a St. Anthony of Baltimore, the man stuck to home and town throughout the enticing music.   In 1911, John Adam Thayer, formerly of *Everybody's,* acquired control of the *Smart Set* from Col. W. D. Mann of *Town Topics;* shortly after he offered the editorship to its literary critic.   This meant removal to New York and Mencken, with a now traditional gesture, refused.

By 1913 the editorship of the *Smart Set* had passed into the hands of Willard Huntington Wright.   That year, he proposed that he, Nathan and Mencken do a series of articles for the magazine on the great cities of Europe, especially those that were gay as well. Mencken, who had been abroad for the second time in 1910, covering the same route that he had traveled over two years earlier—England, France, Switzerland and Germany—got to work on Munich and London.   The first appeared in the April, 1913, issue of the magazine; the second, in that for June, 1913.   Why the London one should have been signed George Weems Peregoy remains to this day a mystery, even to the inventor of the pseudonym.   Next spring Wright and Nathan went abroad and returned with a few more cities in their steamer trunks.   These appeared in due course and were then collected for book publication.   The appearance of *Europe After 8:15* in 1914 coincided with international matters of such far greater consequence that it fell flat upon a market in which it now brings a premium.

The outbreak of the war was the signal for new indiscretions in Mencken's "Free Lance" column. Wilson became the latest symbol of national fraud and an unremitting assault was launched upon the bogus neutrality of the president. By early November of the same year Mencken was denouncing Wilson as an Anglo-maniac and predicting that he would eventually drag the country into war. The prediction, of course, came true; that, however, belongs to a later epoch in Mencken's career. Circumstances were steering him from journalism into magazine work. He had acquired, as in due course we shall see, an interest in the *Smart Set,* and had to be frequently in New York. Grasty, moreover, had left the *Sun.* Magazine work and newspaper duties were proving too much, even for Mencken's seemingly inexhaustive energies. He held on as long as he could, partly out of friendship for the successors of Grasty, but in October of 1915 handed in his resignation. His career as a newspaper editor was over. His connections with the *Sun* were not, however, completely severed, any more than were his interests in and collaboration upon the large dailies of the country. He still contributed two or three signed articles per week to the editorial page of the paper, with which he has been associated down to the present day; he was soon to serve it as a war correspondent in Germany. Yet his days in the editorial sanctum (holy name for that unchurchly den!) had come none the less to an end with his resignation and with the consequent cessation of the "Free Lance." Henceforth that free lance column was to become synonymous with every page for which the fellow would write.

In Baltimore, the effects of the column have been permanent. Although Mencken lost almost every fight that he waged, his thunderstorms cleared the atmosphere considerably. He accustomed a hide-bound, sluggish town to a flaunting freedom of discussion that stopped short only of the libel laws. Time and again he himself was libeled—and it was part of his precarious business to know the law of libel—but made no move to seek redress. The denunciation flattered him. It was the best of proof that he was succeeding at his chief amusement in life,—annoying conventional dullards, or, as he is wont to put it in his irreverent letters, "stirring up the animals." If he never defended himself against even the most palpably unjust of the numerous accusations, it was simply a sort of superior vanity. This vanity, indeed (alas, what are mere words!) has taken the Christian form of turning the other cheek and of heaping coals of fire upon the offenders' heads. Holding grudges is as wearying to the flesh and as degrading to the mind as indignation; *ergo,* do favors for your enemies and let them imagine that you are magnanimous, when all the time you are tickling your eccentric pride. This, too, is a kind of flame, and the Menckenian vanity exposes itself to the fires of the generosity and the magnanimity that it abjures.

The fact remains that this citizen, in whom no civic spirit dwells, has acclimated in his native city the boon of untrammeled press and speech. During the hysteria of the war, not a single man was jailed for his views in Baltimore, nor in the whole State of Maryland. To this very day the *Sun,* and especially the *Evening Sun* defends the right of free speech with all necessary ferocity. That policy was born of the "Free Lance" column.

III

Mencken's style had come to maturity in his early newspaper days. He is inclined to believe that by 1907 he was writing substantially as he does today, and on the whole an examination of his early work supports this judgment. Yet, as I shall show in a consideration of his earliest books, his style, in its essence, was fairly born mature; in his very first book of prose (1905) a paragraph here and there, removed from its context, could be passed off as the work of Mencken today.

That style, clear image of the man, owes many of its characteristics to the journalistic circumstances in which he developed it. It is the direct, forceful expression of one trained to think quickly, to make ready decisions, to plan proportions and effects. It reeks, not of the midnight oil, but of whirring cylinder-presses and the ink of giant rollers. There is printers' ink in Mencken's blood. He enjoys the very clicking of the typewriter, to this day doing his own typing in preference to the service of any stenographer, however competent. The arduous days on the *Herald* taught him to think before writing, thus reversing the usual case among reporters. So, too, the readiness with which his material was transformed from black marks on white paper into hot lead, cold type, and, finally into printed columns, has left him with an impatient desire for that same quick transformation of everything that he writes. The rush of the newspaper-office still stimulates him. In this, at least, he is the newspaper man that he calls himself.

His days on the *Herald,* the *News* and the *Sun* provided him with rare opportunities for the expression, the testing, and the revision of his ideas. The experience of the "Free Lance" column was particularly valuable. No man could have lasted through that five years' gruelling unless he had intellectual stamina of uncommon quality. Under the high pressure of instant combat, Mencken was forced to make very careful examination of the ideas that he held. Meeting any comer in this free-for-all, being buffeted in every direction by every sort of controversialist, he was toughened by the blows, sharpened in wit by the arguments. He emerged one of the foremost polemical writers of his day.

It is this journalistic training, the downfall of weaker spirits, that strengthened the natural abilities of Mencken and gave them athletic outlines. It implanted in him a bias for brevity, a hostility toward long words and sprawling discourse, an eagerness to reach at once for the heart of a matter and spread it forth clearly to the view. For these habits of mind and style there are other, more deeply-rooted reasons; I am concerned, for the moment, only with indicating the effect of his newspaper career. Now, all these virtues—like all virtues—have their less attractive side. A bias for brevity may at times betray one into superficiality; a hostility toward involved discourse may slight matter because of manner; eagerness to catch the attention may sink to a level of concession that fails to distinguish between the berated mob and its berator. So, too, the eternal hunt of the journalist for new words and combinations, unless carefully controlled, becomes habitual exaggeration, distortion, caricature.

The deeper causes of these attributes of Mencken's style are best studied and speculated upon in his earliest books, in his numerous personal paragraphs, in his later comment upon his creative beginnings. His first volumes are the earth and waters of his world as it rose from the mists of the journalistic Genesis. Mencken, thus entering literature by the back door of the newspaper office, restored the tradition of the family to its scholastic status.

FREE LANCE DAYS ON THE
BALTIMORE *Evening Sun,* 1913

PORTRAIT BY HENDERSON, 1913

CHAPTER SIX

*Ventures into Verse—Mencken and Poetry—
George Bernard Shaw: His Plays—
Mencken and the Theatre—The Philosophy of Friedrich Nietzsche—Men vs.
the Man—Europe After 8:15—Drinking
as Art—Mencken and Music*

I

MENCKEN, it is important to remember, was
born into a family that for the two generations
next preceding had been indifferent to religion. Even
on the distaff side, if there had been no acquiescence in
the full implications of this heterodoxy, neither had
there been anything like the stubborn opposition of dog-
matism. To the women, church-going was in the first
place a form of irregular social visiting,—a pastime
unrelated to any literal or symbolistic acceptance of the
ritual. The boy himself, subjected to the familiar
hocus pocus, absorbed only the poetry of the words
and music; even as a man he is sensitive to the spectacle
and to the religious fairy tales as æsthetic experience.
This training, however, did not inculcate in him any of
those metaphysical doctrines of which the independent
personality, reaching adolescence, must rid itself through

131

torturing hours of debate and despair. Mencken never knew the religious crisis. He never suffered the soul-wracking experience of having a familiar parental world suddenly snatched from under him, leaving him adrift in the empty spaces of quest and query. Armored by heredity against the assaults of the emotions, he was further strengthened by the rare emotional exemptions of his household. There was nothing feminine about this boy, as there almost inevitably is in the early career of the artist. His pursuits, from the very beginning, were as masculine as his reactions. Delicate nuances eluded him; he saw in terms of the primary colors, but it was a clear, a personal vision.

In this, of course, there were losses to offset the gains, or, to employ a more scientific vocabulary, there were compensatory adjustments. By nature, the youth was on guard against his emotions. His poetry, where one might reasonably expect the suppressed "weakness" to show, is predominantly masculine, unemotional, even anti-emotional. Later I shall have occasion to study the contradictions of this emotional life more intimately; for the present, I wish to point out that one of the great sources of artistic expansion ran dry very early in Mencken's career. Religion, both as belief and as the material for sublimation into art, has been denied him. What has been sublimated is not the religious feeling in itself, but the boredom and indifference of the child. The critical attitude toward religion early became an amused, an indifferent attitude toward all of life. That, essentially, it has remained. The juvenile worldliness of the verses is transformed, in a surprisingly short time, into the mature sardonic spirit of the book on Shaw and the argumentative aristocracy of the book on Nietzsche. Thenceforth, through trial, error and triumph, the world is Mencken's oyster.

II

Ventures Into Verse is one of the books that Mr. Mencken has tried to live down. His growing renown made the attempt impossible. Though only one hundred copies had been printed, of which the publisher took half; though half of Mencken's fifty were given away to newspaper friends and the rest sent out for review; though the only sales recorded numbered two copies, shipped to a bookdealer in Portland, Maine, there are still a few extant. The attitude of reviewers in 1903 was nothing if not generous. The *Sun* (New York) went so far as to say that "Many of these verses . . . might have been written by the author of *Barrack Room Ballads.*" Professor Pattee thinks so to this day, nor is he far from right. The *Nation* was hardly as flattering as the rest of the country. No one, it seems, detected, along with the influence of the contemporary Britisher, that of an earlier, lighter hand. Yet Mencken, pounding out with his fist the masculine metres of him who later was to find the female of the species more deadly than the male, was, at the same time tapping with his fingers the more fragile rhythms of Robert Herrick, the seventeenth-century ladies' man.

Today the little book brings $60 to $75 in the market, —more than half of what the budding poet had contributed to the cost of publication. It is far more heard of than seen, though Professor Pattee managed, for his essay in the *Sidelights On American Literature,* to exhume a copy and quote one of the more successful of the Kiplingesque invocations.[1] The copy in the New York Public Library is a photostat, the original having been stolen a few years ago. Because of this rarity, and even more because of the light that this firstling throws upon the later career of the young man, I shall quote liberally from the collection. I shall print also, for the first time, a number of other poems that may have been excluded from the original gathering as being too genuinely amorous in origin. Mencken at twenty-three (which, I believe, he has called the age of choice) was already an opinionated bachelor. Already he had left poetry behind for fiction and journalism; but his book caught up to him and has pursued him ever since.

First, for the poems that did not find a place in *Ventures Into Verse.* They are predominantly of a tender, even passionate character. I have already quoted a sonnet from 1898; to 1900 belongs a song written originally for a cantata, *Ruth;* that piece never reached far enough to provide a musical setting for words that lend themselves especially to such treatment:

SONG

Love toils among the reapers,
　And wanders in the town;
Love knows no roof to shelter him,
　Nor couch to lie him down.

[1] Pattee's book was published in 1922 by Scribner's.

Love walks upon the waters,
    And fares into the hills;
Love makes himself a hiding-place
    Among the daffodils.

Ah, love, what lane so winding;
    Ah, love, what road so long,
That down its path you come not
    With your laughter and your song!

To 1901 belongs one of those strangely retrospective
poems that youth is fond of writing as if from the
vantage-coign of eighty or ninety years. It is called

THE OLD TRAILS

As a bird that wandereth from her nest, so is a man that
wandereth from his place.—Proverbs xxvii, 8.

Let us seek the old trails,
    That led us years agone:
Rambling from the little hills to where we saw the sea;
    Steep they were and bold trails
    And gleaming in the dawn—
And there, behind their furthest bend, was Home to you and me!

When we left the old trails
    The world was all before—
Coasts that lured and promised us and stars that showed the way;
    All the roads were gold trails
    And ev'ry shimmering shore
Called us—scarlet, wanton-eyed!—and who could disobey?

Now we seek the old trails,
    Searching where they run:
Grass and weeds have swallowed them, and brick and stone in turn;

> Lost they are and cold trails—
> Time and wreck have won!
> When the years have shut the book—then, at last, we learn!

A year later, and Mencken is singing his swan-song as a bard.

SONG

Yea, there was moonlight, when we walked together;
 Moonlight and fairy light,
 Soft light and airy light;
Shimmering the road along, and dancing o'er the heather—
You and I at evening, walking hand in hand.

Still shines the moonlight; no more we walk together;—
 Yellow light and pale light,
 Glooming light and stale light;
Shadows by the clouds cast, and signs of stormy weather—
Cold falls the moonlight upon a desert land.

This is one of the last poems he wrote.

The contents of *Ventures Into Verse* are, in general, cruder in outlook and in execution. This wise youngster is not to be caught napping. He knows all the old jokes and has a few new ones. He's a he-man, singing the song of brawn and brain. Before he has heard of Nietzsche he has put woman into her place as the amusement of the warrior in his hours of leisure from the battle. If he has a moment of amorous weakness, he hides it behind a jest. Life is a joke and this verse is the laughter. Thin laughter, for the most part, yet ringing with the overtones of the man that lurks between the rhymes. Uneven laughter, too; now it is merely a vaudevillian cackle of the very sort which some of the lines berate, now a grim, sardonic guffaw at the vanity of human wishes. Just as the *Warning* and *Preliminary Rebuke* foreshadow the lower buffooneries of the man, so does *Finis,* with which the book closes, forecast such a shattering burlesque as *Death,* which stands out as one of the finest bits of grim humor in contemporary letters. From the conventional and technical standpoint, Mencken might easily have become a successful versifier; that he had a touch of true poetry in him is revealed more clearly by some of the pieces he left out than by those he chose to include. The strangest trait of *Ventures Into Verse* is that it reveals a marked resistance to the very impulse which gave birth to the poetic ambition. It is less a book of poems than a struggle against poetry.

My selections are intended to convey a rounded impression of the book; I give the good, the bad and the indifferent, and examples of almost every mood.

There come, first, the *Warning* and *Preliminary Rebuke:*

WARNING

Most of the verses that follow have been printed before and the author wishes to acknowledge his thanks for permission to reproduce them, to the editors and publishers of *The Bookman, Life, The New England Magazine, The National Magazine* and the *Baltimore Morning Herald.* Some are imitations—necessarily weak—of the verse of several men in whose writings he has found a good deal of innocent pleasure. The others, he fears, are more or less original.

THE MAN MENCKEN

PRELIMINARY REBUKE

Don't shoot the pianist; he's doing his best.

Gesundheit! Knockers! have your Fling!
Unto an Anvilfest you're bid;
It took a lot of Hammering,
To build Old Cheops' Pyramid!

Of the stanzas written with the echo of Kipling in his ears, three stand out; a *Ballade of Protest* even won Professor Pattee, who, thinking on the man that might have been, turned its refrain against Mencken himself.

TO R. K.[1]

Prophet of brawn and bravery!
Bard of the fighting man!
You have made us kneel to a God of Steel,
And to fear his church's ban;
You have taught the song that the bullet sings—
The knell and the crowning ode of kings;
The ne'er denied appeal!

Prophet of brain and handicraft!
Bard of our grim machines!
You have made us dream of a God of Steam,
And have shown what his worship means.
In the clanking rod and the whirring wheel
A life and a soul your songs reveal,
And power and might supreme.

[1] First published in *The Bookman*, December, 1899.

Bard of the East and mystery!
   Singer of those who bow
To the earthen clods that they call their gods
   And with god-like fees endow:
You have shown that these heed not the suppliant's **plea,**
Nor the prayers of the priest and devotee,
   Nor the vestal's futile vow.

Singer, we ask what we cannot learn
   From our wise men and our schools;
Will our offered slain from our gods obtain
   But the old reward of fools?
Will our man-made gods be like their kind?
If we bow to a clod of clay enshrined
   Will we pray our prayers in vain?

THE SONG OF THE OLDEN TIME

Powder and shot now fight our fights
   And we meet our foes no more,
As face to face our fathers fought
   In the brave old days of yore;
To the thirteenth inch and the needle gun,
   To the she-cat four-point-three
We look for help when the war-dogs yelp
   And the foe comes o'er the sea!

Oho! for the days of the olden time,
   When a fight was a fight of men!
When lance broke lance and arm met arm—
   There were no cowards then!
Sing ho! for the fight of the olden time,
   When the muscles swelled in strain,

THE MAN MENCKEN

As the steel found rest in a brave man's breast
And the axe in a brave man's brain!

The lance-point broke on the armor's steel,
  And the pike crushed helmet through,
And the blood of the vanquished, warm and red,
  Stained the victor's war-steed, too!
A fight was a fight in the olden time—
  Sing ho, for the days bygone!—
And a strong right arm was the luckiest charm,
  When the foe came marching on!

Oho! for the days of the olden time,
  When a fight was a fight of men!
When lance broke lance and arm met arm—
  There were no cowards then!
Sing ho! for the fight of the olden time,
  When the muscles swelled in strain,
As the steel found rest in a brave man's breast
And the axe in a brave man's brain!

A BALLADE OF PROTEST

To the address of Master Rudyard Kipling, Poetaster

For long, unjoyed, we've heard you sing
  Of politics and army bills,
Of money-lust and cricketing,
  Of clothes and fear and other things;
  Meanwhile the palm-trees and the hills
Have lacked a bard to voice their lay;
  Poet, ere time your lyre-string stills,
Sing us again of Mandalay!

Unsung the East lies glimmering,
  Unsung the palm trees toss their frills,

Unsung the seas their splendors fling,
   The while you prate of laws and tills.
   Each man his destiny fulfills;
Can it be yours to loose and stray;
   In sophist garb to waste your quills?—
Sing us again of Mandalay!

Sing us again in rhymes that ring,
   In Master-Voice that lives and thrills.
Sing us again of wind and wing,
   Of temple bells and jungle thrills;
   And if your Pegasus e'er wills
To lead you down some other way,
   Go bind him in his olden thills—
Sing us again of Mandalay!

Master, regard the plaint we bring,
   And hearken to the prayer we pray.
Lay down your law and sermoning—
   Sing us again of Mandalay!

There are moments to counteract these martial strains; moments such as those in *The Transport General Ferguson,* when the Tennyson warriors whose duty it is to know not why, turn in their tombs and "wonder what they've got to do it for." In general, however, the view is distinctly Nietzschean, years before Mencken has heard of the superman.

For 'tis ever the weak that must help the strong,
Though they have no part in the triumph song,
And their glory is brief as their work is long—
   (Sing ho! for the saints of war!)

—A WAR SONG

So, too, the *Sklavenmoral,* with its compensations of a better and more equitable world above, is ironically hymned in *Faith:*

> The Gawd that made the ocean
> An' painted up the sky,
> The Gawd that set us livin'
> An' takes us when we die,
> Is just the same to ev'ry man,
> Of high or low degree,
> An' no one's better treated than
> Poor little you and little me.

The imitations of Herrick are not nearly so successful as those of Kipling. They are banal and miss entirely the delicacy of the original; now and then, by the time Mencken's fan has playfully descended to tap milady's cheek, it has turned into a slapstick with a lower goal. He coarsens the texture; if a Latin pun may be permitted, he turns Herrick's *carpe diem* into *carpe deam.* It is the beauty of the divine lass, rather than the poetry of the moment, that beguiles him.

ROUNDEL

> If love were all and we could cheat
> All gods but Cupid of their due,
> Our joy in life would be complete.
>
> We'd only live that we might woo
> (Instead, as now, that we may eat),
> And ev'ry lover would be true,—
> If love were all.
>
> Yet, if we found our bread and meat
> In kisses it would please but few,

Soon life would grow a cloying sweet,
    If love were all.

THE RONDEAU OF RICHES

If I were rich and had a store,
Of gold doubloons and louis d'or—
    A treasure for a pirate crew—
    Then I would spend it all for you—
My heart's delight and conqueror!

About your feet upon the floor,
Ten thousand rubies I would pour—
    Regardless of expense, I'd woo
        If I were rich.

But as I'm not, I can but soar
Mid fancy's heights and ponder o'er
    The things that I would like to do;
    And as I pass them in review
It strikes me that you'd love me more
        If I were rich.

A MADRIGAL

How can I choose but love you,
    Maid of the witching smile?
Your eyes are as blue as the skies above you;
How can I choose but love you, love you,
    You and your witching smile?
For the red of your lips is the red of the rose,
And the white of your brows is the white of the snows,
And the gold of your hair is the splendor that glows
    When the sun gilds the east at morn.
And the blue of your eyes

Is the blue of the skies
　Of an orient day new-born;
And your smile has a charm that is balm to the soul,
And your pa has a bar'l and a many-plunk roll,
　So how can I choose but love you, love you,
Love you, love you, love you?

Of far better stuff is the other *Madrigal* for which
Mencken has written a robust musical setting; college
humor gives way to a mannish confession that leaves one
no less a man:

Ah! what were all the running brooks
　From ocean-side to ocean-side,
　　And what were all the chattering wrens
　That wake the wood with song,
　　And what were all the roses red
　In all the flowery meadows wide,
　　And what were all the fairy clouds
　That 'cross the heavens throng—
　　And what were all the joys that bide
　　In meadow, wood and down,
　　To me, if I were at your side
　　Within the joyless town?

Likewise, behind the Chaucerian spelling of *A Paradox* is a feeling that could not quite be masked in man-
nerism; there must have been a girl here, much nearer
home than *The Canterbury Tales:*

A PARADOX

Dan Cupyd drewe hys lyttle bowe,
　And strayght ye arrowe from it flewe,

Although its course was rather lowe,
    I thought 'twould pass above my heade—
In stature I am shorte, you knowe.

But soone upon my breast a stayne
    Of blood appeared, and showed ye marke
Whereat ye boy god tooke hys aime;
    I staggered, groaned and then—I smyled!
Egad! it was a pleasante payne!

The stanzas that close the collection chant an abiding cynicism. They are even, in a Menckenian way, didactic. Yet if we had to pigeon-hole him, his place would be much nearer to the second and third men of his rhymes than to the first.

FINIS

There was a man that delved in the earth
    For glittering gems and gold,
And whatever lay hidden that seemed of worth
    He carefully seized and sold;
So his days were long and his store was great,
    And ever for more he sighed,
'Til kings bowed down and he ruled in state—
    And after awhile he died.

> *Oh, blithesome and shrill the wails resound!*
> *Oh, gaily his children moan!*
>   *And the end of it all was a hole in the ground*
> *And a scratch on a crumbling stone.*

There was a man that fought for the right,
    And never a friend had he,

'Til after the dark there dawned the light
    And the world could know and see;
Oh, long was the fight and comfortless,
    But great was the fighter's pride,
And a victor he rose from the storm and stress—
    And after awhile he died.

> *Oh, great was the fame but newly found*
> *Of the man that fought alone!*
>   *And the end of it all was a hole in the ground*
> *And a scratch on a crumbling stone.*

There was a man that dreamed a dream,
    And his pen it served his brain;
And great was his art and great his theme
    And long was his laurelled reign;
But after awhile the world forgot
    And his work was pushed aside,
(For to serve and wait is the mortal lot)
    And then, in the end, he died.

> *Oh! brown on his brow were the bays that bound*
> *And far was his glory flown!*
>   *And the end of it all was a hole in the ground*
> *And a scratch on a crumbling stone.*

Mencken, seeking to suppress his first book, exhibited on the whole an excellent faculty of self-criticism. Its value inheres, almost entirely, in its psychological illumination.

In any larger, truly vital sense of the word, Mencken is a poet,—not only in the Greek sense, but in the sense of one who seeks and revels in beauty. But always, on his quest, he is companioned by a powerful giant of common sense,—too sensible if not too common. Today he is suspicious of the poet. The poet is a sublimated magician. He lulls you to sleep with music, and then works his incantations upon your helplessness. Poetry, to him, is the infancy of the race, the adolescence of the individual. It is not without significance that he is more happy in his estimates of poetic movements than in his views of the separate poets comprising them. The movements are largely political, sociological, philosophical entities that may be criticized in terms of ideas; the poets are human puzzles which must be evaluated in terms of emotion. And Mencken, right or wrong, is always on guard against emotion. Love, the poetry of sex, finds him equally skeptical. Yet, just as his reasoned skepticism of love hardly blinds him to the beauties of the over-poetized sex, neither does his suspicion of the poet deafen him to the strains of the song.

"Once," he writes, in "The Poet and His Art" (*Prejudices,* Third Series),

after plowing through sixty or seventy volumes of bad verse, I described myself as a poetry-hater. The epithet was and is absurd. The truth is that I enjoy poetry as much as the next man—when the mood is on me. But what mood? The mood, in a few words, of intellectual and spiritual fatigue, the mood of revolt against the insoluble riddle of existence, the mood of disgust and despair. Poetry, then, is a capital medicine. First its sweet music lulls, and then its artful presentation of the beautifully improbable soothes and gives surcease. It is an escape from life, like religion, like enthusiasm, like glimpsing a pretty girl. And to the mere sensuous joy in it, to the mere low delight in getting away from the world for a bit, there is added, if the poetry be good, something vastly better, something reaching out into the realm of the intelligent, to-wit, appreciation of good workmanship. A sound sonnet is almost as pleasing an object as a well-written fugue. A pretty lyric, deftly done, has all the technical charm of a fine carving. I think it is craftsmanship that I admire most in the world. Brahms enchants me because he knew his trade perfectly. I like Richard Strauss because he is full of technical ingenuities, because he is a master-workman. Well, who ever heard of a finer craftsman than William Shakespeare? His music was magnificent, he played superbly upon all the common emotions —and he did it magnificently, he did it with an air. No, I am no poetry-hater. But even Shakespeare I most enjoy, not on brisk mornings when I feel fit for any deviltry, but on dreary evenings when my old wounds are troubling me, and some fickle one has just sent back the autographed set of my first editions, and bills are piled up on my desk, and I am too sad to work. Then I mix a stiff dram—and read poetry.

The personal significance of this passage lies in its insistence upon poetry as a crafty assault upon weakness. There is a self-control which Mencken never willingly relinquishes. And to him, characteristically, the best examples of this weakness of emotional surrender are those in which the intellect has at least reared the structure. Yet Mencken, as critic, forgetting the theories, practises better than he theorizes. By his own definition, such critics as Carlyle, Macaulay and Arnold become poets, for, "they could make the thing charming, and that is always a million times more important than making it true." Truth is an ideational concept; charm an emotional. But who has said that there is no such thing as poetical truth? Another paradox that is reconciled to its self-contradiction. In Mencken, the reconciliation is imperfect. He sees the poetry of truth; he does not quite see the truth of poetry. The root of the matter, as he has written elsewhere concerning the critic's choice of criticism rather than of "what is called creative" writing, lies in "temperament—perhaps more accurately in hormones—with accident of education and environment to help."

III

It is this early predilection for ideas as against emotions, this early suspicion of the female as the betrayer into emotion, that led Mencken to Shaw for his début into the world of criticism. Between the Baltimorean and the Irishman there is a strange affinity, for all the differences that divide them. There is, for example, this same masculinity, this same suspicion, this same preoccupation with ideas, this same trend away from the feelings toward an abstract contemplation of man that is heightened, rather than lessened, by actual participation in the hurly-burly. When Shaw describes Dick Dudgeon of *The Devil's Disciple* he is, paring away the disguising details, describing himself; and when Mencken quotes that description, unconsciously he does—again allowing for irrelevant details—the same for the author of *George Bernard Shaw: His Plays.*

Dick Dudgeon is a Puritan of the Puritans. He is brought up in a household where the Puritan religion has died and become, in its corruption, an excuse for his mother's master passion of hatred in all its phases of cruelty and envy. In such a home he finds himself starved of religion, which is the most clamorous need of his nature. With all his mother's indomitable selfishness, but with pity instead of hatred as his master-passion, he pities the devil, takes his side, and champions him, like a true Covenanter, against the world. He thus becomes, like all genuinely religious men, a reprobate and an outcast. Once this is understood, the play becomes straightforwardly simple.[1]

Here is an ambivalence of which the Baltimorean is compact. He even reads himself into Shaw. Thus, on page xiii of his Introduction:

Popular opinion and himself to the contrary notwithstanding, Shaw is not a mere preacher. The function of the dramatist is not that of the village pastor. He has no need to exhort, nor to call upon his hearers to come to the mourners' bench. All the world expects him to do is to picture human life as he sees it, as accurately and effectively as he can. Like the artist in color, form, or tone, his business is with impressions. A man painting an Alpine scene endeavors to produce, not a mere record of each rock and tree, but an impression upon the observer like that he would experience were he to stand in the artist's place and look upon the snow-capped crags. In music it is the same. Beethoven set out, with melody and harmony, to arouse the emotions that stir us upon pondering the triumphs of a great conqueror. Hence the Eroica Symphony. Likewise, with curves and color, Millet tried to awaken the soft content that falls upon us when we gaze across the fields at even-tide and hear the distant vesper-bell—and we have "The Angelus."

---

[1] Shaw, of course, is full of that self-revelation and that self-discussion which I have called *Shawtobiography*. His Blanco Posnet is a later Dick Dudgeon, similarly saved at the last moment from the noose, similarly "going soft" to the point of self-sacrifice, similarly an American. *The Devil's Disciple* and *Blanco Posnet* give Shaw dead away.

The influences playing upon Mencken at the time are clear; they are, chiefly, Mark Twain, Rudyard Kipling, Friedrich Nietzsche and Thomas Huxley. The peculiar character of Shaw's new art is set against the background of Charles Darwin; the artist is related, not only to his physiological and psychological differentia, but to his ancestral and sociological past and to his immediate environment. "What else is talent but a name for experience, practice, appropriation, incorporation, from the times of our forefathers?" he quotes from Nietzsche, going on to say in *By Way of Introduction:*

A century is a mere clock-tick in eternity, but measured by human events it is a hundred years. Napoleon Bonaparte, born in 1786, became an officer of artillery and gravedigger for an epoch. Born in 1868, he might have become a journeyman genius of the boulevards, a Franco-Yankee trust magnate, or the democratic boss of Kansas City. And so, contrariwise, George Bernard Shaw, born in 1756 instead of 1856, might have become a goldstick-in-waiting at the Court of St. James or Archbishop of Canterbury. The accident that made him what he is was one of time. He saw the light after, instead of before Charles Darwin.

Young as he was, however, he was not deceived into making this the basis of what we might call today a behavioristic school of literary criticism. He brings no weights and measures for the fatuous task of determining the quantitative analysis of heredity and environment; intuitively he recognizes that what makes the artist is his origin *plus* that unpredictable entity which is the sum of these parts, an entity which, in defiance of the laws of geometry, is yet a whole greater than the sum of its parts. "No two men see the same thing in exactly the same way, and there are no fixed standards whereby we may decide whether one or the other or neither is right." That simple sentence lifts the problems of criticism up from behaviorism to the plane of a psychology that uses every resource of biology without surrendering to it.

Here, too, in his most unmaidenly maiden criticism, Mencken intones two of his characteristic motifs: antagonism to the ethical principle in art, and antagonism to the masculine fallacy in life. For both, Shaw provides him a facile text. The quotation from page xiii sets down likewise a view of the Irishman which Mencken has since considerably modified.

Stating the relation of the dramatist to his play, Mencken thus early indicates his own essentially æsthetic attitude toward that vaster stage, the world. "The dramatist, properly speaking, is not concerned about the outcome of the struggle. All he is required to do is to draw the two sides accurately and understandingly and to show the conflict naturally. In other words, it is not his business to decide the matter for his audience. . . ."

Just as clearly, in his approving comment upon the Shavian outlook, as set forth in *Arms and the Man* (not only the arms of Virgil's lines, but the softer arms of woman!) Mencken sows the seed of his own ironical *In Defense of Woman*. "Ninety-nine men in every hundred, when they go a-courting, fancy that they are the aggressors in the ancient game and rather pride themselves upon their enterprise and daring. Hence we find Don Juan a popular hero. As a matter of fact, says Shaw, it is the woman that ordinarily makes the first advances and the woman that lures, forces or drags the man on to the climax of marriage." This callow young editor grows eloquent on the subject of what he calls, later in the book, "the marriage comedy." By the time he reaches *Man and Superman,* he has worked himself up to such a pitch that he bursts forth into a paragraph that I would indicate as the first example of the mature Mencken. The climactic passage of *George Bernard Shaw: His Plays* is not merely a brilliant coloratura solo; it is not simply a dazzling pyrotechnical display; it is not only an incipient critic running amuck with the language; it is not solely a phantasmagoria of tropes and turns. It is first-rate criticism couched in a voice that has not been heard before. Through this book on Shaw, Mencken speaks largely and unconsciously for H. L. M. In this passage on *Man and Superman,* sailing like Columbus for India, he discovers America; at the height of his expository enthusiasm for the Irishman, he discovers and reveals himself:

Measured with rule, plumb-line or hay-scales, "Man and Super-man" is easily Shaw's *magnum opus.* In bulk it is brobdignagian; in scope it is stupendous; in purpose it is one with the Odyssey. Like a full-rigged ship before a spanking breeze, it cleaves deep into the waves, sending ripples far to port and starboard, and its giant canvases rise half way to the clouds, with resplendent jibs, sky-sails, staysails and studding-sails standing out like quills upon the fretful porcupine. It has a preface as long as a campaign speech; an interlude in three scenes, with music and red fire; and a complete digest of the German philosophers as an appendix. With all its rings and satellites it fills a tome of 281 closely-printed pages. Its epigrams, quips, jests, and quirks are multitudinous; it preaches treason to all the schools; its hero has one speech of 350 words. No one but a circus press agent could rise to an adequate description of its innumerable marvels. It is a three-ring circus, with Ibsen doing running high jumps; Schopenhauer playing the calliope and Nietzsche selling peanuts in the reserved seats. And all the while it is the most entertaining play of its generation.

Maybe Shaw wrote it in a vain effort to rid himself at one fell swoop of all the disquieting doctrines that infested his innards. Into it he unloaded Kropotkin, Noyes, Bakóunin, Wilde, Marx, Proudhon, Nietzsche, Netschajew, Wagner, Bunyan, Mozart, Shelley, Ibsen, Morris, Tolstoi, Goethe, Schopenhauer, Plato—seized them by the heels and heaved them in, with a sort of relieved "God help you!" The result is 281 pages of most diverting farce—farce that only half hides the tumultuous uproar of the two-and-seventy jarring sects beneath it. It is a tract cast in an encyclopedic and epic mold—a stupendous, magnificent colossal effort to make a dent in the cosmos with a slapstick.

A dent in the cosmos with a slapstick! Here is half of Mencken's signature.

Discussing the character of Marchbanks in *Candida*, Mencken, with a wry face, waved farewell to himself of two years before in a supercilious sentence. "He inhabits a world a mile or so above the pink clouds of the sunset, and writes vague, immaterial verses of the sort that all of us invent and some of us set down in pen-and-ink when we are young." Mencken's verses, as we have seen, were hardly Marchbanksian; they had been abandoned, however, for good. His newspaper work had become too heavy and his interest in prose, as a more difficult medium, had grown. "Any literate boy of

nineteen," he has told me, "can write passable lyrics,
but I doubt that any man has a sound prose style before
thirty." I do not see that these contentions, even if
true, involve the inferiority of poetry. I mention the
abandonment of poetry because Mencken was soon, despite his brilliant beginning, to desert dramatic criticism
with like fickleness. Since his resignation in 1909 as
theatrical critic for the Baltimore *Sun,* in the columns of
which he had struck so many valiant blows for Shaw,
he has written on the theory of the drama, practised it as
a playwright and elucidated it as an editor, yet he has not
been in a theatre more than a dozen times. It is almost
unbelievable. It is all that a Methodist could ask!

The drama has indeed become for him a sort of
adolescent poetry to be avoided.

"The drama," he has written, in "Reflections on the
Drama" (*Prejudices, Third Series*)

is the most democratic of the art forms, and perhaps the only
one that may legitimately bear the label. Painting, sculpture,
music and literature, so far as they show any genuine æsthetic or
intellectual content at all, are not for crowds, but for selected
individuals, mostly with bad kidneys and worse morals, and three
of the four are almost always enjoyed in actual solitude. Even
architecture and religious ritual, though they are publicly displayed, make their chief appeal to man as individual, not to man
as mass animal. One goes into a church as part of a crowd, true
enough, but if it be a church that has risen above mere theological
disputation to the beauty of ceremonial, one is, even in theory,
alone with the Lord God Jehovah.

Let us pause for a moment to note the unadulterated
æstheticism of Mencken's supposititious visit to Church.

"I don't go to church for the religion," said a prominent South American Catholic to me, "I go for the spectacle. It's such a good show." Life, again, in the Menckenian sense, as a show. So, too, Mencken's normal woman, with her innate sense of beauty, "insofar as she has any religion at all, moves irresistibly toward Catholicism, with its poetical obscurantism."

The drama, however, "as representation, is inconceivable save as a show for the mob, and so it has to take on protective coloration to survive. It must make its appeal, not to individuals as such, nor even to individuals as units in the mob, but to the mob as mob—a quite different thing, as Gustave Le Bon long ago demonstrated in his 'Psychologie des Foules.' Thus its intellectual content, like its æsthetic form, must be within the mental grasp of the mob, and what is more important, within the scope of its prejudices. *Per corollary,* anything even remotely approaching an original idea, or an unpopular idea, is foreign to it, and, if it would make any impression at all, abhorrent to it. The best a dramatist can hope to do is to give poignant and arresting expression to an idea so simple that the average man will grasp it at once, and so banal that he will approve it in the next instant. The phrase 'drama of ideas' thus becomes a mere phrase. What is actually meant by it is 'drama of platitudes.' "

Now, all this is sound, but it concerns, at bottom, not so much the drama as the theatre; the theatre as a social institution, not the drama as an artist's, therefore an individual's, creation of beauty out of passion. Mencken is striking, as usual, at the mob. That the drama should not be, primarily, a hatchery of ideas is as evident as the fact that all art originates in emotions, not concepts. The most intellectual structure ever reared by man's mind may be reduced, by the skilful psychologist, to a few platitudes. Scratch an idea in art and you get an emotion. And the emotions are the most ancient platitudinarians of them all! The mob desires the obvious; even in the acknowledged masterpieces it responds only to obviousness, and this is as true of the mob reading at home in seclusion as it is of the mob massed in an auditorium. More: the person who loses his individuality by the fact of mere presence among the mob, sinks for just so long to the mob level. Mencken, in whom revolt against the mob is an inevitable aspect of his own fierce pride in personality and independence, justly heaps scorn upon the theatre, which is the home par excellence of the mob as audience. The real drama, however,—which exists as art, whether a comprehending hermit reads it in a woodland retreat or ten thousand morons applaud their misunderstanding of it in a theatre,—is a matter entirely different. It is, like all art, the product of an individual; it addresses, like all art, an individual. And of it, Mencken rightly asks what one may ask of all the arts: "the unrealities that are its essence," the "romance that never was on land or sea," the "buffoonery that is at the bottom of all we actually know of human life." The conscious embroideries of man in any of the arts can affect, after all, the visible structure, the obvious thoughts and emotions; the masterpiece grows beneath the surface, hidden as much from the master as from his humblest admirer.

IV

The Philosophy of Friedrich Nietzche, first published three years after the book on Shaw, achieved for
Mencken an analogous crystallization of ideas. In the
Shaw book, Mencken formulates a hard, tough-minded
attitude toward woman; in that on Nietzsche, he supports, though by no means with the enthusiasm that
informed the dramatic essay, such an attitude toward
life. His early prejudices against the herd and against
the compensatory religion of that herd assume philosophic coherence. Christianity, the doctrine of the
weak, justifies the failures of the mobman; the anti-
Christianity of the Superman justifies the triumph of the
superior. But Mencken, though he did not then see
that Nietzsche's philosophy was born in appreciable
measure of a personal weakness just as surely as was
Christianity born similarly of a secular inferiority, is not
led astray by the German's vaticinations. He assimi-
lates what is sound; he rejects what is shaky. The book
is chiefly expository; as criticism it discriminates with a
mature intelligence. As exposition it is remarkably lu-
cid; as criticism, it is, to me, stronger not on the philosophical, but on the æsthetic, side. Here was the cue
that Mencken caught too indistinctly. There are moments in which the German anti-Christ is rather a super-
Christ, knowingly sacrificing himself for a visioned
race of supermen yet unborn. This race is his after-life,
as impossible as any heaven dreamt of in the philosophy
of priest or bonze or rabbi. His belief in the doctrine
of eternal recurrence is as childish as any myth that ever

consoled a devotee. His very superhumanity is a wish-
fulfilment in the Freudian manner, with loud overtones
of Adler. He could yield to wilful prejudices as easily
as the softest sentimentalist. He is that which no philosophy or philosopher can transcend: a cosmic poet and
prophet, building a stern Utopia out of the all-too-human
stuff of mankind. That he went mad, as Mencken
rightly contends, attests the weakness of his organism,
not of the thoughts that were born of his brain. These
live an independent existence.

Mencken's philosophy is an anti-philosophy. Because
he has translated Nietzsche, and because, at the age of
twenty-eight, he wrote upon the German visionary one
of the finest expository studies devoted to his labors, he
has been readily classified as a Nietzschean. To be sure,
he shares the epigrammatic quality of the master, and his
impatience with the Philistine. Not for him, however,
the Nietzschean flight into the clouds, the Nietzschean
irrationality that seems at times to transcend rather than
to outrage reason. Not for him the Nietzschean lapses
into the metaphysical. Nietzsche himself has spared his
followers the errors that had to be made. The truth is
that philosophical systems, good or bad, make Mencken
impatient. And, in my opinion, rightly. They awaken
suspicion. They are an easy ascent to the heaven of
certainty. A system ever threatens to degenerate into a
theology. Croce, it seems to me, after having built up
a formidable system, laying tome upon tome like story
upon story of a vast edifice, has blown the structure to
atoms with a single paragraph of his penetrating study,
La poesia di Dante. I have alluded to it more than

once, and in the most varied connections; it will bear repetition. Commenting upon the word "illogica," Croce writes that it means "not entirely harmonized," and that it applies to the system of every man and every philosopher, who always possesses some aspect "not harmonized," not logical. This aspect, he goes on to say, is precisely the source whence springs the new thought or the so-called new progress. It is indicative that Croce, in this very passage that treats of the illogicality of Dante's system, parenthetically applies the observation of the systems of all men.[1] Artistic personality thus becomes a triumph over logic. Here we have, in so many words, the passive, potential negation of all philosophical systems. It is an attitude which Mencken exemplifies. It connotes a vast receptivity and a comparable power of rejection. It is the apotheosis of the Great Uncertain.

In his *Nietzsche,* discussing the controversy between Nietzsche and Wagner, Mencken affords us a pretty example of his essentially æsthetic attitude toward art and life alike. He sides with the composer against the philosopher. "Nietzsche's whole case against Wagner is based upon a fallacy. . . . It is true enough that his book contains some remarkably acute and searching observations upon art, and that, granting his premises, his general conclusions would be correct, but we are by no means granting his premises. Wagner may have been a traitor to his philosophy, but if he had remained loyal to it, his art would have been impossible. And in view of the sublime beauty of that art we may well

[1] *La poesia di Dante,* Bari, 1921. Gius, Laterza & Figli. Page 55.

pardon him for not keeping the faith." Artists, indeed, do not keep faiths; their business, chiefly, is not a petty fidelity, but creation; not intellect, but emotion; not truth, but passion. Perhaps life, as an art, is rendered barren by all our pompous systems, representing, every one of them, a sterile triumph of the intellect over the emotions; here, too, as in the lesser arts, the great use of the intellect should be as a none too rigid guide, not as a self-important chaperone. There is life in feeling; in all thought there is a touch of death. In between lies art, reveling in paradox, where life and death work their will below the conscious level. There are persons in whom that subterranean conflict rises just above the surface; their paradoxical lives are a symbol, as it were, of the unceasing struggle. Mencken is one of these symbols, reveling in the consciousness of the fray. He is amphitheatre, surgeon, patient, audience, all in one.

For the rest, as far as concerns Nietzsche, I have always considered him in the light, not of sociology but of psychology; not as a law-giver but as an artist.

V

In *Men Vs. the Man* the prejudices acquired from his father's talk, the philosophy strengthened by a study of Nietzsche, the gift of polemics that was being developed in his newspaper life, come to flower in a humorous exchange of letters upon the science called dismal. Here Mencken appears plainly in the rôle of a pugilist who, even though he lack the power to administer a knockout, can win on points. Here he is the son of the father, who, confronted with the Knights of Labor in the middle eighties, played one of his cruellest tricks.

August Mencken paid his men union wages, but he refused to treat with walking delegates, inside the shop or out. During this strike the Cigarmakers' Union had a large fund, which it pitched against the endurance of the Baltimore bosses. All floating cigarmakers were sent to Philadelphia, then the paradise of certain employment. Mencken père, knowing that at the city of brotherly love no further proof was asked of a workingman than the possession of a cigar-board, set about collecting every left-over board he could assemble. The cellars of every factory were piled up with such boards, abandoned there by drunkards or wanderers; these the cigar manufacturer distributed to a riff-raff of tramps, sailors and any other such derelicts that he could find, shipped them off to the Union headquarters to get free train tickets to Philadelphia, and in the end thus wrecked the strike fund. As his signature to the deed, he finished by sending along a one-armed man in testimony of the fraud. A buffoonery in the grand manner that tickled him inordinately!

This cruelty,—this echo of the Nietzsche who hated most of all the Socialists, because they had implanted an infertile discontent into the bosoms of workmen by nature intended for an inferior caste—is to be found in Mencken's answers to La Monte's epistles. Reducing the arguments to their smallest compass, we have Mencken, on the one hand, contending that Socialism overlooks certain ineradicable characteristics of the human animal, and certain immutable laws of the biological process. Going further, I believe that these characteristics and laws deserve to be fostered and obeyed rather than opposed, for to their influence we owe all that we have of progress.

His aristocracy is not the ancient fetich of hereditary privilege; it was Napoleon Bonaparte's error that he tried to perpetuate such supremacy in his descendants, overlooking thus a "new idea" which had come into the world, namely,

that an aristocracy must constantly justify its existence.

A member of such an aristocracy, which to Mencken is composed of efficient men of the highest caste

makes it his rule to accept the world as he finds it, and to work out his own salvation with a light heart. His joy is in effort, in work, in progress. A difficulty overcome, a riddle solved, an enemy vanquished, a fact proved, an error destroyed—in such things he finds the meaning of life and surcease from its sorrows.

Our contemplation of the cosmic process he would purge of all human emotionalism.

It is, indeed, utterly unemotional, and its lack of emotion is its principal characteristic.

In fine, individualism raised to the nth degree. La Monte's contention, on the other hand, without repudiating the more general bases of Mencken's individualism, is that

I am a Socialist, not because I am an enemy of aristocracy, or because I undervalue it, but because I wish the proportion of aristocrats to reach the highest possible maximum.

. . . .

So that, my dear Mencken, it is in the name of Individualism, strange as it may appear to you, that I call upon you once more to become the comrade of   Yours faithfully,   R. R. La M.

Mencken, however, did not hasten into the arms of La Monte. His politics of 1909 remain, essentially, those of 1925, although he may—after branding the La Follette platform as idiotic—vote for La Follette on the score that his opponents have been so mendacious in their campaigning. Is it Capitalism that Mencken has been defending, or Individualism, which is a bird of a different species? Has not a great part of Mencken's service to the nation—however little he may be moved by a desire for public service—been his unrelenting warfare upon the extreme forms of individualism that may be assumed by capitalists bent on retaining their power? Is not his repudiation of the Napoleonic conception of aristocracy similarly a thrust at another extreme of individualism run rampant?

What is the personal flower of this individualistic revolt? The aristocrat. Not so much the inherited title as the man of proved superiority. Mencken cherishes the prejudice of blood; to the blue blood of the false, titular aristocracy, however, he opposes the red blood of the true. His aristocrat has conquered, as the last great conquest, himself. This aristocracy, as we may expect, has not yet attained to the serene contemplation of its own excellencies. It must discover function in opposition.

It demands contrast. It requires a dramatic statement of its virtues. It requires a statement, just as dramatic, of the popular vices. The values, however, have been transvaluated; his virtues appear as vices, his vices as virtues. He stands the world on its head; or, to see the spectacle from his post of observation, he places it back upon its feet.

The anti-Christian of the religious sphere becomes the anti-Socialist of the economic. After shattering man's illusions of a heaven above, he proceeds to batter down man's illusions of a heaven on earth. Utopia in the clouds; Utopia on *terra firma*. It is as if, in his individualistic determinism, Mencken would have man find his own salvation, even if partial salvation might be ushered in the sooner by collective effort. Here, however, lurks an inconsistency. Collectivist effort, whatever the "ism" under which its cohorts will be marshalled, will never bring heaven to an earth which nature has doomed, considerably, to hell. Man may rationalize biology; he is, none the less, but the creature of a creation. Yet man rose from the animal through the revolt of the superior. Man, under what we call civilization, rises to true aristocracy through revolt against herd standards. That revolt may be eased by collective action. What, indeed, does Mencken do when the censors go gunning after one of his favorite authors? He circulates petitions with all the energy of a garmentworker collecting strike funds. Collective action that has for its aim the enthronement of the mob-rule called democracy deserves all the scorn that Mencken has heaped upon it. Collective action that has been contaminated with standardized, ethic-ridden religious thinking, places itself in the same class. Any collective action, however,—whatever its roseate claims and illusions,—that will have as effect the removal of artificial economic barriers to self-preservation and self-expression, makes the path to valid personal aristocracy so much the easier. As a supporter of Capitalism, Mencken is incongruously contemptuous of its logical products. He is, because of his sheer honesty in his depiction of it, one of the most valuable allies that the anti-capitalistic factions have ever happened upon. Popular vote is not soon likely to mean popular rule; the class in power will see to that. But our governing classes, too, are unworthy of the power they usurp. A democracy educated to the point where it triumphs over the fact of its own numerical superiority, is as yet a mirage of the future, a poem in terms of sociology. That we are all born free and equal is so much patent bosh. The most we can ask of society is that it provide an opportunity whereby inherent superiorities shall not be stifled under the burden of economic injustice. No government can ever make strong the weak; no government can ever permanently eviscerate the strong. Mencken's scorn for the democrat, the mobman, the subman—one of his most solid and inspiring contributions to our national thought—is the natural scorn of conscious superiority for envious inferiority. It is also, by implication, a vision. It could be more humane without sacrificing any essential quality; it does not happen to be. Again a matter of glands. Within the mobocracy there are minorities more or less consciously striving, in association, to make easier the path toward fullest expansion of self. That is a stride in the direction of valid aristocracy. The Menckenian vituperation of the mob, the Menckenian assault upon collectivism are in themselves so surely the product of his exaggerated individualism that they are of value, chiefly, not as sociology but as an anarchistic, psychological reaction. I have met Socialists who found him far more stimulating than Karl Marx or than even the far better stylist, Engels; Mencken, in a word, was just the free-functioning individual which they expected a Socialistic society to produce; or, to put it less optimistically, that individual would, under a less grinding economic order, find it easier to arrive. Mencken says he does not cherish the sentimentality that the minority has rights. But he cannot say that they do not represent a break away from conformity. I look to no form of society for the production of great men; the best that even Utopia could do would be to give the vast majority its creature comforts. By that same token, however, it would release the energy of the superior for their superiority. It was Poe, after all, not Mencken, who harbored the illusion that genius thrives in poverty.

Let us call this new dispensation aristo-democracy, or what you will. But let us not ask too much of it. Progress has been largely an illusion; always, however, there are men and women—a shining few—who must outstrip their fellows in the race toward the mirage. Theologians may speak of goals; the mob may believe; the elect know only of uncertain, adventurous roads along which there is an occasional glimpse of beauty.

"It is the instinct of true aristocracy," says Mencken (in his notable essay upon "The National Letters," *Prejudices, Second Series*), not to punish eccentricity by expulsion, but to throw a mantle of protection about it—to safeguard it from the suspicions and resentments of the lower orders. Those lower orders are inert, timid, inhospitable to ideas, hostile to changes, faithful to a few maudlin superstitions. All progress goes on on the higher levels. It is there that salient personalities, made secure by artificial immunities, may oscillate most widely from the normal track. It is within that entrenched fold, out of reach of the immemorial certainties of the mob, that extraordinary men of the lower orders may find their city of refuge, and breathe a clean air. This, indeed, is at once the hall-mark of an aristocracy—that it is beyond responsibility to the general masses of men, and hence superior to their degraded longings, and their no less degraded aversions. It is nothing if it is not autonomous, curious, venturesome, courageous, and everything if it is. It is the custodian of the qualities that make for change and experiment; it is the class that organizes danger for the service of the race; it pays for its high prerogatives by standing in the forefront of the fray.

This is a *locus classicus* of the Menckenian canon. See how it rises into an un-Americanese eloquence, borne upward on the tide of his well-controlled fervor. See how the ethical overtone quivers above the aristocratic fundamental: "for the service of the race": (This is a Nietzschean "lapse"; the German, too, had his fond thoughts of a superior posterity.) There is affirmation here: but there is protest, revolt.

Revolt of the dynamic against the static.

Revolt against the mob, with its quantitative standards; its psychology of inferiority.

Against the Philistine, the Puritan: base standards and censorship incarnate. Democracy, the body of the mob; Puritanism the mind and soul of mobdom.

Against levels; against conformity; against "right-thinking"; against all tradition-for-tradition's-sake.

And lastly, supremely, the revolt against self.

The circle is now complete. The right to differ, not only from one's fellow man, but from one's self. The right to inconsistency. The right to be wrong. The right of self-contradiction on the way to the new synthesis. The *perpetuum mobile* of the spirit. The play of indeterminism in a circle of determinism. A cycle of uncertainties in which birth and death are the recurrent motifs.

The Menckenian aristocrat knows power and its prejudices; he has not yet learned pity and its predilections; not, like a Havelock Ellis, transmuted relaxed power into a fructifying pity that does not relinquish any prerogative of power; not, like a Thomas Hardy, blended that pity with a tonic irony. Even today, to Mencken, a Debs is, like all lesser Socialists, a fool. A fool? Why not a poet? If life is a dream, is not one dream as good as another to live and die by, so it be a dream served with the loyalty of one's own higher sanction?

Mencken's assault upon the mob has impressed itself indelibly upon American life. He has pricked the bubble of that farce which has been called Democracy. He has altered the conception of *Vox Populi* even among the most liberal of the intelligentsia. And so doing he has performed a service that more than counterbalances the harshest of the criticisms that he has leveled, whether against the nation as a whole or against the internationalists of the world. There remains the saddest jest of all: the very Socialists who have been most of-

fended by his gibes are made up, not of the masses whom
they have thus far failed to enlist in their own interests,
but of a distinct, even a civilized, minority. As La
Monte might have added, the Socialists have more in
common with a Mencken than they have with the resist-
ing working-class. And as Mencken may not deny, his
individualistic cruelty is untempered by social pity only
in an abstract way. Who was it, for all his doctrine of
killing off the weak, that sent milk twice a month to the
starving babes of war-scarred Europe? Thou art the
man!

VI

From Germany comes not only Socialism, but beer.
And not only beer, but *Gemütlichkeit*. To Mencken, as
is clearly evident in *Europe After 8:15*, drinking is an
art, not a trough; it is, one might say, a fluid music
played upon the palate, not a potion to drug the senses
and lead the way to escape from life. There have been
a few who, drunk with their own imaginings, have set
down Mencken as a drunkard. Well, if that be the
case, one might echo Lincoln's answer to the tender
ladies who objected to having as general a drinker such
as Grant. Where might a fellow find that brand, and
then turn out an annual volume of work such as pours
forth from Baltimore, putting the sober fraternity to
shame?

Drink, of course, may represent escape; it may stand
for that very evasion of reality which so many "realists"
prate against in literature, only to practise it in life. It
may represent, moreover, the secret softness of the hard-

ened literati who, after filling column upon column with diatribes against the sentimentality of our fiction, have recourse to the bottle, where they do what Huck Finn would call their own "sentimentering." Drink, in a word, is to such superior fellows as these a "literature of escape." They find, *in vino,* not *veritas,* but *illusio;* they forget that if truth lies at the bottom of a well, it is a well of spring-water, not of synthetic gin.

For this gentry Mencken entertains no feeling of brotherhood. He can look down on them with all the scorn of a temperance lecturer. He knows, as they will never know, the true meaning of the mystic word uttered by Rabelais' Oracle of the Bottle. He is a true brother to the high-priestess Bacbuc. His drinking is not the last refuge of despair; it is no sea in which to drown adversity. Rather does it add charm to woman and song; rather is it, indeed, part of the music of living.

Of *Europe After 8:15* Mencken wrote the Preface, the chapter on Munich, and the beginning and end of that on London. Turn to the dithyramb on Munich (as sheer writing, in my opinion, one of the finest things that Mencken has done thus far) and you can fairly taste the floods of beer he sings about. Here is a Rabelaisian gusto; here is an all-but-intoxication of words. A step higher would be either music or Katzen-jammer. This is eating, drinking, and making merry; here is emotional expansion, but under an indulgent in-tellectual control. Here is an intoxication of the spirit, attuned to a remarkable sobriety of the mind. If this be drunkenness, make the most of it! I quote a char-acteristic passage.

Let us not, however, be unjust to the estimable Herr Wirt of the Hoftheater Café, with his pneumatic tread, his chaste side whiskers and his long-tailed coat, for his drinking urns, when all is said and done, are quite the smallest in Munich. And not only the smallest, but also the shapeliest. In the Hofbräuhaus and in the open air *bierkneipen* (for instance, the Mathäser joint, of which more anon) one drinks out of earthen cylinders which resemble nothing so much as the gaunt towers of Munich cathedral; and elsewhere the orthodox goblet is a glass edifice following the lines of an old-fashioned silver water pitcher—you know the sort the innocently criminal used to give as wedding presents!— but at the Hoftheater there is a vessel of special design, hexagonal in cross section and unusually graceful in general aspect. On top, a pewter lid, ground to an optical fit and highly polished—by Sophie, Rosa *et al,* poor girls! To starboard, a stout handle, apparently of reinforced onyx. Above the handle, and attached to the lid, a metal flange or thumbpiece. Grasp the handle, press your thumb on the thumbpiece—and presto, the lid heaves up. And then, to the tune of a Strauss waltz, played passionately by tone artists in oleaginous dress suits, down goes the Spatenbräu— gurgle, gurgle—burble, burble—down goes the Spatenbräu—ex- quisite, ineffable!—to drench the heart in its nut brown flood and fill the arteries with its benign alkaloids and antitoxins.

Well, well, maybe I grow too eloquent! Such memories loose and craze the tongue. A man pulls himself up suddenly, to find that he has been vulgar. If so here, so be it! I refuse to plead to the indictment; sentence me and be hanged to you! I am by nature a vulgar fellow. I prefer "Tom Jones" to "The Rosary," Rabelais to the Elsie books, the Old Testament to the New, the expurgated parts of "Gulliver's Travels" to those that are left. I delight in beef stews, limericks, burlesque shows, New York City and the music of Haydn, that beery and delight- ful old rascal! I swear in the presence of ladies and archdeacons.

When the mercury is about ninety-five I dine in my shirt sleeves and write poetry naked. I associate habitually with dramatists, bartenders, medical men and musicians. I once, in early youth, kissed a waitress at Dennett's. So don't accuse me of vulgarity; I admit it and flout you. Not, of course, that I have no pruderies, no fastidious metes and bounds. Far from it. Babies, for example, are too vulgar for me; I cannot bring myself to touch them. And actors. And evangelists. And the obstetrical anecdotes of ancient dames. But in general, as I have said, I joy in vulgarity, whether it take the form of divorce proceedings or of "Tristan und Isolde," of an Odd Fellows' funeral or of Munich beer.

So much for Munich beer. And now, if you wish to catch a glimpse of Mr. Babbitt abroad before Sinclair Lewis discovered him at home, go back to the beginning of the book,—to the Preface In the Socratic Manner,—and listen to the conversation of these two Americanos in the process of broadening and mellowing their minds by foreign travel, as per the directions of Dr. Orison Swett Marden. Mark Twain might have signed it without any visible tremor.

VII

If you will permit me to translate it into Menckenian terms, I'll grant you that *Wine, Woman and Song* would make as good a motto as any for the life and miracles of the unsaintly Henry. Wine,—that is, the joy and charm of drink, not its Circean swinery; woman,—that is, the joy and charm of sex, not its domestic drudgery and its matrimonial muddle; song,—that is, the joy and charm of music, solvent of the emotions and the intellect, goal (as Pater said) of all the other arts, candent image of the flux that is life.

"The world," Mencken has written in one of his numerous fragmentary essays in self-revelation, "presents itself to me, not chiefly as a complex of visual sensations, but as a complex of aural sensations. The fact explains many of my prejudices and weaknesses—for example, my defective appreciation of pictures. It explains something a good deal more elusive: my peculiar taste in women. I seldom give much heed to the faces and forms of women, and I never notice their clothes. But when a woman has a low-pitched and soft voice, with a good clang-tint, she is free to consume my wealth and waste my time whenever the spirit moves her." What is this but a subtle variation of the theme of wine, woman and song, couched in terms of tone? But music, like wine, must be charm, not drunkenness. He measures superiority, as he has written in *A Tip for Freud,* "in terms of the capacity to throttle emotions. I esteem a man who invariably keeps his head, even when a crocodile is after him, or the band is playing, or some woman has her arms around his neck." There is yet another hint, called *Notes for an Honest Autobiography,* which focusses attention upon the important—and sadly overlooked—aspect of the man with which I now have to deal.

My one genuine regret, mounting the gallows at last, will be that I was not better instructed in music in my youth. It is the one art that may be made absolutely pure, and that is thus wholly satisfying. I am a bad artist simply because the one art whose technique I have acquired, that of letters, is unsuited to expression of the sort of ideas that naturally occur to me. Letters deal only incidentally with æsthetic ideas; their main concern is always with philosophical and moral ideas. One cannot write a poem or novel or a drama that is wholly without philosophical content or moral content, but one may easily write such a symphony or string quartet. Philosophical ideas always strike me as dubious and futile, and moral ideas simply enrage me. If I could write a string quartet I'd put things into it that I really feel and believe in. But I lack the necessary technique and am too old to acquire it. Thus I shall go down to infamy without ever having expressed myself freely and fully. It is sad, but damme if I know what is to be done about it.

A composite patter on the paradoxical qualities of Mencken would read almost like Mr. Gilbert's "receipt for that popular mystery known to the world as a Heavy Dragoon." It would moreover bristle, as does another of the Englishman's patter songs, with multitudinous quills of "information vegetable, animal and mineral," with the advantage on the side of the Baltimorean as against the versatile but somewhat dated Major Stanley. For Mencken's knowledge, though he's plucky and adventury, has surely been brought down beyond the beginning of the century. Yet how many of his readers would include, in such a summary, a life-long devotion to music? Music, the most emotional of the arts, and Mencken, the least emotional of men? Yet if there is one art that has cast its spell over all the others with which the fellow daily concerns himself, it is music. Curiously enough, the phenomenon seems to have been noticed by his literary enemies rather than by his friends. Only the other day the staid Mr. Sherman, from his desk on the New York *Herald-Tribune,* was descanting upon the musical influences that appear so frequently in Mencken's work, and suggesting—strange course for hostility!—

analogies to none other than Heine. The truth of the matter lies deep in the well of the Menckenian personality. I have never considered the man as being really deficient in emotion; I believe it today less than ever. His tip to Freud is a tip indeed, and far more Viennese than Baltimorean. Mencken's protestations of his unemotionality are themselves uttered in the language of emotional exaggeration. Perhaps he has reason to fear his emotions; perhaps he has certain emotional "blind-spots," as it were. I would wager that the secret of Mencken's literary unemotionality lies in just this unsuspected and little investigated province of his career: his musical studies, ambitions, frustrations and compensations.

The man, early renouncing poetry and painting and music, crushed his emotions rather than conquered them. They will out by devious channels. The outwardly calm Mencken is in reality a battleground of ancestral influences and environmental stimuli, of emotional temptations and intellectual control. The struggle appeared in the very days of his creative experiments.

In music, I believe, is to be found the explanation of Mencken's peculiar attitude toward the emotions today. In his music more than in his early poetry is the refuge of those emotions that he mistrusts in letters. He flouts them all the more because they are so safely stored away in unwritten compositions. I believe that he has felt, and felt intensely, every emotion that he has mocked, and that, because he has not worked the various emotions off in the various arts of his nonage, he retains the remotest suggestion of fear with relation to them. Hence the impression I am always getting that he feels the necessity of a certain surveillance.

Mencken's relations to music, however, are by no means those of the composer manqué. He has been, non-professionally, a practising musician since his earliest newspaper days. Greater even than the influence of Carter and Owst has been that of the conductor Theodore Hemberger, whom Mencken met in those same distant days and still sees weekly. He began, in 1902, to play trios with Al Hildebrant, 'cellist, and Sam Hamburger, violinist. Out of this trio grew a club that now numbers about fifteen men. Once a week this band has met and played for more than twenty years, in a spirit of bonhomie and music for its own sake and the amusement of the members. Execution is secondary; so is etiquette. During the two score years of their catch-as-catch-can performances they have ranged the entire field of music, new and old. Nothing, from the symphony to the waltz, has eluded the eyes of these good fellows. Symphonies are played on two pianos, string quartet and wood winds, with the quartet sometimes doubled. Thus it happens that every member of the club is on the closest speaking terms with not only the classical repertory but many scores by the lesser composers.

Not even the rigors of prohibition succeeded in disrupting the club, and even today, it is safe to assume, there is plenty of beer and buffoonery. Another remarkable thing about the association is that, during the hysteria that attended the war, men belonging to the different nationalities at grips on the field of battle, with decided and divergent opinions upon the conflict, sat side by side week after week, united in their common love of the art. "Because," as Mencken explains, "they were civilized."

Mencken's knowledge of the art, he avers, is spotty and rent by gaps. He is far more familiar, for example, with the orchestral repertory than with the pianistic. He avoids piano recitals. He believes that he is too ignorant to attempt any mature writing, but even now makes an occasional arrangement for the club. The old ambition, however, may yet move him, as we shall see. As regards his outlook upon the musical world, he has phrased it in a letter so remarkable, sent to me as a mere afterthought, that to paraphrase it would be lèse-littérature. Accordingly having omitted only a paragraph or two of a personal nature, I transcribe it hereunder. It is my belief that it makes one of the most interesting letters written in this country since Huneker drank his last seidel of beer.

The letter, dated May 6, 1925:

Of my tastes in music: in the main they are very orthodox. I put Beethoven first, even ahead of Bach—mainly, I suppose, because I have heard more of him than of Bach. It seems to me that the first movement of the Eroica, Beethoven's first formal defiance of the old symphonic music, remains unparalleled today. Even Beethoven never wrote anything more colossal. The funeral march following seems to me to be, by contrast, almost banal. But of all the Beethoven symphonies I like No. 8 best. It is light, but anyone who regards it as trivial is simply a damned fool. Two things attract me to Beethoven: first his immense dignity; second, his superb workmanship. He is never hollow and sentimental—and he makes more of a few bald notes than most composers make of first-rate melodic ideas. Consider the first movement of the Fifth and the slow movement of the Seventh.

He is the musical scientist par excellence. He never trusts to mere inspiration. All his effects are achieved by sheer brain power.

Next to Beethoven, as a master of the larger forms, I put Brahms. His first symphony is almost incomparable. Incomparable? Then what of his second and fourth? Two masterpieces! I like his third rather less. His "Deutsches Requiem" belongs in the front rank of choral works. I put it beside Bach's B minor Mass. Compared to it, all the familiar oratorios are shabby stuff, fit only for Methodists. Early in life Brahms wrote a trio, opus 8. I believe that its first subject is one of the most beautiful melodies ever written. Only Schubert ever went beyond it.

Of Schubert I hesitate to speak. The fellow was scarcely human. His merest belch was as lovely as the song of the sirens. He sweated beauty as naturally as a Christian sweats hate. What I marvel at is the neglect of some of his best music, for example, the Tragische Symphonie. Its slow movement is certainly almost as good as the slow movement of the Unfinished. Yet it is seldom played. So with his trios and his other piano music. I once travelled eighty miles to hear his octet. The horn player failed to show up, and I had to play his part on a piano. His quintet, opus 163, is another masterpiece. His two piano trios, opus 99 and 100, are both too long—but what fine stuff is in them! Take a look at their slow movements. Schubert's songs I have heard, of course, but I greatly dislike singing, and so I enjoy them less than I ought to. There is more music in his "Deutsche Tänze" than in the whole of Debussy. The fact that these little waltzes and Ländler are very simple deceives many. But so is the Parthenon simple.

Of Mozart I say little. Like Schubert, he is beyond critical analysis: he simply happened. Why are his smaller symphonies so little played? At least six of them are perfect. The big orchestras apparently play only the Jupiter and the G Minor. In the same way most of the Haydn symphonies are forgotten. Everything that Haydn wrote, including especially his string quartets, should be played publicly at least once a year in every civilized city of the world. It would make people ashamed of listening to the maudlin obscenities of Stravinsky and company.

Of Schumann I like best his first and fourth symphonies. The second seems dull to me. The third lacks coherence, though it is very lovely in spots. Mendelssohn I like in spots—for example, the scherzo of the Scotch symphony. I greatly admire a number of secondraters: among them, Goldmark and Dvořák. Goldmark knew how to be sentimental without shedding crocodile tears. Dvořák wrote a great deal of fine stuff in the smaller forms—for example, his Slavonic Dances. I think they are much better than the Hungarian Dances of Brahms—more ingenious and far more beautiful.

Of the men still alive, I believe that Richard Strauss is easily the first. He is the only man who has offered a serious challenge to Wagner as a dramatic composer—I don't mean a theater-composer. He builds up a climax with immense skill, and handles the orchestra better even than Wagner. His music is not often lovely, but it is always moving. But he knows how to write a tune—when he wants to. The first act of "Der Rosen-kavalier" is worth all the Italian operas ever written. Of all his work, I prefer "Elektra" and "Tod und Verklärung." I also like such parts of "Feuersnot" as I have heard; unfortunately, I don't know the whole opera.

Wagner was probably the best musician who ever lived, as Schubert was the greatest genius who ever wrote music. His command of his materials was unmatched in his time, and has never been surpassed, save by Richard Strauss. His ideas, of course, were infinitely better than Strauss's. In "Tristan und Isolde," for example, he displays so many, and they are so good, that the effect is almost stupefying. I believe that "Die Meister-singer" is the greatest single work of art ever produced by man.

It took more skill to plan and write it than it took to plan and write the whole canon of Shakespeare. Wagner's defect is that he is often theatrical, and hence a mountebank. Think of his Char-Freitag music in "Parsifal." It actually describes a romantic but plainly illegal act of love.

Puccini, I believe, has been underestimated. He was the best of the wops. His aim was to entertain well-fed folk after dinner —and he did it very competently. "La Bohème" is surely not a great work, but anyone who fails to get pleasure out of it must be tone-deaf. Verdi, I believe, is not to be heard sober, but with a few whiskeys under my belt I enjoy the last act of "Il Trovatore." Chopin is another composer who is best heard after seeing a bootlegger. His music is excellent on rainy afternoons in winter, with the fire burning, the shaker full, and the girl somewhat silly.

The so-called moderns interest me very much, for I am fond of experiments in the arts. But I'd rather read their music than hear it. It always fails to come off: it is Augenmusik. So far as I can make out, Stravinsky never had a musical idea in his life —that is, in the sense that Schubert and Mozart had them. He makes up for his lack of them by tuning his fiddle strings to G-flat, D-sharp, B and B-sharp, and playing above the bridge. That such preposterous rubbish is solemnly heard and applauded is sufficient proof that a sucker is born every minute. I believe that not more than ten per cent of the people who go to concerts are actually interested in music, or get any genuine pleasure out of it. They are simply interested in mountebanks, i. e., fiddlers, caterwaulers, etc. When the composer happens to be a mountebank also they are doubly pleased.

I never go to hear virtuosi if I can help it. Even Kreisler tires me after an hour. It offends me greatly to see a performer getting applause that belongs to the composer. I take little interest in conductors, though I know a number of them and like them as men. Their importance is immensely overestimated. A flute player with a severe Katzenjammer can do more to spoil a concert than even a Damrosch. Of all the conductors I am familiar with I like Muck the best. He is a good musician and respects composers. His conducting is intelligent, painstaking and in good taste. He does not give a show; he plays the music. His competence naturally makes him unpopular with the frauds who constitute a majority of Boston Orchestra audiences, and at the first chance, during the late war, they fell on him. Some time ago I heard the Boston Orchestra in New York, under Koussevitsky. It was like meeting a beautiful woman of the year 1900—now middle-aged, simpering, and hideously frescoed.

I seldom go to the opera; it is to music what a bawdy house is to a cathedral. The spectacle of fat women sweating, with their mouths wide open, is very offensive. I believe that most of the best music so far written is in the form of symphonies for grand orchestra; I'd rather hear it than any other kind. I greatly enjoy chamber music, especially when I am helping to play it. I believe, with Franz Kneisel, that most string quartets would be improved if they had parts for bull fiddles, and were quintets. Some of the loveliest music in the world is written for string quartets—but it inevitably begins to sound thin after an hour or so. Too much of the music is above middle C.

I know very little about piano music, and seldom play the piano alone. Piano music, in the main, seems to me to lack dignity. Even the Beethoven sonatas fall below old Ludwig's usual level. But maybe I underestimate them because most of them are beyond my technique. That may also explain my feeling that Chopin is a sugarteat. As a boy I used to like Moskowski. I got over it when I began to smoke.

French music, in the main, does not stir me; it is pretty, but trashy. I believe that Vincent D'Indy is one of the worst composers ever heard of, with Massenet close upon his heels. Bizet I like very much better; he at least did not simper. I like some of the new Russian music—I mean, of course, the pre-Stravinskian music. Tschaikovsky, when he tried to be solemn, became merely bombastic, but he could write lovely tunes, and he put many of them into his smaller stuff, for example, the Casse-Noisette suite. He should have written fewer symphonies and more waltzes. Which brings me to Johann Strauss. I believe that he was a musician of the first calibre—a man vastly more talented than, say, Mendelssohn. "Geschichten aus dem Wiener Wald" is not merely good; it is a masterpiece. Beethoven would have admired it, as Wagner, Schumann and Brahms admired it.

Why German music should be so much better than any other kind I don't know. I have often wondered. The English theoretically should be good musicians. They have good ears, as their poetry shows, and they excel at team-work. But most of their music, at least in our time, is palpably fourth-rate. They never get beyond a pretty amateurishness. All their genuinely good composers are non-English—for example, Sullivan (a man of very great talent) and Delius. There are, indeed, only two kinds of music: German music and bad music.

I have spoken evilly of French music. I except, of course, that of César Franck. He was a man of immense talent. But I deny that he was a Frenchman, or that he wrote anything properly describable as French music. He was, in fact, scarcely more a Frenchman than Handel was an Englishman. Berlioz? Well, I'll give you Berlioz. But did he write any music?

Jazz? It may be defined briefly as the sort of music that the persons who go to the opera really like. A few amusing ingenuities are in it; it is clever in the same sense that a caricature may be clever. Some day a composer of genuine talent will put a jazz scherzo into a symphony. A hundred years hence that is all that will be remembered of jazz.

And that's that.

Mencken unemotional? Then why must he measure man's superiority by his capacity to *throttle* the emotions?

We throttle enemies, not harmless opponents. Moral ideas *enrage* him? But this is half-brother to the moralistic attitude of indignation! Mencken, far from lacking emotion, is simply critical of it; and that, as his quondam inspiration wrote, is another story. Fear, relieved or conquered, vents in laughter the excess of energy accumulated for defense. Laughter may retain overtones of that fear, just as it may, even while scoffing with the sense of superiority, betray the uneasiness that is masked by braggadocio. In Mencken's comical treatment of music and its practitioners he practises a criticism as sure of aim and of effect as that which he has devoted to letters. There is, for best example, his one-act play *The Artist,* written in 1909 for Dreiser's *Bohemian,* and issued in book form in 1912 by Mr. Schaff, of Luce and Company. Despite the fact that its action is almost entirely subjective, with not a word supposed to be spoken, it has been done in a number of little theatres. Beneath the foolery, as usual with Mencken's most reckless buffoonery, lies the sober criticism of a corrosive intelligence. This is the representation of a concert, but not in terms of the romantic gush poured into type by deliquescent enthusiasts who take music instead of opium or cocktails. This realistic observer removes for his reader the roofs of the audience's heads, (even as Le Sage's Asmodeus enabled Don Cleofas to look through the roofs of people's houses), to see what is really going on inside. The result is as corrective as is, in its more burlesque fashion, that parody of an annotated Symphony concert programme which is called From The Programme of a Concert. It is easy to see that Mencken had

Boston in mind; and Mr. Philip Hale, the learned commentator of the programme books of the Boston Symphony Orchestra,—a fellow as full of fun as of learning
—was quick to reprint the take-off in the selfsame
books that had been so laughingly parodied. Finally,
turn to the Litanies of the Overlooked, and pray with
Mencken for deliverance from the rosary of musical
pests strung upon this paragraph of obsecration.[1]

We do not always slay the things we love. We may
beat them, like the Russian peasant; we may ridicule
them, like the Baltimore neo-patrician.

It may or may not be significant that Mencken, today,
his interests visibly broadening and his character, without losing any essential traits, becoming mellower, is
undergoing another revival of his creative interest in
music. He contemplates, for example, the writing of
such a string quintet as he describes in his letter, with
a part for the bull-fiddle to relieve the effect of bottom-
lightness. There is, moreover, to be a book upon eight
composers, in which Mencken will trace the influence
that the chosen men have exerted upon his life and writings. Beyond a doubt Brahms will be well represented.
For has not Mencken written that "Brahms moves me
far more powerfully than the holy saints?" And has he
not told me, waving his cigar like a burning baton in
time to his discourse, that "if I were sentenced to be shot"
(gallows and the firing-squad seem to haunt his
thoughts!) "my last request would be to hear the first

---

[1] *The Artist* is to be procured in the special Luce edition; it is also
to be found, together with Programme and the Litanies for the Overlooked, in Alfred A. Knopf's edition of *A Book of Burlesques*, 1920.

symphony of Brahms.   Yes, the first; maybe the second."
A costly procedure for the State,—providing a first-class
symphony orchestra to humor the final whim of this supposititious criminal; yet no doubt there are many who
think his end would justify such means, and be well worth
it to the Republic.

Mencken and Music—the grave and the heaven of
his emotions.   *Tod und Verklärung!*   Death and Trans-
figuration!

CHAPTER SEVEN

Magazines—The Smart Set—Cynical Side Issues—The American Mercury—The War and the Peace—Goodman and Knopf—The Later Books—Mencken and Nathan

I

AT the outbreak of the war in 1914, John Adams Thayer, owner of the *Smart Set,* had reached the end of his courage in the face of the difficulties that beset the magazine. Panic set in and as result, the periodical was soon in the hands of the late Eugene F. Crowe, the paper magnate and one of the chief creditors. Crowe, who was associated in various enterprises with E. F. Warner, the publisher of *Field and Stream,* now put Warner into the magazine as publisher, and Warner, in turn, cast about for a new editor. He lighted upon a man very shortly, and in one of those strange, simple ways that often determine a whole career. Returning from abroad on the *Imperator* shortly before the outbreak of the war in 1914,—it was the vessel's maiden trip—he happened to notice that one of his fellow passengers was wearing a surtout made of the same gray homespun as his own. The coats served as introduction, and before long they were comparing notes on London tailors. The other gentleman was Mr. George Jean Nathan, otherwise unknown to Warner. After a few drinks together, they parted at the dock and, as far as they knew, never to meet again. But when Warner, as Mencken tells the story in *A Personal Word,* "looked into the magazine that he was to manage, he found the name of Nathan on the list of regular contributors, and, recalling their brief meeting, sought him out and asked him to take the editorship. Nathan said that he would do it if I agreed to help him. There ensued negotiations, and the upshot was an arrangement that is still in force."

Mencken did not abjure his Baltimore citizenship. The arrangement was that Nathan should be in charge of the office in New York and that Mencken should come up from Baltimore, where he did the scouting for manuscripts, once or twice a month. In every respect the partnership was a finely balanced affair. Warner had made over the same amount of capital stock to Nathan as to Mencken; in the same way, the editors divided their authority and their revenue from the possible profits. By the wisdom of Warner's business policies they were soon released for the most efficient conduct of their special duties. There was a heavy floating debt to be paid off; only a radical decrease in expenses enabled the new régime to pay off within a year the debts inherited from Thayer and establish the magazine on a firm financial basis. They left a $5000 a year office for one that cost $35 a month. They "fired" all assistants except a stenographer. The first year the editors worked for nothing. Authors received checks immediately upon acceptance of their manuscripts, regardless of the eventual date of publication. Printers and paper mills were paid promptly. No new capital was absorbed. Warner was the unquestioned business head; Mencken and Nathan were the unquestioned editorial chiefs. The business office attended to its columns of figures; there was no interference with the columns of print.

The accounts of the method of collaboration given in *Pistols for Two* and in *A Personal Word* are generally exact. "I read all manuscripts that are sent to us," wrote Mencken in the latter pamphlet, "and send Nathan those that I think are fit to print. If he agrees, they go into type at once; if he dissents, they are rejected forthwith. This veto is absolute and works both ways. It saves us a great many useless and possibly acrimonious discussions. It takes two Yeses to get a poem or essay or story into the magazine, but one No is sufficient to keep it out. In practise we do not disagree sharply more than once in a hundred times, and even then, as I say, the debate is over as soon as it begins. I doubt that this scheme has ever lost us a manuscript genuinely worth printing. It admits prejudices into the matter, but they are at least the prejudices of responsible editors, and not those of subordinate readers. We employ no readers, and take no advice. Every piece of manuscript that comes into the office passes through my hands, or those of Nathan, and usually through the hands of both of us."

Mencken could hardly have been expected, in such a pamphlet, to make any reference to the frequent letters that passed between his collaborator and him during this divided rulership with two capital cities. Judging from the letters that I have examined (they belong to the end

of the *Smart Set* days and the admixture of hoaxing does
not invalidate their essence), the correspondence was the
least literary, and the most liquory in editorial history.[1]
To be sure, there was discussion of authors, and incidentally the display of not a little commercial sapience.
There was more, however, of bantering, of alcoholic
formulas; the forms of address were most irreverent,
as were the references to the lions of the hour; there
were abbreviated courses in comparative female anatomy
and in color values as applied to masculine attire; there
were practical jokes planned with all the care of refined
cruelty; there were sour allusions to readers of the
"school-teacher" magazines. We catch glimpses of Nathan inventing new cocktails, hatching up new books,
abominating the "lady Nietzsches," who are "too damned
intellectual" and too little provided with "pretty chatter."
He grows weary, fears staleness, and contemplates marriage to a rich widow. "I shall name the child Henry."
Mencken criticizes the cocktail formula:

The cocktail you mention is defective in principle. The addition of fruit juices to hard liquor is scarcely to be defended.
The device was invented by valetudinarians afraid of the naked
alcohol, and is cherished today by misers eager to save their
stock. Why is the Orange Blossom a third-rate cocktail? Because of the orange-juice. Moreover, your invention is not new.
I drank such a cocktail as you describe in Norfolk, Va., in 1915.
It was there called "The Twelve Apostles," and was said to be
the invention of an Episcopal bishop.

He labors away at page-proofs, cursing God, as usual.

[1] The letters quoted are from an unfinished project that was to have
been called *Two Editors*. They are thus not a little self-conscious and
planned. They are none the less real and characteristic.

He inveighs against the contemporary typesetters, and suspects that their abominable showing is directly related to the entrance of woman into the craft. He expresses his disgust with too much fiction in the magazine:

> It sickens me to see page after page of short stories. The better they are, the harder it is to read them *seriatim*. Give this your thought and prayers.

He even sides with Mother Church on occasion, as in the discussion of a story by a common friend:

> I am against the last H—— story. It is a capital piece of work, but it would offend the Catholics, and set every priest in the land to whooping against us. I dislike to outrage the Catholics needlessly, not only because they are the only lodge of Christians who never tried to get us barred off the news-stands, but also because they are fundamentally very decent, and detest the uplift almost as much as I do myself. The H—— story, of course, is sound and true. It would be idiotic to argue that priests never do such things. I know more than one who has gone much further. But the public generalizes, and the generalization would be false. It would be absurd, certainly, to say that such doings are the rule among them, as petty grafting and bootlicking are the rule, say, among the Methodist clergy. Give H—— a bottle of vermouth, and he will be glad to change the priest into a Presbyterian.

> I am full of aches and malaises. No doubt the final break-up is beginning. . . . I begin to feel very old.

To which Nathan, on July 12, 1923:

> I'll be good and damned if I give H—— a bottle of vermouth to change the padre into a Presbyterian! I'll offer him a pint of Acker, Merrall and Condit's California No. 2, but that's

as far as I'll go to promote literature in America. I appreciate that you had to give Huneker a small witch-hazel bottle full of green Chartreuse to put clothes on his last heroine and that, accordingly, I owe the firm something, but too much is too much. Let me urge you not to forget that it was I—a year ago—whom you burdened with the job of keeping X—— sufficiently pickled to write —— for us, and that the old boy put my cellar back six cases of Pol Roger, three of Macdougal and five of Chambertin 1904. Also let me urge you not to forget that all you gave Walpole when he was over here was a bottle of home-made beer.

Worse still,

The newspaper reviews of *The American Credo* are beginning to come in by the basketful. *A tragi-drame!* They are so far all extremely favourable. This will kill the book. We sit ourselves down and compose a tome that studiously insults every American institution and every Americano that we don't like, and here we find that the whole caboodle of newspapers hops on the beer-keg and agrees with us completely. As I have been fearing, this will mark the beginning of the end. . . . I have a feeling that the newspaper boys and girls, seized with a sudden astuteness, are doing the thing deliberately.

Whereupon Mencken, among other things:

How you can waste time upon such numskull wenches as —— is more than I can make out. The poor idiot can scarcely read and write. I grant you that there is something to be said for women simply as spectacle, but, after all, one quickly tires of looking at them. Their real value is as comedians. It is not that they are imbeciles, like, say, a business man; it is that they are infinitely shrewd and devious. No woman ever says precisely what she thinks. To disentangle their real motives and ideas from the *chevaux de frise* of their postures and deceptions— this is true sport for a man with an inquisitive mind and hair on his chest. The trouble with —— is that she is too stupid to be a liar, *i. e.,* an authentic woman.

A letter from X—— charges me with some incomprehensible infidelity with a rich literary lady. Ah, that it were true!

I have given my best thought to the gin question, but the bootleggers down this way are extortionate. The most honest one that I know says that the *Polizei* are demanding more and more graft, and that he looks for genuine gin to reach $100. a case before long. . . . The other day a wop offered me some Chianti in bulk at $8. a gallon, but one whiff of his cellar was enough to discourage me. It smelled like a slaughter-house during a strike.

In these letters, of course, was much "spoofing." Underneath the buffoonery, however, is a cynical, sardonic criticism of life that is not to be questioned. This self-same highly individual flavor pervades the series of *Prejudices* that was originally supplied by the *Smart Set* reservoir.

There were early hindrances, however, to the complete success of the *Smart Set*. In the olden days of the Mann régime it had published stories that bordered on the verge of the legally printable, and had thus come to be associated with a sort of perfumed pornography. This reputation, like the odors of a broken phial, clung to it, indeed, as late as 1923, when *The American Mercury* had not yet been born and there were still possibilities of rehabilitating the *Smart Set*. Then there was the cocky name itself, another inheritance from Mann, whose heirs and creditors refused to permit any change. Yet again, an English *Smart Set* Company, which reprinted most of the contents of the American magazine, would have been placed in serious difficulties by the abandonment of the old title. So that not even the influence of the new editors was sufficient to blot out from the public's mind the notion of the *Smart Set* as a sort of society fiction magazine.

However, there was work to be done, and the editors set to it with a right good will. Gradually there grew up, in our own day, a *Smart Set* school of readers and writers. The swashbuckling literary reviews, the pert theatrical comment, the smart epigrams, the heterodoxical essays, the occasional plays, the original fiction, the ideational patter of the *Répétition Générale,* the catalogue of national idiocy known as *Americana*—these were things, in large measure, for civilized persons to enjoy, if not always to approve. For the sake of this fare, one could easily endure the banality of the cover,—another inheritance from the days of Mann. Because the editors' departments were at the back of the magazine, it began to be read as are books in Hebrew and Yiddish,—from the rear first. Mencken-and-Nathan became synonyms for all manner of irritating qualities; cocksureness, impropriety, smart-aleckry, uppishness. One irate versifier, goaded to parody by this superciliousness, wrote of "Mencken and Nathan and God." But every knock, as Mencken had foreseen in the Preliminary Rebuke of his little book of verses, proved a boost. Whatever the figures in the circulation books might show, the magazine was making a perceptible dent in the cultural life of the country.

Looking back to those not too distant days, it is possible to evaluate that influence. Thus, the earliest work of Joyce to be heard of in this country—some of the

tales of Dublin life later published by Mr. Huebsch—
appeared in the pages of the *Smart Set,* after their author
had been brought to the attention of Mencken by Mr.
Ernest Boyd. Lord Dunsany here made his bow, and
so founded his American vogue. Americans aspiring to
notice were early printed—if not actually discovered—
by the magazine: Ruth Suckow, Thyra Samter Winslow,
Sherwood Anderson, Ben Hecht, Eugene O'Neill. In the
literary columns Mencken was carrying his war into
Africa; he sought out the academicians and made them his
favorite prey. In the pages of fiction he and Nathan
were aiding the young revolters against the campus
criteria by printing their product.

These authors were, as a group, both encouraged
and disciplined. Encouraged, because Mencken remembered well his own early efforts to sell his writings to
the magazines; the rule of the *Smart Set* office was that
young writers were to be treated with courtesy, and that
rule has been taken over into the offices of *The American
Mercury.* With courtesy, not with indulgence. Yet for
years Mencken was indulgent, too; he would read and
criticize *gratis* the manuscripts of worthy aspirants. Today, of course, that is impossible; and for that matter, he
trusts little to the efficacy of interviews between authors
and editors. Disciplined, because in one thing, at least,
Mencken is thoroughly German: his dislike of professional incompetence. "I never have any respect," he declares, "for a man who does his chosen job badly. There
is seldom any excuse for him. He could improve if he
would work hard—and forget his bad luck in being born
an ass. My work for ten years past has thrown me into

contact with many authors. I have never got to be friendly with a bad one. I detest such fellows. They put me to unnecessary labor, revising their copy and trying to get sense into their nonsense. My aversion to them is almost physical. To me a Greenwich Villager —that is, an author who is bad and who tries to conceal it by sneering at those who are good—positively smells badly."

Despite his interest in experimentation, Mencken reveals his conservative bias in his insistence that an author prove his mettle by doing good work in the old forms before he tackles a new formula. "Among the so-called modern musicians I respect only those who have proved their right to be revolutionists by writing sound fugues. Among the advanced poets, only those who have good sonnets behind them."

Mencken, remember, is not a "literary" man. His relations with authors, despite the almost inevitable contacts, have been relatively few. He even eschews them, out of a feeling that they interfere with the freest expression of critical opinion. He goes so far as to avoid a too close communion with other magazine editors, despite the long roster that he knows, believing that their problems rarely coincide and that they can prove of little professional help to one another. With the exception of a few literati who are personal friends, his regular associates are drawn mainly from the newspaper room, musical circles and the medical profession.

There were, in these days, side issues, some of a cynically amusing character. Thus, in 1915, needing additional money, Warner, Crowe, Nathan and Mencken decided to start a fiction magazine to sell at fifteen cents. Taking advantage of the presence, in this country, of the horde of French propagandists, they founded, in a satirical spirit, the monthly named *The Parisienne.* A sorry thing it was, as more than one reader will easily recall. But a most successful one, as well; and this, too, more than one reader will understand, if he remembers the strategy employed by the "king" and the "duke" in *Huckleberry Finn,* when they rounded up every yokel in the Arkansas town by announcing that no ladies or children should be admitted to their show. The editors of *The Parisienne* went into the market for stories and novelettes by hacks. Wherever the scene might originally be laid, they changed it on principle to France; the substance must be nothing other than the amours of royalty, with the Mediterranean as an oceanic boudoir, flashing all the appurtenances of *higlif* as visioned from behind the counters of department-stores. On a total capital of $500 it was soon earning $4000 a month. The Comstockians, true to form, attacked it, only to demonstrate its harmlessness and be beaten in court. The judge sustained the magazine's demurrer that the complaint showed nothing improper in the periodical. Mencken, however, soon tired of this tomfoolery, despite the money in it; in 1916 Nathan and he sold out their interest to Warner and Crowe. The transaction placed them on Easy street. Yet they were not through with the fifteen cent *higlif.* Having first entered upon it for cash, they were soon back at it for revenge. Colonel Mann, it seems, upon selling the *Smart Set,* had taken with him the sibilant memory of its alliterative title; soon *Snappy Stories* was on the market, sporting the two long S's that had become the sign manual of that very *Smart Set* cover which, under the terms of the mortgage owned by the Mann forces, could not be changed. Whereupon Mencken and Nathan hatched out the *Saucy Stories*. The *Parisienne* disappeared with the decline of interest in things French, after the return of our troops from France; *Saucy Stories,* however, until June of 1925 pursued its insinuating course. It was a success from the first, but Mencken and Nathan, having sated their thirst for vengeance, again sold out to Warner and Crowe. The game of yokel-catching and boob-bumping must have had a fascination, however. There was sardonic comedy in the venture of baiting the yokelry from the office of the *Smart Set* and feeding their appetites with the trash of The *Parisienne* and the *Saucy Stories.* So back to the flesh-pots turned H. L. and George Jean, this time with that museum of mystery known as the *Black Mask.* Another instantaneous success, with a most interesting subscription list that included a host of national eminences. Perhaps Wilson, with his well-known predilection for detective yarns, beguiled his weary hours with these tales. Once again, after six months of sport, Mencken and Nathan tired of this interlude from their *Smart Set* labors; once again they sold out their interest to Warner and Crowe. The financial purposes had been readily accomplished; Crowe, an immensely wealthy fellow, nearly at the end of his days, with a fondness for the two literary adventurers, gave them an excellent price; this, together with what they had already accumulated, lifted

them permanently out of want.   Magazine adventuring
was now over.

Of all the ventures owned by Warner—today he con-
trols *Field and Stream* and *Arts and Decorations,* both
money-makers—the *Smart Set* proved the least profitable.
By 1918 Mencken, whose natural interests from the first
had been of a wide and varied assortment, had lost his
original enthusiasm for the magazine.   The circulation
gradually declined; it was losing a small amount of
money.   There were periods when no editorial salaries
were drawn.   The highest Mencken ever received was
$50 a week; this meant that his *Smart Set* work was
practically unpaid, as the expense of coming to New York
in the long run exceeded his salary.   From time to time
the proprietors and editors bought in some of the out-
standing bonds, sometimes at very low prices, though
they had always paid interest.   When in 1920, the remaining bonds became due, they had them extended for
five years.   On the death of Colonel Mann they were able
to acquire his bonds, too, a relatively large block at a
low price.   The fresh start allowed to them by thus
shaking the burden of interest-payments proved to be
only temporary.   When the circulation had sunk below
30,000 Mencken proposed to Nathan that they either sell
the magazine or abandon it.   Hearst was approached,
but refused to nibble.   Hereupon they had recourse to
Warner.   Nathan, who had been entrusted with full
powers, at the moment of sale added the proviso
that if Warner resold it within a year, Mencken and he
were to share in the proceeds of the new sale.   Surely
enough, Hearst was soon nibbling after the magazine

and, as a result of protracted negotiations, finally bought it. It took about a sixth of the proceeds to clear the periodical of debt, and each of the former editors had a fourth interest. The rest is news-stand history.[1] To-day the *Smart Set,* after a short interregnum, is a more gaudy edition of its pristine self; Mann and Hearst shake hands across the grave.

II

I should like to point out that the subsequent breach of interest between Mencken and Nathan was more than dimly forecast in the pamphlet of 1922, *A Personal Word,* the object of which was to increase the subscription list of the waning magazine. (Its net result, for all Mencken's persuasive eloquence, was less than twenty subscriptions.) There, on page 6, Mencken wrote: "We differ in many ways. For example, Nathan is greatly amused by the theatre, even when it is bad, whereas I regard it as a bore, even when it is good.[2] Contrariwise, I am much interested in politics, whereas Nathan scarcely knows who is Vice-President of the United States. But on certain fundamentals we are thoroughly agreed, and it is on the plane of those fundamentals that we conduct the *Smart Set,* and try to interest a small minority of Americans." I shall show

[1] Nathan and Mencken got out exactly 110 issues of the *Smart Set,* from November 1914 to December 1923, inclusive.

[2] Here let me express an authorial and personal regret that the pruderies of print do not permit me to transcribe, literally, Mencken's conversational meditations upon the biological reactions of the proverbial bald-headed man in the front row at a musical comedy leg-show.

presently, that even with regard to these fundamentals, there were essential differences of personality. As a matter of simple fact, the Mencken and Nathan partnership was chiefly one in those aspects of the men that caused but a single sector of the circles of their natures to overlap.

This editorial incompatibility, as distinguished from their friendship, was to become increasingly evident after *The American Mercury* had been launched on its course. The *Smart Set* having begun to disintegrate, Mencken chafed more than ever under the restrictions of the magazine. He took the matter to Mr. Alfred A. Knopf, who had become his publisher in 1917. Knopf, coincidentally, had been cherishing a passion to start a first-class magazine of his own, and proposed that Mencken edit it. When the news was carried back to Nathan, he suggested that it might be a good idea for Knopf to take over the *Smart Set,* and for a time negotiations proceeded in that direction. It was decided, however, by Knopf *père et fils,* that too much effort would be involved in any attempt to rehabilitate this losing proposition, with its vexatious name and its shady past.

This out of the way, and the path made clear for the new venture, Knopf repeated his suggestion that Mencken assume the editorship. Just as Nathan, however, had accepted the editorship of the *Smart Set* on the condition of Mencken's co-operation, so Mencken now stipulated Nathan's collaboration as the condition of his acceptance. Long before, they had dreamed in the old *Smart Set* days of a weekly, to be called, after a suggestion in Wells's *The New Machiavelli, The Blue Review.* It had been given up because it threatened to swamp them under too much work. *The American Mercury* thus contained elements of a compromise with this abandoned Weekly. It carried over from the *Smart Set* a few regular features: Nathan's theatrical review, Mencken's literary article, the national Follies known as *Americana,* and, finally, the editorial observations upon the human comedy, *Répétition Générale,* which were rechristened as *Clinical Notes.* Otherwise, the change was radical. Fiction all but disappeared. Poetry, never prominent, suffered a reduction in the ranks. On the other hand, the serious (but not solemn) essay upon matters of sociological and intellectual importance gained an unexpected hearing; it assumed, in fact, a sort of primacy. This, clearly, was the reflection of Mencken's broadening interests. Nathan never cared, nor does he now care, for such ramifications of the American scene. Nor has the matter of technological detail incident to the make-up of a magazine ever held out any attractions to him. To Mencken, however, the drudgery of make-up is an old tale of the newspaper rooms. The mounting problems of printing and handling of manuscript and scouting for the kind of writer *The American Mercury* desired were bound to emphasize the differences that lay at the bottom of their fundamental agreements. By the end of 1924 it was clear that a re-arrangement would have to be made. After much discussion,—a strange interplay of argument, in which Mencken envisaged the case from Nathan's point of view, while Nathan performed the same trick for his partner,—it was settled that Mr. Nathan, after the issue of July, 1925, should withdraw as co-editor, remaining as contributing editor. In such a manner he was freed for the intensive interest that holds him to the theatre and to the drama of the world, while Mencken was released for his extensive delvings into all the isms and ologies from aerodonetics to zymurgy.

As the magazine stands, then, it is, in all but the format, which was designed by Knopf and Elmer Adler, largely the work of Mencken. Even the articles, at first, were often patiently revamped by him in his effort to raise them to a certain *Mercurial* standard. Already, a *Mercury* school, or rather group, begins to grow, in danger only of echoing the chieftain's themes and mannerisms. Already, too, and much sooner than the most sanguine of the founders hoped, it is a financial and intellectual success, in the very forefront of its class. The most optimistic expectation had been a circulation of some 10,000. Yet the first issue had to be reprinted twice (17,500 copies in all) and copies of it bring at the present date (June, 1925) as much as $25. At the end of the first year the print order was nearly 60,000.

III

Parallel with the years that led from the *Smart Set* to *The American Mercury* runs Mencken's career as a traveler in Europe, a newspaper correspondent, and a writer of books.

From the first, Mencken had entered the war in his own private fashion. His resignation from the *Sun* in 1915 must have been received, however regretfully, yet with some relief by that newspaper. Things were warming up in the international arena. In 1916, when Wilson came up for re-election, Mencken led a relentless attack against the man and his policies, advising all persons who were against the war, and in particular all German-Americans, to vote against this contemporary symbol of national fraud.[1] As usual, he was on the losing side. And, as was natural, he was readily listed as a German patriot.

To make matters worse, he was sent, in 1916, to

[1] Curiously enough, for all his disgust with political life, Mencken once was nearly nominated as candidate for the office of Vice-President of the United States, and with none other than Wilson as running mate! The story goes as follows:

In 1912 the Democratic National Convention was held in Baltimore, and one of the candidates for the Vice-Presidency was James H. Preston, mayor of the city. The Evening *Sun* was bitterly opposed to him. In Maryland, there is a primary in each party to determine its choice for President and Vice-President. Having no opposition, Preston did not enter his name; thereby he thought to save the $50 entrance fee. Since there were no other candidates in his party there would be no primary, and so the Maryland delegates, who were all for him, would be free to vote for him in the convention. Charles H. Grasty, then publisher of the *Evening Sun,* hit upon a Machiavellian scheme. It was to wait until the last moment, and then enter Mencken's name as a Democratic candidate. A primary would then have been necessary, and, as the only candidate entered, Mencken would have been chosen, and the Maryland delegates would have been bound to vote for him in the convention. On the last day for entering, Mencken was on the ocean, bound for Europe. Grasty had got Mencken's authority to act as his agent, and arranged to send him a wireless if the scheme worked. But at the last minute Preston entered himself, and so it fell through. If it had succeeded Grasty could have got Mencken several hundred votes on the floor, for he was an ardent Wilson man and had a lot to do with Wilson's defeat of Champ Clark. The Wilson men would have given Mencken a run in order to annoy Preston, who was a Clark man.

Germany as correspondent for the Baltimore *Sun*. That was to prove an exciting experience. He traveled on a Danish ship, via the Orkney Islands, to Norway and Denmark. February of 1917, when the United States broke off relations with Germany, found him on the Eastern front, near Dvinsk, with the German Eastern Army under General Eichhorn. The cold was arctic: 40 degrees below. Thereupon he returned to Berlin, only to discover that, under German military regulations no correspondent could leave the country until six weeks after his return from the front.

"I settled down to spend the six weeks in Berlin. Meanwhile, Ambassador Gerard and his staff were preparing to go home, and a number of American correspondents were planning to go with them. The latter were known to be excessively anti-German. Certain other correspondents, who proposed to remain in Germany (some of them stayed for six months thereafter), thought that it would be a good idea to get me out, so that I might counteract the efforts of the German-eaters. They accordingly made representations to Ludendorff, who was running everything, and orders that I should be permitted to go at once reached Berlin a few hours before Gerard's special train was scheduled to depart. The General Staff gave me a place on it, and so I left with Gerard, but not as a member of his party.

"After a few days in Berne, I proceeded with him to Paris. All sailings from Northern European ports had been suspended on account of the U-boat proclamation, but it was reported in Paris that Spanish liners were still running. No one had apparently ever heard of a Spanish liner before. Gerard and the other correspondents began telegraphing to Madrid for reservations. It appeared quickly that these telegrams were being held up by the French censors; no replies were forthcoming. So I quietly departed for Madrid, and there, by the aid of the American Embassy, got a room on a Spanish liner sailing from Corunna five or six days later. I thus beat Gerard and the other correspondents home by a week. I wrote my stuff on the ship—50,000 words in 10 days—and filed it when I reached Havana. It was printed serially over a period of two weeks. But it did no good. The war was already on by the time I got to Havana. In fact, some of my stuff had to be killed; no American newspaper, at that time, would print it. Nevertheless, it was the truth.

"A day out from Havana I received a wireless from the Baltimore *Sun* saying that a revolution was on in Cuba, and that there was a heavy censorship, and the American press was getting only government canned-goods and the even less reliable press-matter of the revolutionary junta in New York. I was ordered to stop off in Havana and find out the truth. I had a friend there, Captain Asmus Leonhard, of the Munson Line. I sent him a wireless, and his launch met the ship when we reached port. A few hours later he had introduced me to all the chief government officials, from President Menocal down. Meanwhile, I had met Dr. Hermann M. Biggs, formerly Health Commissioner of New York, on the ship. (He had been in France as head of a commission to study tuberculosis in the French Army.) Biggs, it so happened, had many acquaintances in Cuba, and among them were some of the leaders of the revolution. He gave me access to them. (They were leading very secluded lives in Havana.) Thus I got at both sides, and soon had all the facts. I sent my stuff to Key West by passengers on the daily ferry-boat, and there it was filed, and so reached the *Sun*. In this business the New York *World* joined the *Sun*."

It had been an arduous adventure, with sudden climactic changes to accentuate the swiftly changing complexion of international affairs. In Scandinavia, North Germany and Russia, Mencken had frozen in the very heart of Winter; thence he had been thrust from Germany to sunny Spain; and finally, from this ancient motherland to the tropical scenes of Havana. "I shall never forget waking on the Paris-Madrid sleeper as the train neared Bayonne. I had been freezing in snow-wastes, and sleeping in remote Lithuanian farm-houses; now I was in a comfortable bed, and looking out at the blue waters of the Bay of Biscay." The old zest for travel, however, was definitely blunted by these adventures. Mencken got off the boat at Key West all but singing "My Country 'Tis of Thee." When, in 1922, he returned to Europe for a three months' tour of England, Holland, Germany and Bohemia, it was with a sense of weariness; the old glow was gone. It was on this trip that he interviewed the Crown Prince of Germany at Wieringen, Holland, for the Baltimore *Sun,* spending a day with him on his lonely island and discovering him to be a rather different fellow from the caricatures of the American press.

On his return from the front, in 1917, Mencken was considered virtually a German spy. And, to add to the humor of the situation, most of the German-Americans at the same time held him in suspicion. He became the object of governmental espionage. He was supposed to be in the Kaiser's pay, and slated for a royal decoration after the war. His mail was heaped high with anonymous threats, with denunciations; paid spies and spies who labored out of patriotic love alike drew up resounding reports upon his maleficent activities. Their labors, however loving and patriotic, could not have been very skilful or effective, for Mencken himself got possession of carbon copies of some of these reports. He even drew up a report against himself! The document is probably on file at this moment in the archives of the Department of Justice at Washington, appearing as that of a man told off to investigate him. The brains and acumen that went into the making of the reports may be gauged from the accusation of one idiot that Mencken (anno Domini 1917) was an intimate personal friend of "Nitsky, the German monster." (Nietzsche, born 1844, died 1900!) A long series of reports dealt with Mencken's relations to Captain Paul Koenig, commander of the German U-boat *Deutschland,* which had brought a cargo of dyes to Baltimore in 1916. The fact is that Mencken there and then met Captain Koenig for the first time; their friendship was quick to form and it is warm to this day.

The war tested Mencken, as it tested all men. It lost him many friends, some of whom have since made unsuccessful efforts to renew relations. It made him new ones, and he is convinced that the change worked to his benefit. It confirmed him in old opinions and rid him of the last vestiges of patriotic feeling. Today, like and yet so unlike a Romain Rolland, he dwells above the battle; more exactly, in it yet not of it, an unmoved mover; a man without a country, yet not an internationalist. His view of the war is essentially what it was in 1924: a

cowardly and dishonest business, set off by England in order to break down the advantages that Germany got by being more competent. . . . I believe that the so-called neutrality of the United States before 1915 was dishonest and disgraceful. I believe that the true interests of the United States were on the side of Germany—that if we had joined Germany in hamstringing England and destroying France, we might have divided the trade and the wealth of the world, and been secure for a century. Now we must face a struggle with England, and the chances are that she will, as usual, come into it with overwhelming allies, and give us a beating. We sided with England principally because she got control of the sea, and so made it profitable for us to act as her *Kriegslieferant*. I believe that this dishonest neutrality will come home to roost the next time we go to war. Wilson set very evil precedents. Not the least of them was the seizure of enemy private property. We'll lose vastly more next time than the Germans lost last time.

To Mencken personally the war proved a godsend in camouflage. He was spied upon; his mail was opened; he was under surveillance; his enemies had their fling, striking at him when he couldn't answer back. These clouds, however, evaporated and left only the silver. Purging him of his remaining patriotism, it set him free of the last tenuous bonds. His very enemies advertised him into a new eminence, and Mencken, with the touch of Barnum in him, was not slow to take advantage of the publicity. He became, moreover, the blunt and effective spokesman of the inevitable reaction. Mencken the scholar kept his head; Mencken the business-man, who had bought no Liberty bonds during the war, enjoyed the amusement of purchasing them, after the conflict, at 83.

IV

Just as the war brought Mencken to a vastly greater audience as a publicist, so did the period from our break in relations with Germany to the armistice coincide with his rise to widespread acceptance as an author. *Europe After 8:15,* it will be recalled, had fallen flat upon the book market of 1914. It had brought Mencken into contact, however, with Mr. J. Jefferson Jones, manager of the American branch of the John Lane Company, publishers of the book, and Jones was soon proposing a volume by Mencken *solo.* The result was a couple of ventures: *A Book of Burlesques* and *A Little Book in C Major.* Both were made up of salvage from the files of the *Smart Set,* and both, as Lane publications, proved failures.

In 1917, Mencken met an advertising man in New York. His name was Philip Goodman and he loved good food; moreover, he was a "stevedore" in the beery old Baltimore tradition. A friendship quickly grew up, and it soon appeared that Goodman, weary of the advertising game, was ambitious to become a publisher. He had a vision of a revolution in publishing,—of selling books through country drug stores and other such retail agencies. He had inaugurated his publishing career with Nathan's *Bottoms Up* and now wanted Mencken to do a book or two for him; within a month and a half two books were ready for his experiment. They were *Damn: A Book of Calumny,* which had been put together in a week, and *In Defense of Women,* which required some six weeks for careful revision. The books were made up of old material from the *Smart Set* and newspaper articles; the latter fell with the collapse of Goodman's selling scheme. Goodman, after one or two other experiments, abandoned the venture and returned to advertising. Later still, he struck a gold mine as a theatrical producer (*The Old Soak, Poppy*). The friendship has continued; Goodman, in Mencken's opinion, writes as well as he eats and drinks; in fact, during 1920 or thereabouts they exchanged a series of letters that may some day see print.

Meantime, here was Mencken still stumbling about in quest of the right publisher. He had, without realizing it, met him and published through him before dealing with Goodman. In the middle of 1917 he had come upon his man,—Mr. Alfred A. Knopf of New York. What Meekins was to Mencken's journalistic career, what Schaff had been to his authorial beginnings, Knopf proved to his commercial and cultural success. The first book for which they contracted was *A Book of Prefaces,* arranged for on July 9. The volume, to be sure, got off to a slow start; it had sold but 1257 copies down to January 1, 1919, after which it picked up. The sales are of minor importance; *A Book of Prefaces,* although the two

Goodman books were published after its appearance, marks the beginning of one of the most significant of contemporary collaborations between author and publisher. Mencken brought new prestige to the house of Knopf; to the books of Mencken, Knopf brought a business acumen that was heightened by a flair for experiment, commercial adventure, novelty, individualism.

What this meant may be quickly demonstrated by a few figures. *A Book of Burlesques* and *A Little Book in C Major,* brought out by Lane in 1916, had by 1919 reached the total sales, respectively, of 885 and 789. When Knopf acquired the rights the *C Major* epigrams were taken over in part for a revised *Book of Burlesques.* This, issued in January, 1920, had in the first half-year sold 859; in 1924 alone some 1662 copies were disposed of. The book is still a steady seller. So, too, *In Defense of Women* had originally been issued in 1918, and, down to June 28, 1919 had sold some 849 copies; hereupon Goodman disposed of the remaining sheets to Knopf, who soon reset and reprinted the book. Result: in 1922 alone, some 3882 copies were sold, not to speak of an English edition and a translation into German.

In the meantime Mr. Knopf had also become the publisher of Mr. Nathan, and the sudden emergence of Mencken and Nathan is by no means unrelated to their own canny sense of showmanship and self-advertising. They are both excellent publicity men, and one of their finest "stunts" was that strange amalgam of truth and nonsense called *Pistols for Two,* written by that geminate myth, Owen Hatteras, and published in 1917. The plan was Mencken's, and he wrote somewhat more than half of the pamphlet; he and Nathan shared the expense of printing with Knopf. At first it was distributed *gratis;* the demand soon grew so great that the price had to be raised to fifty cents, then to a dollar. Today the pamphlet commands five to six dollars in the market of bibliographical rarities.

In 1919 appeared Mencken's *The American Language.* The series of *Prejudices* began in 1919, II appearing in 1920, III in 1922 and IV in 1924. It is planned to issue a volume biennially as long as interest attaches to the series. At the time I write (June, 1925) the fourth of the series, which has gradually broadened in scope and in appeal, is the most popular of them all. In 1920 appeared *Heliogabalus,* a buffoonery in three acts, of which Mencken wrote most of the text, profiting by numerous suggestions from Nathan. Later in the same year *The American Credo* came out; this was Nathan's idea. Most of the items were collected by him; the Preface was added by Mencken. A four page appendix of which about one hundred copies were issued at Christmas, 1922, for the amusement of friends, is of such a nature that it would make the public prints turn red and perturb the guardians of our moral republic. Accordingly, it is sought passionately by all collectors; it is, however, one of the most difficult of the Mencken-Nathan jocularities to procure.

The American Language, though published in 1919, dates back almost ten years, to Mencken's days on the Baltimore *Evening Sun.* During October, 1910, he had printed an article entitled "The Two Englishes," follow-

ing it up shortly with another on "Spoken American,"
and, on the next day, with one called "More American."
On November 5th the subject was renewed with "American Pronouns," and on the morrow, with "England's
English." At once he began to be flooded with correspondence from all over the country; in the meantime, he
continued the collection of material concerning Ameri-
canisms, and, in the August, 1913, issue of the *Smart Set,*
set forth his findings in a rather extended article.
Whereupon descended another deluge of correspondence,
sweeping Mencken into the composition of a book upon
the subject. The first edition, in 1919, was printed from
type and was gobbled up almost upon publication; before
the 1500 copies had been sold the retail price had been
raised from the original $4 to $6 and then to $10.
Plowing through the mass of material that now began to
pour in from all corners of the world Mencken managed
to prepare a revision in time for December, 1921. The
second revision was interrupted by his trip to Europe in
the summer of 1922; by February, of 1923, it was on
the market, a fat and formidable tome. The making
of the index alone required some eight to nine thousand
cards. Nor is the end yet; other editions, eventually,
will appear.

The series of *Prejudices* was suggested by Richard
Lankhuff, a Cleveland bookseller. He had told Knopf
that it might be a good idea to collect *Smart Set* reviews
every two years; Knopf, agreeing with him, had transmitted the suggestion to Mencken, and before long the
series was under way.

Some time before the conception of *Heliogabalus,* out

of a joint admiration for the play that Percival Pollard had introduced to English readers in his *Masks And Minstrels of Modern Germany*,[1] Mencken and Nathan had made an American version of Ludwig Thoma's *Moral*. The first act of the original was so manifestly impossible for American audiences that the translators were put to inventing a new one to fit in with the subsequent action. In the meantime the manager who had suggested the work went bankrupt; other producers liked it personally but fought shy of its peculiar demands, averring, for example, that they could get no leading man for the play. *Moral,* in fact, asked its masculine "star" to present himself in a most ignominious rôle, that of an Anti-Vice Society President exposed as the protector of a highly fashionable bordello. Almost every leading man on Broadway was approached; to a man they declined. The play was then withdrawn.

Heliogabalus has a different history. It is, in the first place, the one book deliberately planned by Mencken. The basic idea was his; Nathan mapped out the play and developed the plot. Whereas his other volumes have grown out of the newspapers and magazines with which he has been connected, and have, as often as not, been touched off by external suggestion, *Heliogabalus* is a drama that owes its origin to Mencken's old scorn for the dramatists. As he has related in Mr. Frey's Bibliography, "One afternoon Nathan and I were sitting in his apartment at the Royalton, in Forty-Fourth Street, New York, and fell into a discussion of play-writing. We came to the conclusion that writing a play was a

---

[1] Published by John W. Luce & Company. Boston, 1911.

much smaller job than writing a book, and decided to write one to prove it. I contended that a so-called plot was unnecessary. 'Very well,' said Nathan, 'but where is your character?' I had just been re-reading Edgar Saltus' *Imperial Purple,* and Heliogabalus came to mind. We then went to Rogers', in Sixth Avenue, for dinner. By the time we got it down *Heliogabalus* was planned, and six weeks later it was finished. . . . Writing it turned out to be absurdly easy—in fact, a sort of holiday from criticism. I ceased to respect dramatists from that time. Their work, I am convinced, is child's play." [1] As a piece printed for private circulation it proved an immense success. The authors announced, upon publication, that they would never authorize its performance in America until the United States had become civilized. (All in all, a safe défi, since the play as written would never be permitted to adorn the "boards.") Yet at once, because of that very statement (shrewdly made, perhaps, with just such a reaction in view) various offers were received for the stage rights. One manager, indeed, offered $10,000 down in addition to the stage royalties. Mencken and Nathan, however, with pockets as full as their wine cellars, stood their ground. *Heliogabalus* has been translated into the German; several times it has almost been produced, but the days of 1920 and 1921 were hardly the season for such expensive scenery as the production would demand.

To 1920 belongs another of the advertising pamphlets that did much to further the interest in Mencken.

[1] See *A Bibliography of the Writings of H. L. Mencken.* By Carroll Frey. Philadelphia. The Centaur Book Shop. 1924. Pages 5–6.

TAKEN AT A. A. KNOPF'S SUMMER HOME
AT PORTCHESTER, N. Y. 1923

It is entitled *H. L. Mencken,* and consists of a Fanfare by Burton Rascoe; The American Critic, by Vincent O'Sullivan (these had been, incidentally, the first two men to write of Mencken at any length) and a bibliography by F. C. Henderson. The thirty-two page pamphlet was very soon exhausted and thus joined the peculiarly large number of rarities in the career of one of our most prolific penmen.

There remains, then, to speak of the Free Lance Series, suggested by Knopf and named by Mencken after his famous column on the *Sun.* Of these, six appeared: *Ventures in Common Sense,* by E. W. Howe, 1919; *Youth and Egolatry,* by Pío Baroja, 1920; *The Antichrist,* by Nietzsche, 1920; *We Moderns,* by Edwin Muir, 1920; *Democracy and the Will to Power,* by James N. Wood, 1921; and *In Defense of Women,* by Mencken, 1922. Despite the attractive print and format, despite the eclectic selection, despite Mencken's prefaces to each book, the series as a whole proved a failure and was abandoned.

v

The Mencken and Nathan association goes down as one of the most interesting in the literary history of England and America. It created an atmosphere all its own; it impressed itself upon a phase of our letters. Yet it was, on the part of each, but a phase of more individual labors. It was the innate, cynical levity of these men that united them; the end of the association, as an intellectual adventure, was bound to come as soon as more serious interests intervened. Even in their likeness the men were different. This I had brought out some months before there was any inkling of the breach, in a critical study of Mr. Nathan,[1] from which I now quote an attempt to make clear the difficult distinctions that dwelt within a seeming identity.

The truth is that when one has pronounced the Mencken-Nathan outlook essentially aristocratic, æsthetic and antinomian, one has but stated the case in philosophic terms that admit of personal differentiation. Mencken and Nathan thus agree that there is hardly any meaning to life; that whatever meaning there is derives from the impression upon life's metal of a strongly personal seal. Existence becomes, for the undifferentiated herd, the blurred rationalization of a being little removed from the vegetable and the mineral kingdoms. For differentiated man, the artist, it resolves itself into a spectacle,—a show to be judged, not in terms of crime and punishment, but in terms of beauty wrested from inertia and decay. The herd follows rules; the artist, arrogating to himself the prerogatives of the world's supposed creator, creates them, evolves them, breaks them, refashions them, all in his own image. Such a herd has the cowardice of its instincts; such an artist has the courage of his intuitions.

In Mencken and Nathan the process of personalized revolt does not stop at artistic intuition. They would understand as well as feel. Like Poe, they would be at once artists and critics of the artist within them. Like him, again, though in lesser degree, they would lift the

[1] See my *George Jean Nathan; A Critical Study.* Girard, Kansas. Little Blue Book Series, No. 843.

very process of unconscious mentation into the light of critical scrutiny. To understand all is likewise to scorn all, if ever so lightly. Of such a dualistic attitude Mencken and Nathan furnish an illuminating example. In all forgiveness there is a touch of superiority, of scorn, of snobbery, if you will. Not only is this snobbery an avowed attitude in both Mencken and Nathan, but in Nathan it assumes its more pronounced aspect. Why the snobbery? Great art, which has been deeply felt, has also been deeply understood. It scorns us and forgives us at the self-same time. Having probed too deeply for unalloyed pleasure, they recapture the lost pleasure through the joy of criticism; the sacrifice of emotional surrender is counterbalanced by the gains of intellectual conquest.

Perhaps I complicate too much a matter that at bottom is relatively simple. These attitudes have not been reasoned out by Nathan and Mencken, and then adopted as a program. They represent an instinctive response which has afterward been disintegrated into its psychological components.

Note, now, how these twin attitudes, at first sight identical, split into their personal elements.

Nathan, less than Mencken, is a creature of ambivalence. In all the things against which the "Antichrist" of Baltimore inveighs, there is a core of something that attracts him even as it repels. He cachinnates at the electorate, then sweats through the pompous, ponderous pandemonium of their political conventions with glandular glee. It is difficult, on the other hand, to imagine Nathan perspiring through a community conclave. When he has damned it, he sits back and lets it go to hell. Mencken pricks the Puritan with the nib of his pen and holds him up to ridicule before the public gaze; yet in his hot pursuit of the species there is an implicit ethical ardor almost as strong as that he derides, for all the divergence of direction. Nathan, having called the fellow a swine, leaves him curtly to his sty. I am not, for the moment, discussing the justice of these views, though I find myself in philosophic, if not verbal, harmony with them. I am concerned to show how, in each of these men, the views are inevitably colored by the personal lens.

Contrast, for example, the response of Nathan and Mencken to the late war. To each of these civilized gentlemen the war, *sub specie æternitatis,* (and what a grim irony there is in the Spinozan phrase!) took on the appearance of a crazy pageant. Here was the *reductio ad absurdum* of our vaunted civilization, of our boasted Christianity; here was a welter of slogans and slaughter, with the glorified commoner marching to the shambles under gaudy banners and to gaudy tunes, a living—and a dying—monument to the colossal stupidity of the human race. Here was shrieking proof, behind all the battle fronts, of that universal folly which Mencken and Nathan were, rather than combating, deriding. As against their aristocracy of honor and intelligence, here was a democracy of guile and ignorance. As against their individualistic æsthetics, here was rampant ethics in mass formation. As against their intellectual anarchism, their merry antinomianism, here were emotional regimentation and dour-faced conformity.

Yet Mencken, inevitably drawn to the objects of his

aversion, haunts battle-fronts, as we have seen, with the same glee that carries him through the pages of the *Congressional Record* and the major political conventions. Nathan? Let me quote from the Foreword to *The World In Falseface*:

What interests me in life—and my years have . . . marched across the frontier of forty—is the surface of life: life's music and color, its charm and ease, its humor and loveliness. The great problems of the world—social, political, economic and theological —do not concern me in the slightest. I care not who writes the laws of a country so long as I may listen to its songs. I can live every bit as happily under a King, or even a Kaiser, as under a President. One church is as good as another to me; I never enter one anyway, save only to delight in some particularly beautiful stained-glass window, or in some fine specimen of architecture, or in the whiskers of the Twelve Apostles. If all the Armenians were to be killed tomorrow and if half the Russians were to starve to death the day after, it would not matter to me in the least. What concerns me alone is myself, and the interests of a few close friends. For all I care, the rest of the world may go to hell at today's sunset. I was born in America, and America is to me, at the time of writing, the most comfortable country to live in—and also at the time of writing the very pleasantest—in the world. This is why, at the time of writing, I am here, and not in France, or in England, or elsewhere. But if England became more comfortable and more pleasant than America tomorrow, I'd live in England. And if I lived in England I should be no more interested in the important problems of England than I am presently interested in the important problems of America. My sole interest lies in writing, and I can write as well in one place as in another, whether it be Barcelona, Spain, or Coon Rapids, Iowa. Give me a quiet room, a pad of paper, eight or nine sharp lead pencils, a handful of

thin, mild cigars, and enough to eat and drink—all of which, by
the grace of God, are happily within my means—and I do not
care a tinker's dam whether Germany invades Belgium or Belgium
Germany, whether Ireland is free or not free, whether the Stock
Exchange is bombed or not bombed, or whether the nations of the
earth arm, disarm, or conclude to fight their wars by limiting
their armies to biting each other. . . . On that day during the
world war when the most critical battle was being fought, I sat
in my still, sunlit, cozy library composing a chapter on æsthetics
for a new book on the drama. And at five o'clock, my day's
work done, I shook and drank a half dozen excellent apéritifs.

That is more Neronian than Byronic. The æsthetic
cruelty of the closing sentences is matched only by their
exemplary honesty, which outrages the sternest ethical
tenets of our accepted code. The man is too honest for
comfort. Mencken's attitude is virtually the same, but
it is colored by a greater natural sociability, I imagine.
Nathan gives the impression that he is intellectually a re-
cluse,—a sybaritic hermit. Quite in conformity with
that topsy-turviness which is to be discovered not only
in his verbal style but in his general outlook, his is a
hermit's withdrawal not from the pleasures so much as
from the displeasures of our common life; what is more,
it is a withdrawal into, not from, the world. Mencken
does not withdraw; he is eager for frays, and were the
sorry world to be remoulded tomorrow nearer to his
heart's desire, he would sigh with a nostalgia for the
errors of mundanity, like an Alexander bereft of worlds
to conquer. Mencken is the active mode of revolt;
Nathan, the passive.

Mencken becomes more and more concerned with

ideas and with the processes of ideation. Nathan plays with the emotions and with their results rather than their processes, though no more than Mencken would he relinquish for a moment the precious control of the intellect over the feelings. Yet less than Mencken he yields to the blandishments of sentiment. His anti-social cruelty is but an aspect of an intellectual severity that finds in himself his first and chief subject.

See how this disparity-in-agreement works out. There is *The American Credo,* one of the joint labors. The Preface runs almost to one hundred pages of solid, sober disquisition upon a suggested science of descriptive sociology. The difference between the Preface (written by Mencken) and the articles of the Credo (written by Nathan) is the difference between Mencken and Nathan. The one by sheer intellectual curiosity intrigued into the very morass which he is mapping; the other, content with dredging up the mire of superstition and credulousness and letting it stand as silently eloquent evidence. The one, delving into sources and origins, with the frown of the investigator and the *Forschungsmensch* merging into the lines of laughter; the other, skimming over the crust, with a sneer just above his smile. The one beguiled by theories; the other, amused by practise. Look at Mencken's forehead; he is a frown. Look at Nathan's nose; he is a sneer. Underneath the frown, laughter; underneath the sneer a smile. And underneath these things, a common hedonism that unites these fellows at the base of their differences.

There was, then, that cryptic composite known as

Mencken-and-Nathan. There is, however, a Mencken that stands on his own two legs in Baltimore, and a Nathan that sits on his own bottom in New York.

The difference between the two men, symbolically speaking, is the difference between their two cities.

CHAPTER EIGHT

*Epigrams and Burlesques—Impuritanism as
a Literary Force—Bachelor's Wisdom—
Unacademic Philology—Roman License
and American Superstitions—Petite En-
cyclopédie à la Mencken*

I

THE epigram is the journalist of philosophy. At its
best, it distils wisdom; at its worst, it is the
sweat-drop of would-be thought, as sour as a trickle of
perspiration. Its excuse is not its truth, but its illuminating brilliancy; it is a rapier thrust through the heart
of things. It is not so much the jewel itself, as a facet
of the precious stone. It is light without heat; even
when patently it lies, it yet has a glitter of a deeper
truth. The epigram is the philosopher as journalist.

Mencken's epigrams are the barbed tips of his anti-
philosophy. To be sure, many a tip is too blunt to fly
farther than the outer skin of the reader. Yet at their
best his epigrams cut deep; they compress in a line a
volume. They are the soul of his wit. Consider, as
specimens, a few only that I have chosen from *A Little
Book in C Major*:

Wife: a former sweetheart.
Love at first sight: a labor saving device.

Whenever a husband and wife begin to discuss their marriage they are giving evidence at an inquest.

The truth that survives is simply the lie that is pleasantest to believe.

An anti-vivisectionist is one who gags at a guinea-pig and swallows a baby.

Men have a much better time of it than women. For one thing, they marry later. For another thing, they die earlier.

The man who marries for love alone is at least honest. But so was Czolgosz.

Man weeps to think that he will die so soon. Woman, that she was born so long ago.

Adultery: democracy applied to love.

Axiom: something that everyone believes. When everyone begins to believe anything it ceases to be true. For example, the notion that the homeliest girl in the party is the safest.

Clergyman: a ticket speculator outside the gates of Heaven.

Fame: an embalmer trembling with stage-fright.

Honeymoon: the time during which the bride believes the bridegroom's word of honor.

The formula of George Bernard Shaw: to put the obvious in terms of the scandalous.

(Again Mencken, defining Shaw, defines himself. What else are his epigrams but the scandalization of the obvious? Is this not, indeed, part of the very technique of all epigrammatization?)

Archbishop: a Christian ecclesiastic of a rank superior to that attained by Christ; see also *bishop* and *archdeacon*.

Democracy is also a form of religion. It is the worship of jackals by jackasses.

Immortality: the condition of a dead man who doesn't believe that he is dead.

The objection to Puritans is not that they try to make us think as they do, but that they try to make us do as they think.

Theology is an effort to explain the unknowable in terms of the not worth knowing.

A Church is a place in which gentlemen who have never been to Heaven brag about it to persons who will never get there.

I am not sure that Theology has ever been better defined, or, for that matter, the institutionalized Church. I am not sure that the sentimentalists in biology will ever appreciate the cruel, incontrovertible, philosophic overtones of that gibe at the Anti-Vivisectionists. And I am not sure that Mencken himself will find, in his epigrams of sex, cloudy evidence as to a certain fear, on his part, of the deadlier of the species. Perhaps his fear of women, or rather his wariness, is based upon a better understanding of them. The feeling, however, is there. Sex, which to some may become a duet, for him remains a duel. A certain immunity, then, he gains; he loses a certain something else that most men, without acquiring that immunity, never find. That certain something has rarely been sung with more beauty than Mark Twain placed in the mouth of his Adam at the grave of Eve: "Wheresoever she was, *there* was Eden." I would not be misunderstood on this score. I have no profound respect for our modern institution of marriage. Marriage, rather than a sacrament, is an art, with its own arduous preliminary technique. Like all the other arts, it is infested by too many quacks and bunglers. As practised today, it is of course little more than a social license for biological relations between the sexes, plus the buncombe of our various idealisms. It is the line of least social resistance. In a word, too many persons marry. I do not mean that it takes a legalized union of a man and a woman to produce the music of Adam's requiem to Eve. Mencken, biting the apple of knowledge, prefers to forsake Eve as well as paradise. His wisdom is a bachelor's wisdom; it would be that, even were there no marriage laws. For there were Eves such as Mark Twain's Adam had before monogamy was invented; there are such Adams and Eves today, despite the marriage laws.

The marriage ceremony, that solemn farce, has been excellently parodied by Mencken in *The Wedding: A Stage Direction.* Too, despite his predilections in favor of hygiene, he ridicules the eugenists in a scherzando playlet entitled *Asepsis,* in which his medical delvings cast up about every illness to which the flesh is heir. Most characteristic of all the Burlesques, however, is that tiny masterpiece of its kind, *Death: A Philosophical Discussion.* This, almost literally, is gallows humor; here, underlying his seemingly wildest nonsense, is the ground bass of sobriety. The slapstick becomes the gravedigger's spade. In a dozen pages he has presented, in all its devastating inconsequentiality, the bovine reaction of our ordinary mortality to the ultimate mystery. A man lies dead; his pallbearers are discussing the departed:

First Pallbearer—Who woulda thought that *he* woulda been the next.

Second Pallbearer—Yes; you never can tell.

Third Pallbearer—(*An oldish voice, oracularly*) We're here today and gone tomorrow.

Fourth Pallbearer—I seen him no longer ago than Chewsday. He never looked better. Nobody would have——

Fifth Pallbearer—I seen him Wednesday. We had a glass of beer together in the Huffbrow Kaif. He was laughing and cutting up like he always done.

Sixth Pallbearer—You never know who it's gonna hit next. Him and me was pallbearers together for Hen Jackson no more than a month ago, or say five weeks.

First Pallbearer—Well, a man is lucky if he goes off quick. If I had *my* way I wouldn't want no better way.

Second Pallbearer—My brother John went that way. He dropped like a stone, settin' there at the supper table. They had to take his knife out of his hand.

Third Pallbearer—I had an uncle to do the same thing, but without the knife. He had what they call appleplexy. It runs in my family.

Fourth Pallbearer—They say it's in *his'n,* too.

Fifth Pallbearer—But he never looked it.

Sixth Pallbearer—No. Nobody woulda thought *he* woulda been the next.

First Pallbearer—Them are the things you never can tell anything about.

Second Pallbearer—Ain't it true.

Third Pallbearer—We're here today and gone tomorrow.

And so on, in vacuous repetition. What more, after all, is there to say? Nothing more, but to snatch beauty from despair and from meaninglessness. Hence, in life, artists; hence, in living, aristocrats.

II

As we approach the spheres of literature, language and philosophy, the Menckenian assault grows more formidable. Not because of a well-planned mass attack, but because of his reckless running fire upon the arts and sciences. Here, too,—perhaps here especially, the paradoxes hold good. He admires craftsmanship inordinately, yet his *Book of Prefaces,* devoted to Joseph Conrad, James Huneker, Theodore Dreiser and Puritanism as a Literary Force, reveals him as, essentially, not the mere appraiser of technical dexterity, but as the æsthetic critic. He pierces to the core of Conrad's Sophoclean *Weltanschauung:* to the core of Dreiser's world of pity and terror; to the core of Huneker's eclecticism. There are excursions, digressions, irrelevancies, statistics,—a lava of comment, pertinent and impertinent, shot from this volcano,—yet underneath, often hidden beneath the hot, flowing stream and the blinding ashes, is the hardy mountainside of solid, æsthetic response. Just as, in the essays upon the bookmen, he is essentially the æsthetic critic of books, so, in his masterly case against the Puritan in letters is he the æsthetic critic of life. It has become a commonplace of Menckenian, as of Shavian and of Nietzschean criticism, to repeat the discovery that at bottom all these men are themselves Puritans. True enough, in its way; yet it is not the fervor that makes the Puritan; it is not even his madness of conformity, though that, in all conscience, is evil enough. It is what he would have one conform to. It is the rigidity in his course. It is his utter confusion of beauty and duty; indeed, his misreading of both. It is, in a few words, his enthronement of an ethic above an æsthetic:

. . . a heresy too palpably false to be long tolerated, but one which, in the brief period it has already endured, may be said to

230

have accomplished more in the corruption of our Poetical Literature than all its other enemies combined. I allude to the heresy of "The Didactic." It has been assumed, tacitly and avowedly, directly and indirectly, that the ultimate object of all Poetry is Truth. Every poem, it is said, should inculcate a moral; and by this moral is the poetical merit of the work to be adjudged. We Americans especially have patronized this happy idea; and we Bostonians very especially have developed it in full. We have taken it into our heads that to write a poem simply for the poem's sake, and to acknowledge such to have been our design, would be to confess ourselves radically wanting in the true poetic dignity and force; but the simple fact is, that, would we but permit ourselves to look into our own souls, we should immediately there discover that under the sun there neither exists nor CAN exist any work more thoroughly dignified,—more supremely noble than this very poem, *per se,* this poem which is a poem and nothing more,—this poem written solely for the poem's sake.

This is not from Mencken; it is from Poe, in *The Poetic Principle,*—Poe in one of his less violent moods —capitals, italics, foreign expressions and all. It is the Poe who has been called by Vincent O'Sullivan the only American critic of the first magnitude who has preceded Mencken,—the Poe in whom, so to speak, we may come across many a Menckenian passage and some familiar Menckenian reactions to the cultivation of letters in this republic. Poe's thesis had to wait for Mencken's essay before it found the proper elaboration by a worthy successor. The thesis, taking it by and large, is as old as Aristotle: poetry for its own sake, beauty as its own excuse for being, and not for that *profit as well as pleasure* which Horace fastened upon it in his Epistle to the Pisos, more familiar to us as the *Ars Poetica.*

231

Mencken on the side of the old Stagirite, matched against
the scholastic More, Brownell, Sherman, Phelps *et alia;*
more Greek than the academicians themselves! A grinning paradox!

III

All religions,—again recalling de Gourmont,—revolve
madly around questions of sex. Freedom from religious
illusion means, per corollary, freedom from inhibited
sex-thinking. This, in substance, is all of what there is
to the charge of immorality so naturally leveled, by the
preachers, against persons independent of the established
religious thought. Just as Mencken's philosophic freedom reveals itself in the central acceptance of uncertainty;
just as, in language, that independence betrays itself in
his occasional addiction to "American"; just as, in religion, it produces a nonchalant atheism, so, in the realms
of love it proclaims the virtues of bachelorhood. Man
free of God, and free of woman. The superior woman,
likewise, tends not toward single-blessedness, but multiple
independence. Monotheism is a figment of theology;
monogamy, a figment of ethics. I know that Mencken,
in public and in private, protests that he is a violent
believer in monogamy, and that he considers it the norm
of all civilized men. There is a play of words here,
however. Mencken winning victories for Christian
sexual virtue is even more dangerous to the cause he
espouses than Mencken winning victories for Capitalism.
To be sure, the man is sane, but he is not "safe." His

232

definition of monogamy, though true to the dictionary, flouts our precious morality none the less. Speaking like a philosopher, it is monogamy in space but polygamy in time. It is, in simple language, "one woman at a time." If that be monogamy, make the most of it. Mencken makes no pretense to celibacy. Yet the popular impression that he is passionately interested in the unfair sex seems grossly exaggerated. In his moments of relaxation he even prefers the masculine conviviality of the *Biertisch*. "If I ever marry at all," he has told me, "it will be on a sudden impulse, as a man shoots himself." Monogamy!

The logical development to which Mencken's views upon sex would lead seems in my opinion to be the social recognition for both sexes of what today obtains surreptitiously for one of the sexes only: central marriage leavened by preferential variety. That is, for such persons as can experience love, which Mencken affects to believe can never come to a man after thirty. For such as cannot, there will be—as there is today in effect, with a somewhat anachronistic stigma—variety pure and simple, or impure and complex. With the propagation of such scientific knowledge as renders the possibilities of contamination and of conception equally remote, enlightened social opinion is bound sooner or later to revise its moral attitudes. In his attitude toward what we may call the new virtue, Mencken is plain and astoundingly logical. If I cite, from *In Defense of Woman,* the following passage particularly, it is because the religious and ethical aspects of virginity are discussed and disposed of in a single breath; as they are inextricably bound in theology, so in logic, do they fall together.

The notion that honor in women is exclusively a physical matter, that a single aberrance may convert a woman of the highest merits into a woman of none at all, that the sole valuable thing a woman can bring to marriage is virginity—this notion is so preposterous that no intelligent person, male or female, actually cherishes it. It survives as one of the hollow conventions of Christianity; nay, of the levantine barbarism that preceded Christianity. As women threw off the other conventions which now bind them, they will throw off this one, too, and so their virtue, grounded upon fastidiousness and self-respect instead of mere fear and conformity, will become a far more laudable thing than it can ever be under the present system. And, for its absence, if they see fit to dispose of it, they will no more apologize than a man apologizes today.

This comes from no mere contemner of women; from no pathological misogynist. Mencken's realistic outlook stamps him, by his own definition, as sharing largely the "feminine mind."

"Human creatures," says George, borrowing from Weininger, "are never entirely male or entirely female; there are no men, there are no women, but only sexual majorities." Find me an obviously intelligent man, a man free from sentimentality and illusion, a man hard to deceive, a man of the first class, and I'll show you a man with a wide streak of woman in him. Bonaparte had it; Schopenhauer had it; Bismarck and Lincoln had it; in Shakespeare, if the Freudians are to be believed, it amounted to downright homosexuality.

Mencken, then, challenges the Hebrew-Christian morality at the source; its monotheism and its monogamy.

With him, the Horatian *mens sana in corpore sana* becomes a free mind in a free body.

IV

The grin of the paradox that Mencken posed in his *Book of Prefaces* opened into a wide guffaw with the appearance of *The American Language*. Mencken the pea-shooting pantaloon, able only to decry his betters, incapable of "sustained effort" (how Poe abominated that tribute to mere plodding!) ; Mencken the anti-Professor, the anti-Academe, the anti-American, discovered as the sculptor of a milestone in the history of our national philology! The professors out-professored! The national idiom raised to the dignity of a language, with a place in the sun all its own! And by an antic fellow who could turn his pea-shooter, like a magic wand, into a pointer without using it as a birch rod!

Just as Mencken is a poet fighting against his feelings, so, not too deep down in his personality is a professor combating the tyranny of knowledge. *The American Language* is, from the psychological standpoint, a remarkable synthesis of the emotional and the intellectual spirit that is Mencken. It is charged with the man's dynamism; it is a gesture of revolt and self-assertion magnified from individual to national proportions; it contains Mencken the jester and Mencken the scholar, Mencken the anti-patriot strangely blended with Mencken the American, in whom are to be heard overtones of an inverted patriotism. It is, in a phrase, Mencken the man, conflicts, contradictions and all, projected against a continental screen.

The investigation of linguistic differentiation is as old as the first two village patriots who ridiculed their respective, if unrespected, dialects. Its application to living nations speaking originally the same tongue and then branching off on independent paths is beset by many pitfalls of an unscientific character, usually political. Take, for examples, Spanish and Portuguese in the old world and in the new. There is an evident divergence; the Portuguese of Brazil is not, precisely, the Portuguese of Lisbon; nor is the Spanish of the various republics in Central and Southern America the Spanish of Madrid. I am not prepared to say that there is yet a "Brazilian" or a "Mexican" language, as distinguished from Portuguese and Spanish. Undoubtedly, however, and this is the important consideration, there is a differentiation due to new surroundings, climate, blending of races, distance, diversity of interests. What time will bring, none may say, although increasingly wonderful means of international intercommunication will doubtless have the effect of lessening the chances for radical divergence.[1]

Now, the same process is inevitably at work in the United States, and Mencken presents the case with fullness, force, clarity, humor and courage. What interests me is not the question whether an "American" language really exists as yet; I do not believe it does,[2] although the lines drawn between dialects and languages are as ten-

[1] It is interesting to recall that Remy de Gourmont, in his enthusiasm for a "Spanish-American" language, coined the adjective *néo-espagnol.* My attitude toward it is the same that I maintain toward Mencken's *American,*—one not so much of opposition as of deliberation. De Gourmont and Mencken alike are not so much wrong as premature.

[2] I notice that the great philologist, Otto Jespersen, in a review of

uous as the words that compose them. But when one recalls the history of languages and the development, let us say, of French, Italian, Spanish, Provençal, Portuguese, Roumanian and lesser idioms out of what once was Latin, one cannot declare too surely that "American" will never be distinct from English. Mencken, with a prevision that is little more than the application of common sense unobstructed by sentimental allegiances, studies the beginnings of that parting of the ways, relates them to differences in national psychology, to historic moments, to changes of milieu,—in a word, he breathes the spirit of life into the letter of language. It is no small service; it gives him—imagine Mencken upon an academic pedestal!—an honorable, and a considerable niche in the gallery of American philology. If proof were needed for the obtuse, upon whom proof and protest alike are wasted, *The American Language* alone would prove that his swashbuckling humor, his sadistic slashing of the established mumbo-jumbos is, though humanly liable to error, founded upon solid scholarship and—whisper it not in the university corridors—upon that human understanding without which scholarship is a sterile and a pestilential mockery.

Only he who has spent nightmarish hours tussling with Cowperian "philologers who chase a panting syllable through time and space," with grammars of Old Spanish and Medieval French, with tomes upon Germanic Mor-

---

The American Language published in *Litteris* (Lund, Sweden), for March, 1925, takes a similar stand. Jespersen also points out that a number of Mencken's own corrections in later years tend away from "Americanistic" extremes toward a more widely understandable English.

phology and Phonology, with treatises upon Vulgar Latin, the Italian Dialects, and what not else that was devised to obstruct man's joy in learning, may appreciate the service Mencken has performed with his gleeful study in linguistic differentiation.

The American Language does, for the idiom of the United States, what the work of the Colombian scholar Rufino Cuervo did for the Spanish of Spanish America, and what such Brazilian scholars as Verissimo and Ribeiro have done and are doing for the Portuguese of Brazil. It is simply the concept of evolution applied to linguistic instead of to animal life. Considered as a personal document, it is, as I have suggested, thus far the synthesis *par excellence* of the man's quirks, quips and qualities.

As Mencken studies in this book and out, so he writes, the "American" language,—"American" in gusto and spirit, however, rather than in speech. Consider what we might call his *Non Credo,*—for Mencken's æsthetic of aggression makes of him a Mephistophelean spirit of denial. *Ich bin der Geist der stets verneint!* The extract I give below was originally a letter written to Rascoe.

I am against all theologians, professors, editorial-writers, right-thinkers and reformers. I am against patriotism because it demands the acceptance of propositions that are obviously imbecile, *e. g.,* that an American Presbyterian is the equal of Anatole France, Brahms or Ludendorff. I am against democracy for the same reason; it is indistinguishable from lunacy. To me democracy seems to be founded wholly upon the inferior man's envy of his superior—of the man who is having a better time. That is also the origin of Puritanism. I detest all such things. I acknowledge that many men are my superiors, and always defer to them. In such a country as the United States, of course, few of that sort are to be encountered. Hence my apparent foreignness; most of the men I respect are foreigners. But this is not my fault. I'd be glad to respect Americans if they were respectable. George Washington was. I admire him greatly. I detest men who meanly admire mean things, *e. g.,* fellows who think that Roosevelt was a great man. I also detest poltroons—that is, men who seek unfair advantages in combat. In my gladiatorial days on the Baltimore *Sun* I never attacked a single man who was without means of hitting back. I controlled space that was dedicated to any one who wanted to attack me. No man was ever refused this space. My objection to Americans is that they like to fight with the enemy strapped to the board. Hence the persecution of Germans during the war, the robbery of helpless alien business men, the American Legion, the American Protective League, the attack on Spain, the wars with Nicaragua, Santo Domingo, etc. This poltroonery is not essentially American, it is simply democratic; the inferior man always shows it.

I am, tested by the prevailing definitions, a bad American. I do not believe this country has the glorious future that patrioteers talk of. It will probably remain second rate for a long time— a mere milch cow for England. Most of the American ideals, so called, that I know of seem to me to be idiotic. If they were sound, I'd probably jump into the nearest river. The sort of country they conjure up would be simply a paradise of bounders, forward-lookers, right-thinkers, all sorts of stupid cowards. I do not believe that civilized life is possible under a democracy.

I am an extreme libertarian and believe in absolutely free speech, especially for anarchists, socialists and other such fools. Once those fellows were free to gabble *ad lib.,* democracy would be reduced to an absurdity; the mob would go stark crazy. I am against jailing men for their opinions, or, for that matter, for anything else. I am opposed to religions, because all of them seek to throttle opinion. I do not believe in education, and am glad I never went to a university. Beyond the rudiments, it is impossible to teach anything. All the rest the student acquires himself. His teacher merely makes it difficult for him. I never learned anything in school.

My scepticism is intolerably offensive to the normal American man: only the man under strong foreign influences sees anything in it save a gross immorality. If the notions of the right-thinkers are correct, then such stuff as mine (and particularly such stuff as I shall write hereafter) ought to be put down by law. I believe that, in the long run, it *will* be put down by law—that free speech is too dangerous to democracy to be permitted. But I surely do not complain about that. The Puritans have a right to determine the laws of their country. And I reject the sentimentality that the minority also has rights.

As there is something of Poe in Mencken's critical attitude, so does his sheer delight in heaping up words suggest the verbal gusto of Whitman. For Whitman, too, wrote an "American" language, just as Poe wrote an "Anti-American" criticism.

Since Mr. Stuart P. Sherman has read his war-prejudices into Mencken's *American Language,* interpreting it in terms of propaganda,—a work "over-ambitiously designed as a wedge to split asunder the two great English-speaking peoples," [1]—it may be worth while to hearken unto a pair of great Englishmen. Neither Hardy nor Ellis wrote the lines I am about to transcribe with Mencken's work in mind; they did speak, however, out of a sense of linguistic flux, out of a sensitivity to the

[1] See *Americans,* Scribner's, 1922. Page 10.

ever-changing spoken and written language of their people and of all peoples. Wrote Hardy, in a letter to William Archer: [1]

> I have no sympathy with the criticism that would treat English as a dead language—a thing crystallized at an arbitrarily selected stage of its existence, and bidden to forget that it has a past and deny that it has a future. Purism, whether in grammar or vocabulary, always means ignorance. Language was made before grammar, not grammar before language. And as for the English vocabulary, purists seem to ignore the lessons of history and common sense.

And Ellis: [2]

> For most of those who deliberately seek to learn to write, words seem generally to be felt as of less importance than the art of arranging them. It is thus that the learner in writing tends to become the devoted student of grammar and syntax. . . . That is, indeed, a tendency which always increases. Civilization develops with a conscious adhesion to formal order, and the writer—writing by fashion or by ambition and not by divine right of the creative instinct—follows the course of civilization. It is an unfortunate tendency, for those whom it affects conquer by their number. As we know, writing that is real is not learnt in that way. Just as the solar system was not made in accordance with astronomer's laws, so writing is not made by the laws of grammar. Astronomer and grammarian alike can only come in at the end, to give a generalised description of what usually happens in the respective fields it pleases them to explore. When a new comet, cosmic or literary, enters their sky, it is their descriptions which

[1] See *The Life of Thomas Hardy,* by Ernest Brennecke, Jr. Greenberg. Page 139.

[2] See *The Dance of Life,* by Havelock Ellis. Houghton Mifflin Co. Pages 172–173.

have to be readjusted, and not the comet. There seems to be no more pronounced mark of the decadence of a people and its literature than a servile and rigid subserviency to rule. It can only make for ossification, for anchylosis, for petrifaction, all the milestones on the road of death. In every age of democratic plebeianism, where each man thinks he is as good a writer as the others, and takes his laws from the others, having no laws of his own nature, it is down this steep path that men, in a flock, inevitably run.

V

Revolt against the human; revolt against the divine. "In all of his writings I have ever read," declared Professor Pattee, "I have found no innuendo directed at Christ himself." The simple fact is that Mencken, true to the individualistic rationalism of his character, is an agnostic. Mere blasphemy, being but the scowling face of true religion, has little place in his scheme of things. Determined confrontation of truth, however, is a different matter. He finds his gods and his devils among their prototype,—man. Strictly speaking, then, Mencken is not an anti-Christ; he is—and there is a difference— an anti-Christian. Perhaps we must qualify even here. Discussing, in his book upon Woman, the ethics of the so-called fair sex, he mentions, *en passant*, "the religion preached by Jesus (now wholly extinct in the world)." Christianity is democracy in the name of God; democracy, under whatever name it may go, is the rule of the mob; ergo, Christianity is the ethics of the weak and the envious; wherefore, it is bad. The logic is as straight as the shortest distance between two points. It needs neither innuendo nor blasphemy; it requires the rare

ability to state, with scientific precision, the results of a
calm observation. It may be made into a melody and
played in thirty-two variations, but the main theme rises
always clear above the rhythmic changes, the harmonic
alterations, the contrapuntal variety.

Mencken does not take his anti-religion any more seriously than his other pleasure-aversions. It may be sought
for, as well as anywhere else, in the buffoonery called
Heliogabalus.

Varius Avitus Bassanius Heliogabalus rules over Rome
in the third decade of the second century, A.D. He rules
also over a harem of wives, all legally his. His orgies
are in the most approved fashion, and if his multiplicity
of wives is at first a source of increased delight (who was
it said that every man carries a harem under his hat?),
it soon becomes a marsh of multiplied domestic troubles.
When Lucia the Galatian, a Christian maiden, is brought
before him as a rioter,—a "soap-box" case,—his judicial
frown, as he gazes upon the fair lass, melts into an ap-
praising smile. Straightway he ushers out Dacia, new-
est and youngest of his wives, and returns to the bench to
try the case by himself. Being a judge of beauty, he
further decides that the court is too public for this affair;
to the star chamber, then, where the sounds of music be-
token ill for Lucia's purity and for the fond peace of the
Emperor's other wives. The Emperor has begun to see
a new light; or, rather, he has found a new flame. Let
her chatter about the spirit, if she will; his mind is on
matters more earthly. And so, while Lucia imagines
that she has brought the Emperor a light, Heliogabalus
takes her for the flame. Another wife for the harem.

A half year goes by, and Heliogabalus is still wooing his Christian wife-in-name-only. To be sure, when a fellow has so many other wives to court, it is rather hard on his imperial highness; Lucia, however, is different. Her Christianity has, as it were, a "kick"; it fillips his pagan senses. Yet her charms have been dearly bought. The Emperor wants poetry; he gets hymns. He wants long, Roman, succulent kisses; he gets a Christian peck. He wants abandon; he encounters chaste reserve. Lucia, too, for all her religion, begins to display some universal attributes of the eternal feminine. Nor are the eleven other wives delighted over the triumph of this Christian usurper. While she evinces jealousy of the pretty Dacia, the ousted mates are plotting a coup. There is a gabbling quarrel, with startling revelations. And Heliogabalus returns to the charms of Dacia. He returns for good; he is sick of Lucia's self-righteousness and maudlin Christianity. He is sick of such martyr-voluptuaries as Simon of Cappadocia, whom he cheats of the martyr's joy by a spiteful pardon. He has had his Christian spree; now back to Roman riot!

The outline omits the one element which gives to the buffoonery its most palatable quality; the dialogue. There are a number of clever and well-managed situations; there are the regulation gibes at the medical profession and at legal procedure. Love is treated in cavalierly fashion, and when Heliogabalus gets drunk at the end of the second act, he hiccups epigrams like those that used to grace the bottoms of the pages in the *Smart Set*.

"Love is the triumph of imagination over intelligence."

"A short preface to a long book."

"Love is like war; easy to begin but very hard to stop."

"A woman in love is less modest than a man; she has less to be ashamed of."

"Love is the delusion that one woman differs from another."

What interests me more than the theatrical qualities of the piece, which would make an admirable libretto for an Offenbach to set to music after he had lost track of his drinks, is the fundamentally serious note beneath all this tomfoolery. For *Heliogabalus* depicts Mencken's attitude of free joy as against the restrictive tenets of the Hebrew-Christian morality. The play, of course, is as modern as today. Though no great shakes as art, it affords a sanitation of the soul that is not far removed from the soul's sanity. It is almost an anti-morality play, heavy with hedonism. All nonsense, of course, yet the learned could base upon these three acts an entire philosophy of life.

VI

Mencken's Introduction to *The American Credo* is implicit and explicit in everything that he has written about his country and its people. The fervor with which he vents his scorn has not deceived his more discerning commentators; I doubt that it much deceives the man himself. Rather, it amuses him. Mr. Wilson, one of his best critics, has regarded Mencken as the "civilized consciousness of modern America, its learning, its intelligence and its taste, realizing the grossness of its matter and its mind and crying out in horror and chagrin." He names Mencken, similarly, "one of the greatest of Americans," and though there is no need to accept the greatness, to doubt the American quality would be shortsighted. Combating or exposing the superstitions that are the average American's substitute for life and thought, Mencken gradually compiles his series of *Prejudices;* these have come to comprise his personal encyclopædia of aversions and admirations, a sort of Voltairean *dictionnaire philosophique.* In the *Prejudices* are to be found excursions into almost everything knowable, definitions couched in a highly personalized idiom. Begun as literary essays, they have taken on, with the progress of the series, the color of Mencken's remarkable repertory of interests. Writing of men, women and things, he writes, all the time, of himself. This he knows; this he wants you to know.

Ask a professional critic to write about himself and you simply ask him to do what he does every day in the practice of his art and mystery. There is, indeed, no criticism that is not a confidence, and there is no confidence that is not self-revelation. When I denounce a book with mocking and contumely, and fall upon the poor author in the brutal, Asiatic manner of a drunken longshoreman, a Ku Kluxer, or a midshipman at Annapolis, I am only saying, in the trade cant, that the fellow disgusts me—that his ideas and his manners are somehow obnoxious to me, as those of a Methodist, a golf-player, or a clog-dancer are obnoxious to me—in brief, that I hold myself to be a great deal better than he is, and am eager to say so. And when, on the other hand, I praise a book in high, astounding terms, and speak of the author as if his life and sufferings were of capital importance to the world, then I am merely saying that I detect something in him, of prejudice, tradition, habit of mind, that is much like something within myself, and that my own life and sufferings are of the utmost importance to me.

That is all there ever is in criticism, once it gets beyond cataloguing. No matter how artfully the critic may try to be impersonal and scientific he is bound to give himself away. I am a critic of books, and through books of *Homo sapiens,* and through *Homo sapiens* of God.

There you have, in Mencken's own words, what I have called his æsthetic of agression. Revolt always in the direction of a greater individual freedom. Does man's sense of the natural mystery crystallize into a dogma of creation? Smash it. Does man's laborious accumulation of fact and fiction about the universe harden into a rock of formulas for pedants? Blast it. Do delicate souls, aware of a reality which they dare not face, weave a mesh of illusion to shield them from the dreaded impact? Slash it. Yet Mencken would eat his cake and have it; he would shatter illusions, and nurture them. He revels in destructive criticism, all the while building up a formidable body of peculiarly personal doctrine. He begins his creative life as a poet, abandons the muse, and after having dallied with her, proves her harshest critic; yet there is indubitable poetry,—call it heroic verse,—in his attitude toward our capricious existence. He berates the pedants and the professoriat, and then sweats for silent years over a ponderous tome, which outdoes the professors at their own game. The man is suspicious of sentiment; suspiciously violent with the overly learned; suspiciously truculent with the commoner. Somewhere in the hidden cemetery of his soul lie

buried a poet, a professor, a lover—if not of mankind, of mankind's potentialities. He reaches his af-
firmations through negations. He says his Yea to life
with many a Nay. His definitions, as often as not, are
denials. All this he calls his vanity; it is, at bottom, his
vitality. His very excesses are jets of nature's own
prodigality. Almost habitually, the man speaks with
evident exaggeration, but rarely are his proportions dis-
torted.

I consider Mencken, essentially, as an aesthetic critic,
and what is more, an æsthetic critic in an almost Crocean
sense of the term. For all his quondam support of what
he called "catalytic" criticism, he remains, in the essentials of his practise, "creative," and in just that sense
which he sought to replace with his word borrowed from
chemistry. (Remark the subtle influence of Mencken's
earliest scientific enthusiasm upon the evolution of his
critical opinion. Had he never dabbled in chemistry as
a boy, this theory might never have occurred to him):

A catalyzer, in chemistry, is a substance that helps two other
substances to react. For example, consider the case of ordinary
cane sugar in water. Dissolve the sugar in the water and nothing
happens. But add a few drops of acid and the sugar changes into
glucose and fructose. Meanwhile, the acid itself is absolutely
unchanged. All it does is stir up the reaction between the water
and the sugar. The process is called catalysis. The acid is a
catalyzer.

Well, this is almost exactly the function of a genuine critic of
the arts. It is his business to provoke the reaction between the
work of art and the spectator. The spectator, untutored, stands
unmoved; he sees the work of art, but it fails to make any in-

telligible impression on him; if he were spontaneously sensible to it, there would be no need for criticism. But now comes the critic with his catalysis. He makes the work of art live for the spectator; he makes the spectator live for the work of art. Out of the process comes understanding, appreciation, intelligent enjoyment—and that is precisely what the artist tried to produce.

There is something wrong here. The critic compared to a mere acid which "itself is absolutely unchanged?" Mencken condemning himself to the office of a sterile, static intermediary? The critic—*i. e.,* an artist in his own right—as intellectual procurer? The lapse was so obvious that Mencken abandoned the catalytic theory shortly after the publication of *Prejudices* (First Series), in which it appears. In *Prejudices* (Third Series), we read, in the "Footnote on Criticism," that the critic, "is not even trying to discharge the catalytic office that I myself, in a romantic moment" (he has his moments, you see!) "once sought to force upon him. He is, first and last, trying to express himself."

We are thus brought back to Spingarn's "creative" critic. And Mencken is just that, however he may eschew the word.. In the same Footnote he refers to his championship of Dreiser. He points out that, when, years ago, he took up the cause of this neglected artist, his own commentators fell into either one of two assumptions regarding his underlying purpose: (a) that he had a "fanatical devotion for Mr. Dreiser's ideas and desired to propagate them," or (b) "that I was an ardent patriot, and yearned to lift up American literature. Both assumptions were false. I had then, and I have now, very little interest in many of Mr. Dreiser's main ideas; when we meet, in fact, we usually quarrel about them. And I am wholly devoid of public spirit, and haven't the least lust to improve American literature; if it ever came to what I regard as perfection my job would be gone." (A slight relapse into catalycism, for give Mencken a master to revel in, and he writes dithyrambs as fluently as ever he erupts into Vesuvian vituperation.)

What, then, was my motive in writing about Mr. Dreiser so copiously? My motive, well known to Mr. Dreiser himself, and to every one else who knew me as intimately as he did, was simply and solely to sort out and give coherence to the ideas of Mr. Mencken, and to put them into suave and ingratiating terms, and to discharge them with a flourish, and maybe with a phrase of pretty song, into the dense fog that blanketed the Republic.

True, as far as it goes; but not far enough, therefore not sufficiently true. Even unfair to Mencken, who, with the touch of masochism that there is in all critics, accuses himself so persistently of vanity that one wonders what modesty he is concealing. Take down his *Book of Prefaces* and turn to the essay on Dreiser. Mencken, of course, is written all over the pages; but so is Dreiser. Why does Mencken plow through every book, though it outrage his fondness for clear speech, sound construction; though it present a view of the world which is not his own? Because he sees beyond Mencken into Dreiser, and beyond Dreiser into life. Because he delights, not merely in a glorified exhibitionism, but in piercing to the core of reality at the centre of the artist's creation. In Dreiser something *lives*. That makes the artist, as it makes the critic. Mencken, so different from Dreiser in almost everything but this elemental approach to fundamentals unencumbered by illusions, has understood Dreiser better than many an uncritical soul who is spiritually akin to our lonely novelist. Why? Because he is not catalytic, but creative; because he has worked his way through all the outer wrappings of the Dreiserian manner straight to the concrete, intuitive origins. I haven't the slightest interest in, or intention of, dragooning Mencken into the camp of the Croceans. I am no campfollower myself; the relation I am indicating on Mencken's part is not one of allegiance but of analogy. In Mencken there is none of the Italian's metaphysical logomachy; the American is far more "practical" than his foreign colleague, less burdened with learning, less swathed in verbiage. Yet, after you strip Mencken of such externalities as sociological, political and philosophical wrappings, you find in him essentially the creative critic; the artist who creates his works out of other men's books as they create their books out of the materials of life itself. All art, therefore all criticism, is autobiography; but not all autobiography is therefore necessarily criticism or art. For this there must be a creative personality; must be, not only life, but significant life,—a definite attitude toward the riddle of existence. Mencken *is* such an attitude; more, he pierces to the roots of such an attitude in the subjects of his criticism. If that is not creative, then find a better word. Was it not Mencken himself who wrote of Huneker, that he had "absolutely no feeling for extra-æsthetic valuations?" Now, Mencken has such feelings; they form, however, chiefly the setting of his æsthetic reactions.

It follows that the limitations of the critic are limitations of personality; so, too, of course, with superiorities.

Croce himself, for all his understanding of the creative impulse,—perhaps because of it,—brings to his reader understanding rather than joy of art. He understands the joy, but in his criticism he communicates the process rather than the creative passion. Perhaps that is as it should be; for the original passion we must return to the work itself. Yet, if to the critic as artist we apply the Crocean method, we may trace Croce's own creative origins to a desire to comprehend rather than to enjoy; he is a spectator, not a dancer, of life. In understanding lies his enjoyment, and yet another paradox is reconciled to its self-contradictions.[1]

---

[1] Eventually, no doubt, the series of *Prejudices* will be pruned away to an irreducible minimum. This is what already is happening in England; in Germany, special selections are being made for translation. It should be interesting to see what these foreign *Prejudices* will look like, for the merely local and journalistic will have to disappear in favor of the essential doctrine.

CHAPTER NINE

Forces and Resultant—The Style—Impact and Reaction—A Theory of Theories— Per Aspera ad Artem

I

MENCKEN,—the essential Mencken,—may be summed up in a half-dozen words: passion for freedom, hatred of fraud. Whatever he has written, whatever he has done, may be traced to these twin aspects of a single function: liberty. To him, liberty means the utmost freedom possible under an orderly society. This is not incompatible with a certain authority; but that authority must be based upon genuine superiority. In our contemporary society such authority in state, in religion, in art, is constantly assailed by fraud, *i. e.*, by inferiority intriguing for dominance in politics, theology, æsthetics. Hence, on the passive side, Mencken's huge delight in the spectacle of living; hence, on the active, his equal delight in plunging into the fray. It is a sorry spectacle at best; at either end, a figment called God and another called Devil; in the middle, wraiths that call themselves men and women, the men chiefly bunglers and the women chiefly biological laws clothed in the latest fashion. What, confronted with such a play, is the attitude of the superior man, the aristocrat? To maintain a certain personal dignity, to function with an unimpeded organism, to laugh without applauding. To hide one's concern at the spectacle if, in a weaker moment, it appears. Why a "weaker moment"? Because the emotions are traitors that must be held in leash by the intelligence. Because the measure of man is the measure of his intellectual control over those emotions. Herein lies his dignity, his liberation from sentimentality, his humor.

The test of Mencken's influence upon his contemporaries, regardless for the moment whether it has been for the good or the bad, is the measure of these qualities that has been introduced by him into our cultural life. By that test, that influence has been incontestably great. Mencken has dramatized himself in terms of American life. He has compelled the discussion of every theme that has been of vital concern to him. Things significant to him have therefore been made significant to the rest of thinking America. Dignity in letters assumed the form of his dignity,—not the weary solemnity of the pedants, but a matter of proper equilibrium between head and heart, hardly incompatible with glee and buffoonery. In Puritan America, he tickled the Muses and it was found that they were none the less beautiful for their laughter. He plucked pedantic beards and it was found that these sober gentlemen concealed much ignorance behind their flowing rhetoric. The exercise of his peculiar, and by no means infallible, qualities cleared the cultural atmosphere of the nation. Indeed, much as he declaims against any desire to be of service, not the least service he lent was to clear intellectual paths as well as the cultural air.

His writings, taking them by and large, have impressed a personality upon the national scene. They have eased the spiritual burdens of the civilized minority—I believe that phrase is his—and helped to create such a civilized generation. This, inevitably, rather than as the result of a program. Mencken, consciously, pretends to no program. His concept of liberty includes every other right worth fighting for. "I believe that any invasion of it is immensely dangerous to the common weal—especially when that invasion is alleged to have a moral purpose. No conceivable moral purpose is higher than the right of the citizen to think whatever he pleases to think, and to carry on his private life without interference by others. If that right is taken away, then no moral system remains; all we have is a prison system. This begins to prevail in the United States."

Carry such a belief into the field of the fine arts and you have an inalterable opponent of all censorships, however discreet. Mencken has rarely been on firmer ground than when he wrote:[1] "It seems to me far better that indecencies should go unchallenged by law than that gangs of fanatics and perverts should police the rest of us. I believe that every form of censorship, however discreet it may be when it starts, falls inevitably into the hands of such fanatics and perverts. They alone are interested in such matters. The rest of us know very well, by experience in this world, that the effect of

[1] In a private letter.

indecency upon normal persons is trivial. I have myself read most of the books that the Comstocks denounce, and yet believe that I can honestly say that they have not influenced me in the slightest. Nor am I alone. Most of the men I respect have read them—and many of the women. I know women who have passed through appalling baths of indecency—for example, by going through the training of nurses—and later abandoned their virginity willingly, and who yet remain self-respecting, intelligent, clean-minded and charming. The effects of such experience are grossly exaggerated by prudes. Some individuals, male and female, are naturally lascivious; others are naturally cold and reserved. I believe that education influences them very little. I greatly dislike the former kind. . . . On the whole, I probably belong to the colder half of humanity. Indecency fills me with none of the dreadful emotions that Comstocks talk of. In the main, it simply tires me."

Again, intellectual control of the emotions, enlisted this time in the cause of emotional holidays.

Mencken would keep the roads free, no matter who travels over them. He is not the partisan of every man whose cause he fights. His combats, even when fought for a man, have been fought even more for this self-same liberty. What the Truth is he does not pretend to know, but all avenues must be held free for it to arrive—and, at the proper time, to leave.[1] Life is a play without any curtain-calls; when the curtain falls, let it

[1] See the *Motivos de Proteo,* by José Enrique Rodó, section CXXVII, entitled "La despedida de Gorgas": "I have tried to impart to you the love of truth; not truth, which is infinite."

at least have fallen upon a spectacle that was worth the passing performance.

There is a paradox here, as almost everywhere else in Mencken,—the paradox that is Truth charging at humanity with both its horns. In theory he is centrifugal, ready for eternal change in the fundamental changelessness of life. In practise he has altered but little since the earliest days. Whereas normal youth fights its way through a welter of emotions to the summit of ideas, Mencken as a writer was born very near that summit. Today finds him fighting his way to a haven of emotions. Should he ever reach it, whether through the potent influence of music or through subtler passages, he will emerge with new and greater power. Here, I imagine he will encounter the greatest combat of his career: against himself. Having said which, I hasten to doff the crystal gazer's turban, holding none the less a sharp eye to the future.

II

Mencken's style is the verbal image of the man. It is a perfect vehicle for his generally unemotional thinking. It has been, I imagine, as much responsible for the attacks against him as have the ideas that have been attacked. A minor *Schimpflexikon* might be compiled of the epithets that have been hurled at him in return for his own.[1]

[1] To the compiler of this proposed *Catalogue of Abuse* I herewith present a few sample imprecations, culled from recondite sources.

A single leading editorial in *The Arkansas Writer* for July-August 1921 yields the following: *bracycephalous Caliban, Black Knight of Slander, imported pervert, intellectual Houyhnhnm, traducer of mankind, pestilential nuisance, German propagandist, common scold, in-*

That style needs no justification, except to the unimaginative. Its very existence, of course, is its own best excuse.

I recall attending once, in an Eastern university of the highest standing, a lecture on Cicero by a visitor from England. The members of the classical faculty had assembled in the modest lecture room, accompanied by a handful of students who had been urged, by none too subtle means, to grace the occasion. The lecture was long and dull; so long, so dull, indeed, that, at the end, one of the heads of the classical department, behind the back of the lecturer but in full view of the students who sat in my section, pinched his nostrils as if to avoid inhaling a nauseating stench. The sight offended me. I would have preferred that the local dignitary perform the pantomime in sight of the English visitor.

Why do I suddenly recall that almost forgotten scene? Because Mencken's style is, in one aspect, the answer to such academic hypocrisy. His pantomime is public. It is uninhibited. It causes a free and healthy laughter, not

sufferable excrescence on the body of American literature, self-appointed emissary of the Wilhelmstrasse, subverter of democracy, a super-egoist, modern Attila.

From the *Jacksonville* (*Miss.*) *Daily News* for May 12, 1925: *prodigious vaunter of verbosity; In truth, 'tis a fulsome compliment to call him an ass. The ass is useful, and Mencken isn't; a cheap and spurious smartness; a mountebank, a perpetual and preposterous pageant, a rantipole, a vain hysteric raging to and fro; a cheap iconoclast; idiotic vanity; puny quidnunc, this jackal in lion's skin, this Hittite, this brazenfaced hierophant; a pariah, an outcast, a literary renegade; vehement, voluble and verbose; a tadpole of the puddle, grown a toad and throned on the stool of his own conceit;* after which, concluding that *it's a waste of lather to shave an ass,* the editorial ends.

the snickers with which, on that day, we received the unprofessorial conduct of the professor. The style of the typical academic, the antithesis to Mencken's unfettered linguistic gusto, is a species of what I may call verbal protective coloration. It shrinks from personal distinctiveness; there is, indeed, no personality to convey. It sinks, by its stylistic conformity, safely into the background of scholastic tradition. It is grammatical, unobtrusive, sheltered in the grove of its own herded humility. Mencken, on the other hand, not without the counsel of the showman and the man of affairs that lurk within him, inverts the academic process. Not for him the shelter of an engulfing background. Sooner a quick death in the open. Whence derives what I call his projective discoloration. He thrusts himself upon the attention. He demands it. In the arena of our letters he is the picador, the banderillero, the matador, all in one. Ideas, even iconoclastic ones, are necessarily limited in number. They are the *raræ aves* of intellectual creation. "An absolutely new idea," he has written to me, "is one of the rarest things known to man." True originality, then, must derive from the impress of personality upon idea; it is in such a sense that the style is the man, and that Mencken, orchestrated in all the keys and every instrumental combination, is his style.

It is an athletic style, trimmed of superfluities. It is frank, direct, hammered almost to an irreducible minimum. It turns ideas into shocks. It produces a prose that resembles now a needle-bath, now a trip-hammer, now a sonata in chromatics. Yet the bath invigorates, the hammer rivets attention, the chromatics never blur the clear progress of the music. It is a contagious style; critics such as Sherman and Pattee,[1] coming to pray with him and remonstrate, are trapped into Menckenizing, or into the very jazziness of style that they berate. Youngsters bent upon hewing out a career seize upon his catch-phrases and carry them out to the furthest decimal. Nay, what shall we say? Mencken himself is capable of imitating Mencken. The serpent bites his own tail.

When Mr. Pattee, however, assigns the provenance of Mencken's style to an O. Henry, finding in that clever gentleman the model for triple comparisons and smart, unexpected endings, methinks he goes too far. And, also, not far enough. If we must hunt for models, the real ones are to be found rather in a Percival Pollard or a Huneker. But specious, academic ones could be found in Cicero, let us say, and Plautus. Cicero's triplex phrases are a commonplace of the classroom, as are Plautus's whip-like curls at the end of a sentence. Yet have these peculiarities been adduced in proof of the essentially journalistic spirit of a Plautus or a Cicero? Surprise, in Mencken, is no mere trick of the newspaperman; it is a picture of the fellow's attitude. His trick of beginning a sentence in all sobriety, only to have it explode in a metaphor or a simile of ignominious connotation is hardly a borrowing from O. Henry. It is the perfect mirror of a leaning toward buffoonery,—a buffoonery that is not only in itself a criticism of life, but an inheritance going back through father and grandfather to an-

---

[1] I have in mind Sherman's essay No. I in *Americans* (Scribner's, 1922) and Pattee's *Tradition and Jazz* (Century Co., 1925).

cestors who had mingled with the dust of earth long before O. Henry was born.

In Mencken, exaggeration is likewise art, not mountebankery. It is, strangely enough, a species of inverted
geniality. It does not, when properly read, destroy
proportions. It is, in its way, poetical, in that it employs
imagery for a heightened emotional effect.

Mencken must not be read by the dictionary. When
he calls a man an "idiot" it is merely his manner of dis-
agreeing with a method or a manner. It refers, moreover, to the specific point under discussion and holds good
for the particular moment. When, as in the *World*
(New York) of June 21, 1925, he declares that "All
that is remarkable in even the most profound painting
may be grasped by an educated spectator in a few minutes," he is not merely confessing his incapacity for appreciating art; he is saying, in his own peculiar way, that
painting is a matter for educated eyes rather than for
the windy metaphysics in which artists are wont to obscure their labors. For Mencken, more than a theorist,
is a practitioner. He wants, in our parlance, not talk but
action. His own talk is his especial form of action.

Behold, thou art fair, my love; behold, thou art fair; thou hast
dove's eyes within thy locks; thy hair is as a flock of goats, that
appear from Mount Gilead.

Thy teeth are like a flock of sheep that are even shorn, which
come up from the washing; whereof every one bear twins, and
none is barren among them.

Thy lips are like a thread of scarlet, and thy speech is comely:
thy temples are like a piece of pomegranate within thy locks.

Thy neck is like the tower of David builded for an armoury,

whereon there hang a thousand bucklers, all shields of mighty men.

That, I take it, is from a great poem. That, I take it, is full of Solomonian exaggeration. It could be made the text for a sermon in exaggeration. Yet, my contention is that the processes in the case of both Solomon and Mencken are, as creative literature, essentially similar. In Solomon, exaggeration serves as the poetry of emotion; in Mencken, as the poetry of idea.

Another paradox: Mencken, the devil's advocate, is the Prince of Darkness in American literature. It should not be forgotten, however, that another name for the Prince of Darkness is Lucifer. And Lucifer means, The Bearer of Light.

III

The reaction against the work of Mencken assumes two forms: an ethical and an æsthetic. In general, the ethical riposte sounds from the halls of the academies and from the mouths of the elder generation; the æsthetic attack comes from the ranks of the younger critics, the intellectuals and the liberals. Between these two fires Mencken maintains a position that is distinctly his own, now seeming to give aid and comfort to the one, and now to the other. At the base of the ethical attack is a pride of knowledge combined with a sense of righteousness; at the base of the æsthetic attack is a similar pride of knowledge,—a different knowledge, to be sure, but a similar pride,—and likewise a sense of righteousness,—a different righteousness, again, but a similar sense.

One of the deepest remarks that Mencken has ever made is that "æsthetic purpose nearly always turns out, on examination, to be simply moral purpose in disguise. Moral indignation is the hallmark of all so-called æsthetes. Beethoven, they argue today, was not merely a bad composer; it is a degrading thing to admire him." That is profoundly true, if the term æsthete be limited to the members of those côteries that have made of art a snobbish pursuit,—almost a mark of social distinction. It is equally true as a danger-signal to the more earnest and passionate devotees of æsthetic interpretation. It is so true, indeed, that it may be reversed, turned in upon itself:[1] moral passion at times acquires a positive æsthetic value. Implicitly, if not explicitly, Mencken has recognized this in his evaluation of Dreiser, just as unconsciously he has exemplified the original form of his statement in his recognition of such disparate figures as Cabell and Sinclair Lewis. The important word in his statement is not, after all, *æsthetic,* but *purpose.* Let us say, then, that all purpose is moral, and a trap for indignation.

The attacks, on the ethical side, are weak; first, because the position in itself is not strong, and second, because Mencken outgenerals his opponents at every move. The one obvious retort, from Mencken's critical enemies of the ethical camp, should be that Mencken is himself, willy-nilly, largely and importantly an ethical force. This it has been left for his friends, from Burton Rascoe on, to indicate. Instead, his ethical opponents,—the Boyntons, the Shermans, the Pattees *et frères,* some of

[1] As Anatole France was fond of remarking, "No doubt that is true, but so is the contrary."

them highly estimable gentlemen who command one's thorough respect even in the heat of the battle, others content to conduct a warfare in ethics on shady ethical principles,—have concentrated their fire upon Mencken's rampant individualism. Here they are lost; here they play into the enemy's hands. To aver that Mencken is no gentleman, and that only a gentleman may be a critic; to berate him as a traitor to his country; to call him a menace to our younger generation; to nominate him as the hell-mouth of America; to question his scholastic baggage; to do nothing, in short, but call names, is to attempt to bag authenticity with a label. And to do so in language that has been affected by Mencken's own, is to confess a double defeat.

The æsthetic attack, but lately begun, is more pertinent to the issues involved. It comes, moreover, not alone from the younger enemies of Mencken, but from his friends as well. It comes, indeed, subtly from Mencken himself, with his over-insistence upon his lack of emotionalism. I have already said that, to me at least, there is something suspicious in this excess of protest. I have already speculated upon what this may hide, upon its self-protective character. Here, where potentially dwells the new strength of Mencken, dwells also what I perceive to be his true deficiency as an artist: *his relative insensitivity to nuance.* This is directly related, not to his lack of emotions—which is a mere phrase—but to the struggle between his strong sense of dignity and his equally powerful sense of the laughable,—to that element in him of forced dominance of intellect over emotion. For Mencken, too, like the rest of us, is repressed,—repressed even in a Freudian sense,—and repressed, topsy-turvily enough, as to his better rather than as to his worse qualities. To match the psychology of that French play which shows the unsaintly reverse of a saint, he could show us the equally surprising reverse of a sinner.

Mencken, because of his excessive mistrust of the emotions, is too ready to interpret emotional excess in terms of insincerity and humbuggery. Wherefore yet another paradox: although standing for freedom of experiment, although fighting for honest artistry, he is decidedly wary in greeting the "new" and the experimental. His acceptance of our newer cultural values in the arts has been readier in the case of those men whose labors carried a sociological implication or, if only by inversion, an ethical or anti-ethical import. (That this æsthetic weakness may be found even among the most æsthetic of our critics is shown by Ludwig Lewisohn's similar acceptance of Sinclair Lewis, as well as by his own single significant lapse, the novel *Don Juan*.) Mencken's welcome of Lewis is largely conditioned by Lewis's importance not so much in the art of the novel as in the science of sociology. So, too, his early espousal of Dreiser, as well as his later defence, though æsthetic on the whole, were appreciably conditioned by non-æsthetic considerations.

Mencken, measuring man by his control over his emotions, measures his artists in the same manner. Hence his fondness for the man who knows his job, and for the artist who is also the expert craftsman. But art, too, is a very subtle intellectual control of the emotions. And "new" art, for all the emotional excess to which it may give rise, is like all other art, a form of experimental living. It lends itself easily to ridicule, because emotional abandon is one of the conditions of its existence. Not without reason do even the most rational and least emotional of mortals seek solitude for their amours. Here, as the classic example, is the technique of refuge from attack during emotional absorption. The newer art of subjective display offends Mencken almost as much as would public love. Indeed, doesn't he in the extreme of his reactions summon the word "obscene"? It is a double offense: an undisciplined dominance of the emotions and an unashamed exhibition of them. It offends him as manners; it puts before him a spectacle which he is psychologically incapable of appreciating to the full.

I would relate even his cruelty, his critical masochism and sadism,—even his glee in the contemplation of humanity given over to the insanity of war,—to his emotional bluntness. They who cause most pain are they who feel it least.

"As a critic," he asserts, "I regret nothing. I have made some mistakes, but on the whole I have been on the side of sound artists and against frauds. My judgments, as I look back on them, have been pretty good. The men I was advocating in 1908 are all viewed with respect today; the fakes I then attacked are now forgotten. I have been, at times, very cruel, but I do not regret it. A bad writer has no rights whatever. Any mercy shown him is wasted and mistaken."

More softness in Mencken would have made of him a satirist in the vein of Mark Twain, to whom he is in other respects so strangely related. As it is, a certain innate hardness has made of him a mocker, with himself as the ultimate target. (Again the serpent biting his own tail!)

Yet if Mencken undoubtedly has the defects of his quality, he has the rare quality of his defects. His relative insensitivity to nuance makes him often an indifferent judge of the more subjective practitioners of the arts,—of the lyric as against the social poets, of the psychological as against the sociological novelists, of the plangently self-pitying composer and his cacophonously introspective brother as against the self-contained classicists and romanticists of music. Yet by that same token he is freed, by his exemption from these excesses, for the more critical examination of them. One raucous, honest blast of "Fake!" from him is worth a thousand of the timorous essays in which groping criticasters stumble through a darkness of the dictionary for sonorous words with which to drown out the cries of their own incomprehension. For it is the weakness of the æsthete to suspect greatness in dulness and wordiness, and similarly to hold clarity in suspicion of insignificance. Mencken, carrying Voltaire's famous dictum from the realm of style to that of substance, would proclaim that what isn't clear isn't thought; nor felt, as Croce maintains.[1]

When the younger critics call Mencken a mere vaudevillian, a critic for flappers, they fall into the fallacy of their elders. Indeed, was it not the ethical Mr. Sherman, from his Puritan shores, who nominated

---

[1] Yet how frequently is Croce, for all his theory of art as expression, muddy and logorrheic! To the prose of the great Italian I prefer, by far, the clear, harmonious style of his American interpreter, Spingarn.

Mencken as the critic for the *jeunes filles?* And was it not Mr. Munson, from his little tent on the Impuritan marge, and Mr. Calverton, from down where all is not well on the Potomac, who caught up the Sherman echo and broadcast it in turn to the younger group of intellectuals,—the first to the æsthetically-minded and the second to those of the newer sociology and of the behavioristic criticism?

There is fruit for much thought—and feeling—in the words that close the third chapter of Havelock Ellis's *The World of Dreams*.[1] Æsthetic critics and the Puritan-ethical ones, the *nouveaux érudits* of the intelligentsia and the sociologico-proletarian gentry of the Upton Sinclair-Calverton persuasion may alike ponder these wise and humble words in the conceit of their own exclusive methodology. "The phenomena of dreaming furnish a delightful illustration of the fact that reasoning, in its rough form, is only the crudest and most elementary form of intellectual operation, and that the finer forms of thinking involve much more than logic. 'All the thinking in the world,' as Goethe puts it, 'will not lead us to thought.' "

Nor, may I add, will all the feeling in the world lead us to art. The intellectual arrogance of the laboratory critic is matched only by the emotional deliquescence of his softer rival. To be sure, it is easy to manufacture a sort of robot-criticism, which will have all the appearance of validity and lack only the "soul" which is personality. It is easy to call such a thing "scientific"

[1] See, in Ellis's book, published by Houghton Mifflin Co., 1922, page 70.

criticism, and such a criticism a "science." It is easy to postulate the eradication of subjectivity. As easy, in fact, to postulate as it is undesirable and impossible to effect. To control subjectivity is one thing; to delete it is quite another. Until that day when every human being is a perfect replica of the other, criticism no less than creation will remain essentially an art. To attempt to make of it a science is, at bottom, the evidence of a yearning for a unity that nature does not show.

"Nature," Dr. Kallen has written in a profound sentence, "is naturally pluralistic; her unities are eventual, not primary; mutual adjustments, not regimentations of superior force. Human institutions must have the same character. Where there is no mutuality there may be 'law and order,' but there cannot be peace." [1] Kallen wrote with a nation in mind; his sentence may be applied to the realm of criticism: Criticism is not a regimentation of superior logic, it is a mutuality of thought and feeling,—two aspects of living that our vocabulary has split asunder, but which life maintains as an indissoluble and an unpredictable entity.

We may probe to the probable origins of art, whether through the maze of psychological analysis or of sociological doctrine; we may study the effects of heredity and environment upon the creature that is man; we may track these stimuli to their most hidden visceral adumbrations, to their most obvious social sources. This will give us an insight into origins, and, at that, by no means the whole story. But will it, despite all claims, give us

[1] See *Culture and Democracy in the United States.* Boni & Liveright, 1924.

values? Art assumes a fundamental sameness in all human beings, else how is a work to mean anything to one's fellow man? The value of art, however,—an indeterminate value differing with the distinctions that prevent all creatures from being precisely alike, derives from just this element of difference. Granted that even æsthetic values are not permanent; who wants permanency of any sort? Ah, but let us have a scientific method in criticism, even if it be not itself a science! Yes, if you are scientifically-minded. Poe was, yet in his criticism he anticipated more than one of the æsthetic criteria associated with Francesco de Sanctis and Croce in Italy, and with Spingarn in the United States. Mencken himself, so patently influenced by science, yet can yield to the sentimentalities that all prejudices are. To be sure, if all our reflexes can be conditioned into uniformity, à la Watson out of Pavlov, then we are ready indeed for robot republics. In that event we shall need no art, and certainly no critics.[1]

Until then, let us cultivate the illusion—it is as good as any other to live and die by—that existence is made interesting by the personal distinctiveness that rises above the common likenesses; that art and science, like thought

[1] In my sense of the word critic such otherwise highly estimable gentlemen as V. F. Calverton and Upton Sinclair are midwives of a new social order, rather than pregnant creators of values. See *Mammonart: An Essay in Economic Interpretation,* by Upton Sinclair, published by the author at Pasadena, California, 1925, and *The Newer Spirit,* by V. F. Calverton, Boni & Liveright, New York, 1925. It may clarify the issue, and also the difficult nature of the problem, if I say frankly that with reference to the sociological questions involved, I stand as near to the various outlooks of Kallen, Sinclair and Calverton as to Mencken's Capitalism.

and feeling, are not parallel lines but the inter-penetrating planes of a homogenous sphere; that criticism, after it shall have satisfied its lower desires for a specious show of scientificism, remains interesting not for its judgments, not for its method, its "system," not for its apparatus and its paraphernalia and its adventitious aids, but for the revelation of a salient, an alive personality.[1] This is the only sense in which I care to recognize Mencken's "aristocracy"; it is the chief sense in which criticism interests me. Man writing books, man writing about them, is manifesting himself. This fact he may hardly escape, even by way of the laboratory. And if, on some not impossible day, he shall make that escape, whither will it take him? To those wastes that Shaw evolved in the grand finale of his metabiological Pentateuch, *Back to Methuselah.* Of such a death-in-life we well may ask, "where is thy victory?"

Mr. Mencken, for all his specific failings, is wiser than the scientific critics to whom he is temperamentally akin; he knows that criticism and art thrive best in the solitude of one's own higher sanctions, and that it does most good —if it must do good—by ignoring its very beneficiaries and exulting only in its own freedom. This, too, has its ethical implications, but at that place where ethics and

---

[1] "Wherever life is at low ebb system flourishes. Therefore I find significance in the remark of Goldwin Smith in his *Memoirs,* that he could never get much from Emerson's writings because he could 'find no system' in them. Goldwin Smith and his fellow-Oxonians of that day would have been puzzled by Nietzsche's aphorism that 'the will to system is a lack of rectitude.'" See *John Addington Symonds: A Biographical Study,* by Van Wyck Brooks. New York, B. W. Huebsch. 1924. (First edition, Mitchell Kennerly, 1914.)

æsthetics merge,—where one's moral and artistic criteria derive, not from without but from within, responsible to the sternest of masters, oneself.

From the double attack of the ethicists and æstheticists Mencken emerges, not unscathed, surely, yet victorious. What matters a battle lost here or there, if the campaign be won? Fundamentally, in the broader acceptation of the term, Mencken, in both life and letters, is the æsthetician. Freedom and honesty of function is his personal translation of Keats's equation between truth and beauty, of Emerson's excuse for being. He points to no goals; he glories in the beauties of an unobstructed path. There is no martyrdom in him,—nothing of those martyrs who, as Anatole France divined, would under favoring circumstances be themselves the executioners. What is Truth? What, Beauty? What, Goodness?

IV

The entire problem of theories in art leaves me dubious. Can even a theory of art be science? Though it be based upon demonstrable fact, is there not room for the subtle insertion of the personality into the combination of the facts that makes the theory? And does not our illogical self rush into this vacuum with all the inevitability of natural law?

"Poe," said Baudelaire, "is a poet who pretends to have written his poetry according to a poetic theory." The statement, made by a poet, implies a healthy suspicion of all theoretic structures in art. The artist in Baudelaire, when confronted by such a cold-blooded analysis as Poe made of *The Raven* and its composition, naturally revolted against this assumption that creation could be harnessed to a method. It was characteristic of the great brain that was Poe to face even the mystery of artistic genesis as if it were but a greater cryptogram, to be solved by mental application. Poe would raise the very Unconscious itself into the light of the Conscious, and exhibit its mechanism. As a result, *The Philosophy of Composition,* which few accept verbatim and more condemn as a hoax, is neither inspiration nor fabrication. It is, so to speak, creation *ex post facto.* It is almost valueless as general theory, but invaluable as an insight into Poe's necessities as artist, both conscious and unconscious. Poe the theorist is Poe the artist still. He does not, in this famous paper, explain the genesis of *The Raven;* he does, however, throw a strong light upon himself.

Theory is not science; it is art. The man who really believes that he writes or composes or paints according to a theory is self-deceived. Consider, as another example, Wagner. Employing his *leit-motive,* he used them unconsciously as a guide to himself, not to the hearer. The entire series of music-dramas, including the *Ring,* can be thoroughly appreciated without the slightest knowledge of the guiding-motifs.[1] Wagner, developing his theory of the unending melody and of the leading

[1] Little as I agree with Mr. Wm. J. Henderson's view of Wagner as a dramatist (see his *Richard Wagner,* G. P. Putnam's Sons, New York; 1901; fifth edition, 1923), I believe that his suggestion to call the *leit-motif* a *guiding*-motif instead of a leading-motive, is based upon even sounder principles than he adduces. I would even favor the definite adoption of this phrase into the vocabulary of musical criticism.

motif, was responding to a need of his creative imagination. What a sorry figure he cuts today as an allegorist, as a teacher *via* the stage, as a Messiah of the arts. Whatever is vital in him—and what a tremendous world of vitality is in Wagner, what an unending source of wonder and ecstasy!—is in his legacy of tones, unblurred by pedantic commentary, particularly his own.

Yet another example: Dante. The most beautiful poem in the *Vita Nuova* is set in one of the most absurd bits of commentary that ever spattered the pages of a book. And the *Commedia* itself? Its allegory has precisely as much artistic worth as has the allegory in Wagner's vast tetralogy,—which is to say, none at all.

Are we to infer, then, that the artist does not know what he wishes to do? That he does not know what he is doing? In appreciable degree, yes. De Sanctis, the great Italian critic, predecessor and master of Croce, has written that "man does, not what he wishes to do, but what he can." In other words, he may imagine that he is doing one thing, while in reality he is doing another. He is possessed by the genius that he thinks he possesses. His theory is the effort to explain to himself the unexplainable. So explaining, he reveals, as I have said, not the hidden process, but his more conscious self.

If theory is art rather than science,—a thing of the imagination rather than of demonstrable reality,—then philosophy is the poetry of reason. It is therefore to be enjoyed as a play of the mind, if enjoyed at all.

Which brings us back to Poe. Read, if you can, his

Eureka. In this poem—for that, really, is what it amounts to—Poe feeds fat his need of rationalizing the universe. A beautiful theory, if you can understand it. Poe, however, showed how truly he understood it himself by asking, in the preface, that it be considered as the poem it is.

Shall we, then cease constructing theories? Yes, when we cease making music and pictures and poems and stories.

V

Is Mencken a critic at all? Is he, if so, a literary critic? Or is he, rather, a critic of society? Is he peculiarly American? Is he, more than a critic, a humorist, an artist in his own right, regardless of the demonstrable validity of his criticisms? Speculation upon these points has been rife, except among those who airily and ignorantly dismiss him altogether, almost since the man "arrived" with the outbreak of the war.

Mr. Arvin, for example, denies to him the rôle of literary critic, crowning him in compensation with a brighter wreath than that he takes away. While I do not consider Mr. Arvin fortunate in his notion that Mencken, as a reaction from the ethical school of critics, has tended to divorce literature from life, Arvin has written with fine discernment of certain of the man's qualities: [1]

To refuse to Mr. Mencken, however, the thorn-crown of the

[1] See *The Rôle of Mencken,* by Newton Arvin, in the late and much lamented *Freeman* for December 27, 1922.

literary critic, is in no sense to deprive him of literary distinction or to refuse him the recognition of his importance. What he really is, is a social critic, and besides that, a humorist of a very high order. Literature he may look upon as an escape and a refuge from life, and "extra-æsthetic valuations" he may regard with odium; but there is nothing anæmic or effete in his own comment on the life of man, or on the life of the society he moves in. As to promptness of his results, at least, we have had almost no critic in this generation who has written with greater relevance or rightness, or who has been a greater sanative force. Into the sultry atmosphere of the 1910's he came like a gust of fresh air, and ever since has been giving humbug and cant and bigotry a spirited run for their money. He has been a gadfly to the State, a voice crying in the wilderness, a mouthpiece of the Lord. All that is vulgar and cheap and craven in American life has had its due from him; and is certainly less secure than it would have been without him. He has done this, however, not as a Carlyle would have done it; he really has no "Messianic delusion"; but as a freer and more robust Mark Twain. That is to say, he has done it as a humorist; and it is as a humorist, I think, that he may most justly be considered. His book on "The American Language" is one of the most entertaining books ever written by an American, and a great social document besides. In such essays as that "On Being an American," "The Forward-Looker," "Education," "Suite Américaine," he seems to me to have his finger on some of the genuine sources of humour—extravagance, incongruity, unexpectedness, irreverence. I confess to finding such phrases as "the anthropoid majority," "Y. M. C. A. lamassary" and "making botany obscene," exquisitely funny. His style, as a style, is a medium of perfect efficiency; it is vibrant, athletic, vascular. He should take rank among our first-rate prosateurs. He is not a literary critic, of course; but there are plenty of such fish in the sea.

To Frank Harris,[1] Mencken assumes chief importance as a critic of politics.

To say that Mencken is the best critic in the United States is less than his due; he is one of the best critics in English. In his absorption in criticism alone, and in a certain masculine abruptness and careless piquancy of style, he reminds me of Hazlitt, one of the critics who belong to literature. In regard to creative work, especially to stories and plays, his judgment is often at fault, and always leaves a good deal to be desired; but in dealing with politicians and political issues, how sane he is, how brave, how honest, how surely he finds the fitting word, the blistering epithet! And what a delight it is to hear this bold strong voice in the unholy din of sycophants and of the hireling's praise and blame which makes the American press the vilest of Christendom! And kindly Mencken is, too; kindly as only the honest can afford to be; full of the milk of human kindness for all those who choose the upward way.

In the eyes of both Burton Rascoe and Vincent O'Sullivan,[2] Mencken becomes a product typically American. "Mr. Mencken (wrote Vincent O'Sullivan originally in the London *New Witness*), does not derive from England or from anywhere else but the U. S. A. He is as peculiarly American as pumpkin pie or a Riker-Hegeman drug store. In this sense he is the first American critic except Poe." Mr. Rascoe finds Mencken likewise "a natural product of American traditions, American training, American character—a product, perhaps, of reaction against these things, but still plainly a product.

[1] See his *Contemporary Portraits* (*Fourth Series*), New York, 1923, Brentano's. Page 154.
[2] See the pamphlet *H. L. Mencken,* issued by Knopf in 1920.

The delusion of un-Americanism on the part of Americans who have risen above the mob is common enough. There is a notion among critics that Edgar Allan Poe is unrepresentative of America, that he is essentially French."

The notion, as Rascoe shows by citing Remy de Gourmont, has been admirably exploded. Poe, in de Gourmont's opinion, is "much more representative of America than Emerson or Walt Whitman. His spirit has its practical aspects. Deprived of a literary vent, he would have made a stupendous business man, a promoter of the first order." This with equal truth, says Rascoe, might be said of the redoubtable Baltimorean.

The Uruguayan critic, José Enrique Rodó, has seen better than de Gourmont into the peculiarities of Poe's essential Americanism. "None will deny," he has written in *Ariel,* during the course of a discussion of the United States, "that Edgar Poe is an anomalous and rebellious individuality within his people. His select soul represents an inassimilable particle of the national soul, which not without reason dwelt among its fellows with the feeling of infinite solitude. And nevertheless, as Baudelaire has deeply revealed, the fundamental note in the character of Poe's heroes is the super-human temper, the indomitable resistance of the will. When he conceived Ligeia, the most mysterious and adorable of his creations, Poe symbolized in the inextinguishable light of her eyes the Will's hymn of triumph over death."

To Rodó, it will be remembered, the Will was the chisel that had sculptured the American people out of solid rock. "Its salient characteristics are two man-

ifestations of the will: originality and audacity. . . .
Its representative personage, like the superman of
Nietzsche, is named *I will.*"

I confess, however, that despite the truths upon which
such personal descriptions are based, they possess little
appeal for me. The radical mind, itself protesting so
vehemently against the pigeon-holes of the academician,
runs the danger of pigeon-holing itself in its very designa-
tion. Radical; conservative: more pigeon-holes. So,
too, the mind supposedly above irrational national allegiances builds dangerous traps out of its very adjectives.
Of course Mencken is, in his own way, American. But
to me it is far more important that he is Mencken. The
man transcends the nationality.

I would also add a quotation from de Gourmont's
notable, if not infallible, *Marginalia sur Edgar Poe et
sur Baudelaire:*

I do not believe that the American milieu was any more hostile
to Poe than the French milieu to any of our contemporaries. He
had enemies, but also literary friends, admirers; he lived with two
women whom he adored, Mrs. Clemm and Virginia; he made his
living at work which does not seem to have been uncongenial, for
he was fond of writing, not only his tales and his poems, but his
articles. . . . His worth was not recognized, but his relative
superiority was granted; it seems certain that, had he lived, his
final years would have been those of a literary dictator. . . . In
England, indeed, he would have been more highly appreciated;
there is a truly intellectual, a truly aristocratic public in that
country, to whom an original page is a joy and who knows how
to show itself financially grateful. In France, Poe's sufferings
might have been greater. He would, in all likelihood, have been
no more able to earn his living than Baudelaire, Flaubert, Villiers,

Verlaine, Mallarmé. His tales, so rich in ideality, would have been flouted, like those of Villiers, by the mob of democratic readers; and no review or periodical would have accepted his vituperative, vehement criticisms, which brusquely abandon their aggressiveness only to treat, in a style at times too harshly precise, the most abstruse problems of thought and expression.

De Gourmont's remarks do not dismiss the charge of American hostility; they serve to emphasize the proposition that most milieus are hostile to superiority. The larger truth is that Mencken, at bottom is, as a critic, a critic of life. That life happens to be lived in the United States. If he is an anti-patriot it is not *against* America and *for* any other nation, but rather against the basic falsity of that mental surrender which is the one great virtue of patriotism itself. See the evolution of his attitude as mirrored in his macaronic English: the *Boobus Americanus* becomes *Homo Boobiens;* the critic of America is the critic of mankind; there were Philistines in Philistia before they were born in the United States.

Mencken himself is generally free of such clichés. He can rave for reams against the professoriat, yet when truth or beauty issues from its precincts, he seizes upon it eagerly and shouts for joy. If learning is the topic of the day, he bows to the superior learning of the pundits. He writes,—I have read such complaints—as if he had never read his predecessors. Well, he *has* read them, even if he doesn't plaster his pages with exhibitionistic quotations. Is the feeling for beauty then so easily got from apprenticeship to print? He is undisciplined and not mellow. Shall all our voices be pitched in the same key? Shall none exult and shout because we take our pleasures soberly? Rest you happy, sirrah, I am as God made me, and even so shall you take me in this naughty intractable world.

There remains, then, to consider the view of Mencken as an artist pure and simple, yet neither simple nor pure. Mr. Edmund Wilson,[1] in one of the best articles I have read on Mencken, saw comparatively early, through his ruthlessness and rigidity to the artist within. "A genuine artist," he called the Baltimorean, "and man of first-rate education and intelligence who is thoroughly familiar with, even thoroughly saturated with, the common life." Wilson saw the weakness of Mencken's strength, the militant idealism behind his cynical manner, the righteous indignation behind his affected scorn of indignation. So, too, Rascoe,[2] a year later, returning to the man whom he was one of the first to write about at any length,[3] perceived that Mencken had a sentimentality for which his cynicism was largely a defense mechanism. The *Epitaph,* indeed, becomes, before the end, a Resurrection, for Rascoe places Mencken in the company of Voltaire and Montaigne, of Swift and Butler. It is Mr. L. M. Hussey,[4] however, who, relegating all other considerations to a secondary plane, lifts Mencken to the primary position of an artist. The man, he declares, is first of all emotional, not ideational.

[1] See article in the *New Republic,* June 1, 1921.

[2] See *Notes for an Epitaph,* Literary Review of the New York Evening Post, March 4, 1922.

[3] The prominent other is the novelist, Vincent O'Sullivan.

[4] See *The Saturday Review of Literature,* November 22, 1924.

He is to be considered and enjoyed, then, not so much for his ideas as for the personal form with which he endows them. He is, in fact, a creator.

Here, I believe, we approach the core of the matter. The American critic? The phrase is at once too limited and too broad. Its limitations I have hinted at. Its over-inclusiveness is at once evident. There are things in Van Wyck Brooks, in Ludwig Lewisohn, in Joel Elias Spingarn, in John Macy, in Frank Harris, that I do not find in Mencken; there are things, occasionally, in the ethical professoriat that I cannot get from him,—worth-while things, I mean. Brooks, for example, is cautious, sensitive, patient, firm; a lover of clear, melodious speech. Someone has said of him that he is a young man who writes like an old man. Mencken, I imagine, no matter how old, will always write like a young man. Lewisohn is so acutely responsive to beauty that it turns often to pain; the beauty that fails him in life he frames in sentences compact of melody and meaning. Spingarn, too learned to be a pedant, too poetic to be a shouter in the literary market-place, retires into the silences where past and present, old and new, radical and conservative, cancel out their irrelevances and fuse the residue into an æsthetic core.

So, too, there are things in Mencken which I do not find in these men,—outspoken disgust, a healthy suspicion of the social amenities, a devil-may-care zest in living, a flaunting of personality, praisings and blamings unchecked by thought of later revision,—in a phrase, immediate, intuitive reactions.

Hussey is right. Mencken is chiefly an artist,—the

critic as artist,—even, as I sought to show earlier in this study, the creative critic in a Spingarnian, Crocean sense.[1] This affinity to the European æsthetic critics was largely lost to his native critics, who were concerned almost entirely with his significance to the moment and to the immediate milieu. Abroad, however, in the home of Croce, where Spingarn is not unknown, it was readily discerned by Giuseppe Prezzolini,[2] who pierced through the Puritanism and the Americanism of the man to the more universal foundation.

VI

Where, in the line of American authors, does Mencken seem to find his place? Without implying direct influence, which in my eyes is an interesting but minor consideration, I should answer, with Poe and Whitman and Twain. To each of these men he presents interesting resemblances and from each he differs in a radical manner.[3]

[1] I would call to the reader's attention a very important article by Mr. Spingarn on *The Growth of a Literary Myth* (*The Freeman,* May 2, 1923). In it, that notable critic takes Mr. Mencken to task for having invented the so-called "Croce-Spingarn-Carlyle-Goethe theory", which has wrought havoc among the younger American critics. The theory turns out to be very much the creation of Spingarn, through Croce, and hardly much of Goethe or Carlyle. It should clarify, at least, the confusion that has sprung up in many young minds between the creator's manifest purpose and his actual artistic accomplishment.

[2] See *Il Mondo,* for March 16, 1922; article, *Uno stroncatore americano: H. L. Mencken.* Signor Prezzolini speaks of a "genuine" puritanism and a "genuine" Americanism. I think it would be clearer to say "inverted."

[3] Mr. Carl Van Doren, in his *Many Minds* (A. A. Knopf, 1924)

Only a few years ago Mencken, in his second series of *Prejudices,* was commenting upon the small influence Poe has had upon his nation as a writer.

The tide of Poe's ideas, set in motion in France early in the second half of the century, did not wash England until the last decade, and in America, save for a few dashes of spray, it has yet to show itself. There is no American writer who displays the influence of this most potent and original of Americans so clearly as whole groups of Frenchmen display it, and whole groups of Germans, and even a good many Englishmen. . . . It is significant that the critical writing of Poe, in which there lies most that was best in him, has not come back; no normal American ever thinks of him as a critic, but only as a poet, as a raiser of gooseflesh, or as an immoral fellow.

It would be easy to trace a resemblance between Mencken and Poe that is founded upon something more tangible than residence in Baltimore. Through all the differences that divide the amorous visionary from our disillusioned contemporary rises a loyalty to the truth as seen at the moment of writing; they share the gift of volubility, and of vituperation; they abhor the intrusion of ethics into art; they declaim with equal ardor against their countrymen. Poe was a lover and per-

---

places Mencken in precisely this company. "Unlike Poe," he continues, indicating essential differences, "he has in him nothing of the poet and he has written nonsense about poetry. Unlike Whitman, he has not studied the common man at first hand and he dismisses such persons with the insolence of a city wit. Unlike Mark Twain, he despises the miserable race of man without, like Mark Twain, also pitying it." (See page 133.) The contrasts are in large measure valid; they admit, however, of important qualification.

petrator of hoaxes; Poe, throughout his life, maintained a marked psychological allegiance to his mother; he had the makings of a first-rate business man, of a creative magazine-editor; he was peculiarly a man of intense feelings bent upon dominating and explaining and criticising those feelings; his immense capacity for vision and cerebration did not slay a fine sense of the practical, though De Gourmont finds in him a paralysis of the will. Poe was full of contradictions. And this struggling Poe Mencken has understood better than any of our contemporary critics. As early as his *Book of Prefaces,* published three years before the second series of *Prejudices,* we find him writing of the man: "As a matter of fact, there have been intermittent rebellions against the prevailing pecksniffery and sentimentality ever since the days of Irving and Hawthorne. Poe led one of them—as critic more than as creative artist. His scathing attacks . . . keep a liveliness and appositeness that the years have not staled; his criticism deserves to be better remembered. Poe sensed the Philistine pull of a Puritan civilization as none had before him, and combated it with his whole artillery of rhetoric." This selfsame essay on *Puritanism as a Literary Force* is the latest phase of the same hundred years' war. Mencken does not stand as isolate as Poe stood; yet I wonder whether, taking into account the increase in population, he is not virtually as solitary.[1]

[1] For a full discussion of *Poe As A Literary Critic* see my monograph thus named, in the series of Little Blue Books, number 730. Girard, Kansas.

Coming to pure poetry, I find a curious resemblance between Poe and Mencken. Poe, you will recall, ruled out of the province of poetry all passion, which he defined as "intoxication of the heart." His conception of poetic beauty was thus deliberately narrowed. Here, subtly evidenced, is an instance of his reason stifling his imagination in the one province where imagination may rule. Here, too, the virtual passionlessness of his life is mirrored in the cherubic chastity of his poetic theory and practise. For this there must have been psychological, even physical reasons, upon which there has been much speculation with little concrete result. Now, Mencken's attitude toward poetry is similarly characterized by a suspicion of passionate abandon. In him, as lyrical as he may be, there is a rational pull that tethers him to the hither pole of self-control. He enjoys poetry after he has told himself that it is an *illusion consciously entered into.* His surrender is conditional. There is, in Poe, something—nay, very much—of this desire consciously to control the creative impulse. At bottom, such a desire is Utopian. It assumes the impossible,—the ability to discover the unconscious origins of art, to trace its genesis from intuitive chaos to reasoned fulfilment. Poe was cursed by this desire. His various *rationales* offer evidence of it. Mencken is not cursed by it, but he betrays, just the same, vestigial traces of the wish. Mencken is, as Poe was, a strange equilibrium of the reason and the imagination. In Poe, the imagination conquered, though everywhere the reason throws its glaring light. In Mencken, the reason conquered, though almost everywhere the imagination sheds its grateful glow.

In *A Fable for Critics*, Lowell (James Russell, not Amy) has written of Poe:

> There comes Poe with his raven, like Barnaby Rudge,
> Three fifths of him genius and two fifths sheer fudge,
> Who talks like a book of iambs and pentameters
> In a way to make people of common sense damn meters,
> Who has written some things quite the best of their kind,
> But the heart somehow seems all squeezed out by the mind.

It is not a crude evaluation, considering that Lowell had to compress it into pesty anapests. Poe could—and did—teach Lowell a thing or two about versification, in his review of this selfsame *Fable,* as well as in his analysis of Lowell's handwriting (see *A Chapter on Autography*). The proper answer would be, of course —and how well it would suit most of our contemporary novelists!—that it is even a worse plight for the mind to seem somehow all squeezed out by the heart. Then again, I don't think Lowell would, in prose, have said *all* squeezed out by the mind." There is the trouble with writing metrically; one has to say things, true or not, in order to keep the rhythm correct.

Lowell, however, was fundamentally right. There is "fudge" in Poe. Whether it's just two-fifths, I cannot say, having left my graduate in the laboratory. There *is* genius in Poe. Three-fifths? It is a remarkable proportion, even if Poe was disgruntled at the lines. Now, there are fudge and genius in Mencken.

And in Mencken, too, the "heart somehow seems all squeezed out by the mind."

"The great poet," says De Gourmont of Poe in the *Marginalia sur Edgar Poe et sur Baudelaire,* "was an active literary man who often developed to the point of pedantry an inner need to sermonize his contemporaries. It is absurd to picture Poe as a morbid visionary; he was educated to the degree of erudition and his precise, sagacious intelligence had that something about it which Pascal called the geometric spirit. We may suppose that he lived perfectly conscious of his destiny and of his genius."

With the possible exception of the phrase implying erudition (although one may be erudite without much education) De Gourmont has hit upon an explanation that has eluded many of Poe's countrymen. There was a distinct touch of the pedant in Poe, and I believe that it was due, though by no means wholly, to just such a desire to lecture his fellows. It was an evidence of, as it was a relief to, a conscious sense of superiority. Poe's pedantry, however, was not mere professional pomp of knowledge, not mere delight in learning for learning's sake. It was his analytic fervor pushed to extremes. This man, whom De Gourmont accuses of paralysis of the will, in reality dominated his material. He followed it to the very core of its being; he ran along its every ramification. The grammarians did not know their business; neither did the poets, nor the dramatists; Poe, literally, would refashion the world in his own intellectual image. The overflow of his intellect sought out the

288

channels of phrenology, autography, cryptography, rid-
dles—even acrostics.

Was Poe's heart "all squeezed out by the mind"? Or
was it the kind of mind (and heart, for that matter)
which Lowell could not quite understand? "Feeling
with me had never been of the heart," says the one who
tells the tale of *Berenice,* "and my passions were always
of the mind."

Could Mencken's passions be better described?

It is no accident, then, that Mencken, of all contemporary American writers, should restore Poe the critic to
the stature that is his by right.

The resemblance to Whitman is one of manner rather
than of matter; Mencken is not quite, as Edmund Wilson
has suggested, "a gloomy Whitman." He is a Whitman on guard against undignified enthusiasm. He has
a veritable gusto for cynicism. He casts his eye over
the sprawling States; he catalogues their vices with a
verbal zest that no American has displayed since the
good grey poet sang his last. And, strange paradox in
a mesh of paradoxes: while Whitman professed an un-
bounded love for the commoner, he never touched his
heart; Mencken, who unwearyingly proclaims his scorn
for his fellow-Americans, compels their attention.

Mencken, in the history of American criticism, is the
humorist *par excellence.* He is the one commentator
upon our life and letters that stands, in relation to our
criticism, as does Mark Twain in relation to our fiction.
Lacking the softer humaneness of the creator of *Huckleberry Finn,* he is free, on the other hand, of those

inhibitions that preyed upon Clemens. Yet, viewing the matter objectively, should we, without those inhibitions, have had that very *Huckleberry Finn* which Mencken has eulogized since his boyhood contact with it? There are Menckenian inhibitions, too. They have played their rôle in the creation of a notable body of work. The utterly uninhibited artist is a fiction.

Mencken has found his place in American letters as a merry antinomian; as an unmoral humorist; as an intellectual anarchist. His position is unique; he has made of writing and living a vital concern, relevant to everyday life. The great paradox of his nature is that it is essentially lyrical, emotional, artistic. Yet he holds it under firm control—even practises compulsion upon it. His revolt is instinctive, intuitive. To that revolt his control gives a form and a name. Control slew the poet in him. It weighs yet upon his wings. But when it weighted his pinions it endowed him with a second-sight, a piercing vision that is in itself a form of flight,— often an Icarian flight, often a delusive vision, yet unmistakably, if deviatingly, sunward.

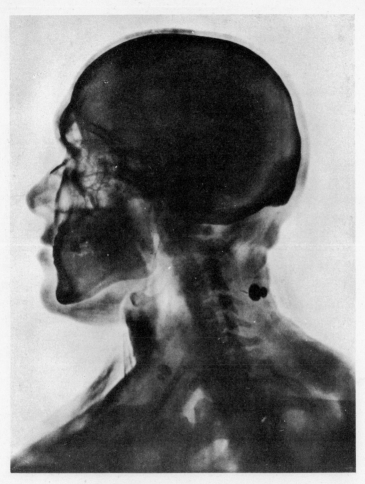

AN X-RAY PORTRAIT TAKEN BY DR. MAX KAHN,
BALTIMORE ROENTGENOLOGIST IN 1921

PORTRAIT TAKEN IN 1922 BY E. O. HOPPÉ OF LONDON

CHAPTER TEN

Da Capo

I

THE gravitation of Mencken into general criticism was not an accident; it was the solution of a personal problem,—even a personal conflict. From drawing and music to poetry, from chemistry and poetry to fiction, from fiction to drama, from drama to the criticism of letters, from the criticism of letters to the criticism of life. Here is a progression away from emotional surrender. Yet not so far away that the emotions dwell beyond reach. Mencken is a man of strong feelings, therefore of prejudices. If he does not consciously surrender to those emotions, he must at least evaluate them, play with them, experience them as feelings, yet with the compensation of dominating them as a critic. Mencken the critic is thus the compromise between his heart and his head. Here are rooted his paradoxicality, his contradictions. He cannot escape his feelings entirely. That he throttles them is a personal fiction; he is at grips with them.

He has reached a point where a change must come, lest stagnation set in. That he has felt this, both consciously and unconsciously, there is important evidence, easily available. Consider, for first instance, his Foreword to Mr. Frey's *Bibliography;* it is in its way a valedictory:

An air of finality always hangs about a bibliography. To me, the author dealt with, it hangs especially about this one, for I have a feeling that most of the books listed are of a sort that I shall not write again—that whatever I do hereafter, if I do anything at all, will differ materially from what has gone before. It is not that I have changed my fundamental ideas; it is simply that my interests have changed. In other words, it is simply that I have passed into the middle forties, and am no longer the artless youth that I once was. That youth was chiefly interested in the gaudy spectacle of human life in this world, *i. e.,* in the superficial effects of ideas. The somewhat oxidized fellow who now confronts you is chiefly interested in the immemorial instincts and emotions that lie under them. So this is a good time, perhaps, to draw a line and take stock. I certainly hope that the show is not over, but there is, I suspect, a climax and a new beginning.

That was in 1924.

Turn back five years. *The American Language* had just appeared in its first edition. Had some of Mencken's critics been less busy with making him out as a propagandist, they might have noticed, in the book, a significant statement,—one doubly significant for its occurrence in a learned, if light-hearted, discussion on philology, and for its nature as an unpremeditated by-product of the work in hand.

In that first edition, at the very end of the book, clos-ing the "Miscellanea," sounds this strangely new Menck-enian music:

In all human beings, if only understanding be brought to the business, dignity will be found, and that dignity cannot fail to reveal itself, soon or late, in the words and phrases with which they make known their high hopes and aspirations and cry out against the intolerable meaninglessness of life.

How simply eloquent, how un-Americanese a passage with which to close a book upon the "American" language! What a *democratic* motif from a superman! What a budding connotation of human pity! It might have been written by Havelock Ellis.

Let me add another instance, from a recent letter. "For the religious spirit itself," wrote Mencken, "I have an active dislike, but it seems to me that, in most cases, it is founded upon defective knowledge—that it is, at bottom, no more than a sign of ignorance—and so I am not inclined to give it too much respect, save when its fruits are noble. I respect a Catholic Sister of Charity much as I respect a Bach or a Michelangelo. But the average pietist, like the average ecclesiastic, seems to me to be not only a fool, but also a public nuisance. Religion is fundamentally opposed to everything I hold in veneration—courage, clear thinking, honesty, fairness, and, above all, love of the truth. In brief, it is a fraud." Here is another remarkable passage,—a central Menckenian contradiction. The man who cries "Be hard!" may yet respect the woman whose very life is the incarnation of "Be soft!" In the Sister, the supreme virtue—as seen by Mencken—is doubtless the honesty of her dedication,—a selfless, even superstitious sincerity, yet a purging honesty. Here, surely, Mencken brings understanding to the business and discovers dignity in simple humanity. But why should the Catholic

Sister of Charity stand alone? Has she not sisters and brothers of every denomination and race and affiliation?

Can we have here a hint of the new Mencken that is emerging from the old? Can it be that the ruthlessness is losing its fettering rigidity? That Mencken's will-not-to-feel may yet become, not a will-to-feel, but at least a greater willingness to feel? There is that saving word, *dignity,* of course, which in Mencken is always bound up with a salutary control of the emotions. I have already indicated, in Croce, a passage [1] that might be used to blow up all philosophical structures, including his own. Here, in Mencken, is a similar passage that might act, through a similar illogicality, toward a similar end. It reads almost like an unconscious confession. It implies, as I say, a new Mencken. It implies, as I have already written, also a fresh struggle with himself. The man has taken on new hues; he gives out new overtones. May we not discover in the innocent sentences from *The American Language* and the letter a hint that joy in one's superiority to inferiors is after all but a sterile and an undignified satisfaction? That it is better to contend with equals than to lord it over slaves? That way lies, not prejudice, but tolerance,—a tolerance not to be confused with the weakness that refrains from criticism out of an uneasy consciousness that there is so much—in oneself—to criticize. A tolerance, in short, that finds *dignity in all human beings, if only understanding be brought to the business.*

[1] See page 160.

Mencken has the understanding. He knows the business. Will he bring the one to the other?

If he does not, he still remains in our national life a salient figure, with failings as great as his virtues. If he does, he may add cubits to his stature. I am not hinting at a softening of the man, or at an abandonment of a philosophy. I have in mind rather the relaxation of a tension, the completion of a circle. I have in mind, not the embracing of a new doctrine, but the release of Mencken's fuller self. I have the feeling, then, that he has been, indeed, himself, but not all of it. I am not concerned with having him, or any other man, become other than he really is. I regard him—the artist—in the light of a work of art, æsthetically. What are the greatest potentialities suggested by his personal endowments? How has he exemplified them; how fallen short? In what direction, given the force that is peculiarly he and none other, is he to move toward a fuller self, toward self-completion?

II

Such a self-completion is really connoted by the skepticism and the eclecticism that Mencken avows. "In all my life," [he says in the letter I have just quoted],

I don't recall ever writing a line that, at the moment, I didn't believe to be true. All this does not mean, of course, that I hold my convictions to be impeccable. On the contrary, I regard them all rather lightly. . . . I am always willing to be convinced; I change my ideas as my knowledge increases.

But I never change them under pressure—never for any other reason than that I have been convinced of their error. . . . I do not
advocate any particular formula or school. . . . The test, to
me, is not the man's programme, but his honesty. If he is making
a sincere effort to do something worth while I am disposed to
allow him a wide latitude in the choice of means. This latitude,
I find, is incomprehensible to many persons. They cannot grasp
the concept of liberty.

Mencken is thus credited, against his wishes, with a
public service. There can be no doubt that his books
have not only stirred up a healthy revolt but have done
much toward the creation of a sophisticated, intelligent,
"civilized minority,"—that they have helped to make life
more comfortable for the non-conformists. It is characteristic of him that he should be more glad of the comfort
than interested in the revolt.

Planned for the immediate future are a number of
books, some on such familiar themes as *Democracy* and
Prejudices, one on a group of composers, others of a
nature that must for the present remain undiscussed.
Two, however, contain the seeds of fresh promise: a short
treatise on *Christianity* and a work to be called *Advice
To Young Men.* One may hazard the guess that the
second will be as startlingly unconventional as its title is
tame. For it is to set forth, without the sermonizing
blather so common in books of the sort, a realistic account
of what Mencken and his kind have found to be the true
wisdom about such things as women, religion, politics,
drink and the rest. A latter-day Socrates, to "corrupt"
the youth of America! What ho, slaves! Brew the
hemlock for this low seducer!

III

It was late in the afternoon of a New York May. I had been closeted with Mencken for three hours. The talk had turned upon his restless life, upon art and science, upon men and women, upon business and pleasure. We had already shaken hands and I had grasped the door-knob, about to leave, when his face lighted up with an unholy glow. "Criticism! Criticism!" he rasped as he stretched his arms in relief after this secular confession. "It's all an illusion! An illusion!"

It is. So, to round out the platitude, is life. It is a useful fiction, as Vaihinger would say. Vaihinger, who in *Die Philosophie Des Als Ob* might have indicated Life as the greatest *As If* of them all! In the meantime, here is Mencken at forty-five, sinking his emotional and intellectual roots in a fecund soil of uncertainty. Let us view him in that same indefinite light. He is something more than an American critic; he is something more than a critic of books. His artistry is the expression of a free personality in terms of the printed and the living environment. It derives from life and flows back into it.

A
MENCKEN
MISCELLANY

Verse, Chiefly from the
Knocks and Jollies
Column of the
Baltimore *Herald*

WAR

The day is not far distant when war, like human sacrifice, will be at an end.—REPORT OF THE PEACE CONFERENCE.

The good king dreamed the dream
And his word went out to all,
 Over the sea
 And under the sea,
And the nations heard his call:
"Have ye forgot the Son
Who made Love conqueror?—
 Peace is the Lord's,
 Go sheath your swords!—
Let us have done with war!"

From the sky-rim came reply,
And the nations called him blest,
 Over the sea
 And under the sea
Answered the East and West:
"We will slay our kind no more,
Our murderings shall cease:
 We have bent the knee
 To the holy Tree
Whose snow-white flower is Peace!"

So fell the good king's word
As a drop of holy balm,
 Over the sea

And under the sea
Sounded a new, brave psalm:
"Praise Him that sent the Son
Who died that we might not die:
We will sweat no more
In the bonds of war
Nor hark to the bugle's cry!"

.   .   .   .

Sudden a trumpet call—
Sudden a flag unfurled—
Under the sea
And over the sea
The echo shakes the world!
And the nations turn to the strife
As the jackals turn to the dead:
Yea, we are Huns
When call the guns
And the snow-white flower is red!

(This was written just after the first Peace Conference, called
by the Czar of Russia for May 18, 1899. It was printed in the
Baltimore *Herald* at the time. When the World War began, in
1914, it was reprinted in the Baltimore *Evening Sun*.)

IM HINTERLAND

Im hinterland, im hinterland,
Where roosters crow and porkers grunt,
And cows engage the toothsome cud,
And carrots bloom and turnips bud,
And ways are rough and speech is blunt,
Im hinterland, im hinterland.
But let a man with fairish front
Set out to do a three-card stunt,

Im hinterland, im hinterland,
And plenteous coin will flow his way,
For every coruscated jay—
    Im hinterland, im hinterland—
Will buck the game and gladly pay
For opportunity to play
His luck ag'in a certaintay—
    Im hinterland, im hinterland;
And that's the way they are today,
And that's the way they'll be for aye—
You cannot civilize a jay
Or from his belfry pluck the hay,
Alas, alack, alackaday—
    Im hinterland, im hinterland.

—Printed in "Knocks and Jollies" column in the Baltimore
Herald, January 20, 1901.

TO G. W.

When Valley Forge is long forgot
And Yorktown's faded from the map;
When none but antiquarians wot
That you were once a warlike chap;
When people know the Delaware
As but a stream of germs and mud,
And think Luzon a village where
The Continentals shed their blood;
When all your monuments are down
And all your ex-valets are dead;
When history says your hair was brown
And curled in ringlets o'er your head;
When people know no longer who
Instructed them in being free,

305

They will remember that 'twas you
That hatcheted the cherry tree!

—Printed in "Knocks and Jollies" column in the
Baltimore *Herald*, February 17, 1901.

A DIRGE

Mum is the man of words,
Silent the loud Nebraskan,
Dumb is the clarion voice that erstwhile
pealed like a bell;
Cold is the fevered brow,
As the ears of a chilled Alaskan,
And closed is the muscular mouth that
one time gaped like a well.

Still is the atmosphere
That the strong lungs agitated,
Dead is the hurtling breeze that swirled
from the Coast to Maine,
And dead is W. J. Bryan,
And to stay dead is he slated
'Till the Salt Creek stern-wheel steamer
comes out of the woods again.

—Printed in Baltimore *Herald*, November 18, 1900,
after Bryan's second defeat.

THE CONNING OF FREDERICK JONES

Certes, the tale is a weepful one
Of Frederick Clarence Jones,
And how he was conned by a heartless blonde,
And how, in remorse, he groans,
And tears his hair in dank despair
And moans in mournful tones.

Ventures *into* Verse

Being Various BALLADS, BALLADES, RONDEAUX, TRIOLETS, SONGS, QUATRAINS, ODES *and* ROUNDELS ❧ All rescued from *the* POTTERS' FIELD *of* Old Files *and* here Given DECENT BURIAL ❧ [Peace *to* Their Ashes]

BY

Henry Louis Mencken

WITH ILLUSTRATIONS & OTHER THINGS *By* CHARLES S. GORDON & JOHN SIEGEL

MARSHALL, BEEK & GORDON :: NEW YORK :: LONDON :: TORONTO :: SYDNEY BALTIMORE ❧ FIRST *(and Last)* EDITION M C M I I I

TITLE PAGE OF MENCKEN'S FIRST AND ONLY BOOK OF VERSE

ACADEMIAE VITEMBERGENSIS
RECTORE
GODFRID. LVDOV.
MENCKEN D.
PANDECT. PROF. PVBL. CVR. PROVINCIAL.
ELECTOR. SCABINAT. ET FACVLTAT. IVRIDIC. NEC
NON IVDICII PROVINCIAL. IN MARCHIONATV
LVSAT. INFERIORIS ASSESSORE

NOmen ſuum profeſſus, atque
in Album literariae huius Reipublicae
receptus, Magiſtratui Academico fi-
dem, obedientiam Praeceptoribus, uitam de-
nique totam, Academiae legibus conuenien-
tem, promiſit

Qvod teſtatur hac ... publico Academiae
ſigillo munitá, ... o recuperatae per
CHRISTVM ſal... ...1 menſe ...
XIII. die

DR. FRIEDRICK OTTO MENCKEN (1708–1754)

The original document in this photograph is in Mencken's pos-
session and is of unusual interest. The student, Leonhard
Ludwig Mencken (1710–1762) was the son of the rector,
Gottfried Ludwig Mencken (1683–1744)

Blonde were her locks as the woven gold,
  And blue were her dreamful eyes,
As the bluest blue of the misty dew
  That clings to the azure skies;
And her lips were as red as the reddest red
  That ever a mortal saw,
And the white of her brow was as white (said Fred)
  As is possible under the law.

Thanksgiving Day was the fateful day
  That Fred and the charmer met
(And alack and alas! till the first of May
  He will think of their meeting yet!)
Oh, blue were her eyes as the azure skies,
  And blonde were her golden locks,
And red were her lips with the ruddy red
  Of a bunch of hollyhocks!

Now, Fred J. was a masher gay,
  And he took the blonde for a prize,
And soon he was holding hands with her
  And making goo-goo eyes;
And ever the blonde quoth, "Freddie, dear,
  Are you sure that you love me true?"
And Frederick sighed as he ever replied,
  To the clinging blonde, "I do!"

Oh, the days have come and the days have gone,
  And it's now the Christmastide,
And the blonde has sworn a whispered oath
  To be Frederick Jones' bride;
And Fred to the savings bank hath chased
  (He is bughouse with delight)
And he draws his coin in a feverish haste,
  To the paying teller's fright.

"She loves me true!" he breathes in joy,
  As he dashes down the street;
"De gazoot is daf!" says a messenger boy,
  As he notes Fred's flying feet.
And where is our hero going to?
  And what is he going to do?
To purchase a tasteful Christmast gift
  For the blonde that loves him true!

To the marts of trade has his path been laid,
  To the Rue de Dim Bazar;
And now he has reached his journey's end,
  Where the bargain counters are:
"What would you, sir?" said a merchant bold,
  And Frederick makes reply:
"I would see some tasteful Christmas gifts,
  And if shown the best, may buy."

And now the merchant shows his stock,
  A heap of treasures rare;
And a diamond pin and a pocket clock
  Have riveted Frederick's stare:
"And how much gold will purchase these?"—
  "A hundred pieces of eight."—
And Frederick's blood did well-night freeze,
  And it made him hesitate.

"Ten pieces down," said the merchant bold,
  "And you take the wares away,
And then, you pay three plunks a week
  Till the first of the coming May."
" 'Tis well," said Frederick Clarence Jones,
  And then he remarked aside,
"By the time I have settled the merchant's bill
  The blonde will be my bride."

So he took the bauble and went his way,
  With a genial smile and fond;
And bright on the morn of Christmas Day
  He hied him to the blonde.
He has rung the bell of her citadel,
  And she answers to his ring;
"Fair maid," says he, "accept of this,
  My Christmas offering!"

She has smiled a smile and he sees no guile,
  She has thanked him o'er and o'er,
She has made him think he's the real thing
  And thenceforth It for sure;
"And do you love me?" he asked her bold;
  "I do!" replies the blonde;
And he plunges into the outer cold,
  With a lingering back look fond.

But, alas! what a mark was F. C. J.!
  And alack! what a rube was he!
For when back he came to press his claim
  The blonde he could not see!
So he up and spoke to the low-browed bloke
  That stood by her dim back door,
"Prithee, where's she at?" Said the bloke, "Take that!"
And he smited Frederick sore!

So, alas and alack! for F. C. Jones,
  And alas and alackaday!
He must pay three plunks of his hard-earned coin
  Each week till the first of May!
And the blonde she weareth the diamond pin
  And the jewel-set pocket clock,
While Fred wears glass and a watch of brass
  And his overcoat's in hock!

THE MAN MENCKEN

Certes, the tale is a saddish one
  Of Frederick Clarence Jones,
And how he was conned by a crafty blonde,
  And how, in his woe, he groans,
And tears his hair in wild despair
  And moans and moans and moans!

SEASIDE

Here, where the small concerns are uppermost,
  And all the earth seems fashionèd for joy,
Here, where the bloodless, lesser sinnings cloy,
  And care nor sits the faces of the host;
Along the bauble-lined and swarming coast,
  (Ho, when the sea calls, what a vain employ!)
  Like children sporting with a trivial toy,
A hundred thousand strut and plume and boast.

And yet beside them pounds the changeless sea—
  Hark! how its surges flog and flay the strand!—
Wild and unfettered, strong, mysterious, free!
  Flinging its old defiance to the land—
A hundred thousand brave its majesty:
  Smiling, it sends them sprawling on the strand!

This belongs to 1901 or 1902.

Two Early Stories

THE COOK'S VICTORY [1]

> "Forced into virtue, thus, by self-defence,
> E'en Kings learn justice and benevolence!"
> —*An Essay on Man.*

Captain Hiram Johnson, of the oyster pungy *Sally Jones,*
thought that buckwheat cakes reached the maximum of delicious-
ness when they were a light, unbroken brown. Consequently,
when Windmill, the colored cook of the *Sally,* placed before him
a dozen which ranged in hue from a dirty, speckled russet to a
charred and lustrous black, he was very angry indeed.

Pushing his chair back from the swinging table, he leaned
against the solitary berth in the *Sally's* cabin and swore earnestly
and loudly.

"What do you mean, you black rascal?" he said. "What do
you mean, suh, by offerin' me such garbage? Huh?"

"Deed it war'n't my fault, cap'n," answered his servitor,
meekly. "Dat dar la'd——"

"Don't you go blamin' it on that la'd!" roared the captain.
"Don't you dare do it!"

"I was on'y a-goin' to say——" began Windmill, but the captain
refused to hear him.

"I paid ten cents a pound fo' that la'd in Balt'mo'," he shouted,
"and you can't find no better nowhere!" He arose and stamped
with indignation. "It ain't the la'd; it's you, you soot-faced,
black-hearted, gin-soaked——" but the captain's anger paralyzed his
tongue, and for a moment he could only splutter and fume.
Windmill eyed him with alarm.

[1] Mencken's first short story to be published. Written early in 1900,
when he was 19. Accepted by *Short Stories* April 28, 1900, and printed
in the August number, 1900.

313

"What did I hiah you fo'?" demanded the captain, with increased vehemence. "What do I pay you sixteen dolla's a month fo'? To cook vittles or to burn 'em up?"

As Windmill—who was thus named on account of the unusual prominence of his ears—made no reply to these questions, the captain proceeded to "learn" him, by precept and example, how to fry buckwheat cakes in the manner of the masters of the art. Stalking to the galley, he gave the feeble nut-coal fire a few savage thrusts with the poker and began larding the pan. Windmill stood by in silence.

"You take a hunk of la'd as big as a quartah," he said, suiting the action to the word, "and spread it over the bottom of the pan. Then you h'ist a spoonful of battah and dump it onto the la'd—so. You see?"

Windmill replied that he saw, and the captain proceeded to complete the operation. First, he gave the crackling cake a few jabs with the turner, to "loosen it up," as he said, and then, when he thought the under side sufficiently browned, he attempted to turn it. But here he met with difficulties. The cake was fast attached to the pan. Finally, however, after the under side had become a rich black, he succeeded in detaching it, and then, with a deft movement, he slid the turner under it and gave it a graceful toss in the air. It rose as one cake and came down in seventeen pieces.

"Thunderation!" he shouted, turning to the trembling Windmill. "What do you mean, suh, by that, suh?" The cook quailed beneath the weight of profanity which followed.

"You must 'a' jogged it too much," he ventured, feebly. The captain's face became a dark, luminous purple.

"Do you mean to criticize me? you black villain!" he asked in a voice which suggested the howl of a storm. "Do you mean to blame it on me when your battah falls to bits?" He shook the pan at the frightened darkey's head. "Overboard with it!" he said, seizing the bowl. "Overboard with it!" And he hurled it bodily through the open skylight and spread its contents about the deck above.

The two dredgers who constituted the pungy's crew dodged the flying batter as it came toward them, and jumped from the dredge which they had been operating in alarm. On peering down the hatch they received salutes which cut their investigations short.

The captain, having thus disposed of his breakfast, remembered that he was still hungry, and being in a desperate mood, resolved to cook his meal himself. Windmill he ordered to stand by for instruction. With infinite pains he mixed a new bowl of material, and with even greater care prepared the stove and pan. As he proceeded step by step he kept up a running fire of sarcastic explanation. At last the first cake neared completion.

Carefully he shifted it to the turner and cautiously he braced himself to flip it. Then he tossed it in the air and it fell intact and right side up—on the stove lid beside the pan. Windmill jumped to the rescue, and was about to lift it from its resting place, when the broad part of the turner, propelled by the captain's muscled arm, collided with the back of his kinky head, and the captain's heavy shoe-tip came into sudden contact with his crazy bone. The face of the captain was again a deep luminous purple.

"Now you've settled your hash for good!" he exclaimed, as the cook danced with the pain of the double blow. "Now you can pack your traps and git ashore! Git! You son of unrighteousness! Git! Move! Jump!"

But the cook didn't "git," and neither did he move or jump. Instead he backed toward the mast and assumed a defensive attitude.

The crew stopped their work and stared dumfounded. Being shanghaied men, who had been lured into a shipping office in Baltimore while too drunk to walk unassisted, and placed aboard the *Sally* while in a state of insensibility, they looked with delight upon the threatened war. It might end in their personal gain. But they knew that the captain carried a remarkably fierce-looking pistol in his hip pocket, and when he slowly drew it from its hiding place they stood at attention with very respectful expressions upon their unwashed faces.

"Ah!" said the captain, with long-drawn emphasis. "Mutiny, is it?" His bushy eyebrows seemed to meet and his beard to stand on end like the fur of a battling tom cat. As he cocked his revolver the cook grew limp, and slowly and fearfully started to wriggle 'round the mast.

"Ease up!" commanded the captain, and then to the crew: "Bring up the irons." The cook halted, and as the captain replaced his revolver in his pocket, began to make a plea for mercy. But the captain was in no mood for compromise. Bringing forth the stump of a cigar from the depths of one of his vest pockets, he lighted it with care, and after blowing a huge cloud of suffocating smoke from his nostrils, said, with solemnity:

"You're a dead nigger." The cook shuddered, and the captain went on: "Yes, you're a goner. You're a mutiner, by Jupiter, a rank, howlin' mutiner. Article two twenty-one, chapter thirteen, verse seven, of the Acts of the Legislature of Maryland in Congress assembled covers you all right. 'And if any man shall commit mutiny aboard any vessel in the Ches'peake Bay or tributaries thereof, he shall be taken to the jail from whence he come, and be there hanged by the neck 'till he be dead. And may God have mercy on his soul.' That's the law—chapter and verse."

At this point the crew reappeared with a pair of ship's irons that had been in the possession of the captain's family since the days when his great grandfather, one Silas Noah Johnson, commanded a Baltimore clipper ship. They weighed little short of fifty pounds, and were covered with rust and dirt. Laboriously the crew pried open the jaws designed to encircle the legs of captives, and fitted them about the ankles of the quaking Windmill.

"Lemme go, cap'n," wailed the latter woefully. "I didn't mean no hahm, cap'n. I wasn't a-goin' to hit you."

"By Jupiter, I know you wasn't," replied the captain with fine scorn. "The idear! You hit *me!* Well, I guess not! But— oh, let it go at that. I think I'll put in at Joneses Point and hang you myself. Hump yourselves, there"—this to the crew, who were painfully trying to lock the irons. "Ain't you got no strength? Shove 'em together!"

The crew, with much difficulty, fastened the irons on Windmill's legs and made the chain fast to the mast. Then they stood by while the captain delivered an harangue on mutiny, hanging and other matters, which bristled with blasphemous metaphors and profane similes.

"Now you get back to work," he said, as he ended and went aft. The crew returned to the dredge windlass and soon had it creaking busily. At times the captain helped them "cull" the oysters which the dredge brought up, and at other times he labored at the wheel.

Windmill had sunk to the deck, and with the irons encircling his legs, sat disconsolate and silent. That he had done nothing to warrant his execution he was sure, but he also well knew that on Chesapeake Bay it is customary for each pungy captain to enact his own laws and execute his own sentences. A year before, one Captain Joshua Kellum, under whom he then served, had put him in irons and refused him all food for three days because he had incautiously displayed a revolver. A man whom he had met when last ashore had been locked up in the hold for forty-eight hours because he had questioned his captain's veracity. Memories such as these made Windmill exceedingly downcast.

At intervals the captain came forward and inspected the irons which bound his prisoner. The latter, more than once, begged to be released. A strong northwest wind had sprung up, and he was becoming numbed by the cold and flying spray. But the captain was obdurate, and to the darkey's plaints he made profane and positive answers.

Now, it must not be supposed that he was by nature an unusually cruel or heartless man. As a matter of fact, when compared to the average pungy captain, he was considerate and kind in the extreme. But on this trip there had been much to vex him.

First, there was the persistent bad luck which had followed the *Sally* since her departure from Baltimore a week before. All the way down the Chesapeake a series of minor accidents had befallen her. While becalmed off Kent Island, the first night out, the boy whose duty it was to "cull" the oysters taken had escaped by swimming ashore. Then the water cask had sprung a leak and it had become necessary to secure another at Crisfield. Then one of the crew, by some unknown means, had obtained possession of the captain's whiskey bottle, and by emptying it had become gloriously drunk. Then a sail had been torn and the bowsprit had cracked and a heavy dredge block had fallen on the captain's foot.

Added to these misfortunes was a greater one: The *Sally* had searched in vain for good ground. On an oyster bed which the captain had discovered on a previous trip, and which he thought that he alone had located, he found a dozen busy tongers. On the Sells' Point beds were scores of Crisfield boats. Everywhere the *Sally* went rivals were encountered. All this had made the captain exceedingly pessimistic.

At nightfall one of the crew, by order of the captain, brought Windmill a huge chunk of stale bread and a can of water. The darkey, chilled to the bone by the damp bay wind—for it had blown up cold during the day—begged for a release from his bonds, but to all entreaties the captain was deaf. When the latter came forward, before turning to light the mast lights, Windmill was in tears, and with much mournful eloquence pleaded for permission to carry his chains below for the night. But the captain still paid no heed to his lamenting.

Before midnight the thermometer began falling rapidly. Windmill, exposed to the blasts of the storm, shivered and quaked like a fever patient. By crouching in the lee of the water barrel he succeeded in escaping some of the gusts of cutting wind, but despite his efforts to protect himself he well-nigh froze. His ears, which many a facetious shipmate had referred to as studding sails, seemed to be dropping from his head, and his arms and legs grew numb. By the time the first faint pink of the dawn showed over the Wicomico shore he was half senseless.

The captain, in his berth in the stuffy cabin, had rested but indifferently. So far not more than twenty-five bushels of oysters had been dumped into the *Sally's* hold. The two men of the crew, who had been signed for ten hours' work a day, had labored, on an average, about fourteen. The pungy had been four days on the beds, and she was now far down the bay, within less than fifteen miles of the Virginia line. Of these things the captain thought while he lay awake, and then he thought of the good beds beyond the border. It was true that dredging over there was forbidden to Maryland boats, but then did he not know that the sloops of the Virginia oyster navy were unable to be at more than one place at one time, and was it not worth the risk?

Twice before the captain had attempted poaching. Once he had been successful in eluding the guards, but once the *Sally* had got a shot through her cabin. He debated the matter in detail and at length, and finally decided to try his luck again.

Bright and early next morning the *Sally* began a slow movement toward the boundary. In the shoal water along the shore a pretence of dredging was kept up until dusk. While the crew strained and tugged at the windlass Windmill shivered at the mast. At breakfast time and again at noon a slab of bread and a can of water had been placed before him, and he had been commanded to eat and drink. After much begging he had been given a tarpaulin by the captain, and with this around him he felt fairly comfortable, though the cold steadily increased.

At sundown the captain approached him, and in silence unlocked his irons. Then he said:

"You've been reprieved." Windmill stretched his limbs with a sigh of satisfaction. "You've been reprieved," continued the captain, "so as you can help. We're goin' acrost."

With these laconic orders the *Sally* got under way, and as the moon appeared she crossed the line and entered the forbidden waters. Windmill was posted in the bow as a lookout, and as the pungy scudded along toward the inshore beds a few miles below the boundary he craned his neck for a sight of suspicious craft. But he saw none, and soon the crew was hard at work.

Before midnight the *Sally* drifted into a lot of floating ice. The captain shouted vigorous orders in a whisper, but by some accident the vessel became hopelessly entangled, and after an hour's hard labor the crew gave up in despair, for the ice held her in a strong and unbreakable grip.

Then the captain rose in his wrath and swore from the shoulder —deep, comprehensive oaths that made even the hardened blasphemers of the crew stare aghast. The water between the small ice blocks about the pungy was congealing rapidly, and soon there was a straight stretch of ice thick enough to bear a man from the *Sally* to the shore. Fifty yards on the other side was the clear water, and toward this the captain purposed moving the *Sally* if every man aboard of her was killed in the operation.

With shovels and oyster rakes the four men attacked the ice, and by dint of much exercise of muscle, began making an appreciable gap in the off-shore side. It was killing work, and after an hour of it the crew demanded a half-hour's rest and a bracer of whiskey. This request the captain answered by striking one of the men in the face with his doubled fist and breaking a rake across the other's legs. The crew interpreted these actions as being a declaration of war, and as soon as both had recovered they made a combined attack on the *Sally's* commander. The jumping and stamping in the conflict which followed made the ice beneath the contestants crackle and tremble ominously, and with mutual accord they transferred the scene of the battle to the pungy's deck. Here Windmill went to the rescue of his superior officer, and while he was engaged in butting the irate crew with his iron-like skull the captain had time to dive into the cabin after his revolver.

Waving it threateningly he sprang on deck. The crew, on catching sight of it, made a simultaneous spring for the ice on the land side, and before the astonished captain had recovered sufficiently to spring after them, they were well on their way to the shore. As he stood speechless on the deck he heard a voice from the darkness hurl back an avalance of profanity such as he alone could have surpassed. Then the sound of the deserter's retreating footsteps died out, and the captain turned to Windmill.

"Lord help us," he said piously. "It's five years in the pen!"

The cook sensibly suggested that it would be well to continue their efforts to dig a way to the open water, and the captain silently lifted up a shovel and started to work. Until the dawn the two labored valiantly. Then the ice began to grow mushy and yielding. Suddenly it gave way beneath Windmill's feet, and he plunged down into the freezing water.

With much difficulty the captain dragged him over the side of the *Sally* and carried him into the cabin. The darkey was nearly frozen and half scared to death by his sudden bath, and for fifteen minutes lay shivering and speechless beside the stove. When he had recovered sufficiently to go on deck the ice was breaking up around the *Sally,* and soon it was plain she would be able to pass out into the channel.

Then began work which was to test the captain's seamanship to the full. Slowly and cautiously the *Sally* made her zig-zag way through the breaking ice toward the open water, completely halted at times by thick pieces, and at other times seemingly on the point of being crushed like an egg-shell in the crackling grind. Windmill helped the captain at windlass and rope and wheel until he fairly dropped with exhaustion. His cold hours on deck in chains and his dip into the freezing bay had well-nigh killed him outright, and now, when there was added the fatigue of a night without sleep, it came about that he was in exceedingly unjoyful and rebellious frame of mind.

Just as the *Sally* broke into the channel a sail appeared to the southward, and while the pungy painfully toiled through an acre of drift ice, the vessel, which turned out to be a sloop, gained on her steadily. The captain shaded his eyes to look at the new-comer, and as he did so a puff of smoke spurted from her bow. Then between the smoke and the *Sally* the choppy water was lashed as with a whip in half a dozen places, and as he heard a faint deep "boom" it dawned on him that the sloop was firing on him.

"Lord save us!" he said. "It's the Virginia police boat!"

With his foot he prodded Windmill. The darkey had sunk to the deck and was leaning against the mast.

"H'ist yo'self, you black rascal!" he shouted. "We'll have to run for it!"

As he spoke another spurt of smoke spurted from the sloop's bow. Again the water was lashed, and at this time up to a point much nearer the *Sally's* stern than the first time.

The captain, hardly noticing the fact that the cook did not budge, fell to with tremendous energy. Blocks rattled, ropes strained and sails flapped and bellied, and soon the *Sally* was fairly under way. Then of a sudden and without warning a lift broke, and the mainsail fluttered to the deck. In a minute the captain had rudely repaired the parted rope and was straining with all his might and main in an endeavor to hoist the fallen canvas. But the block was rusty and the sail heavy with spray, and despite his gigantic efforts he could not move it. Meanwhile the *Sally* drifted and plunged hither and thither, and the sloop came nearer and nearer. At intervals he heard a "boom" and saw the lashing of the water. Then he bethought him again of Windmill, who still reposed by the mast.

"Here, you enemy of righteousness," he shouted, "h'ist yo'self and lend a hand! Git a-hold of this rope!" But Windmill only turned over lazily and said:

"How many years in de pen is it?"

"Five, you rascal," bawled the captain. "Lend a hand at this lift!"

"I think I'll take de five," said Windmill. "It's better dan hangin'!"

The captain's face was a study, as for the third time it became a deep luminous purple. He raised his foot to kick the darkey, but just then a shot struck the water not ten yards away, and in consequence he decided on a hurried compromise.

"Your sentence is commuted," he bawled, with much profanity, "to life imprisonment."

But Windmill was unsatisfied.

"Dat's more dan five years, ain't it?" he said, seeking shelter from the nearing shots on the forward side of the mast.

The captain exploded in a perfect hurricane of wrath.

"I'll make it ten years at hard labor," he yelled.

"Too much," said Windmill.

"Make it seven."

"No, sah."

"Six."

"No."

"Five."

"I'll git dat much hyeh in Virginny."

The captain began to plead.

"Lend a hand," he said pathetically, "and we'll say a year in jail."

"No sah," said Windmill, rising. "I hain't goin' to no penitinchry an' I ain't goin' to no jail. I ain't done nothin' to nobody, an' nobody ain't goin' to hahm me. Dem people ain't goin' to lock me up. I didn't come down hyeh on my own hook. You's de cap'n; not me."

While this long speech was in progress a shot struck the water so close to the Sally that a sheet of spray was dashed over both the captain and the cook. The latter now began to feel fear, and was glad enough to fall to when the captain said:

"Lend a hand, you rascal! You're pardoned!" But first he demanded a clear understanding.

"No hahm ain't a-comin' to me?" he asked.

"No," said the captain. "Now git a-hold of the lift."

"I ain't a-goin' to no jail?"

"No! Git a-hold of the rope!"

"I ain't——"

"Git a-hold of the rope!"

Whereupon Windwill seized the rope, and the mainsail of the *Sally* rose upon the mast, and as a gust of wind bellied it the pungy shot forward. Then Windmill took the wheel, and the captain prepared to reply to the shots of his pursuers. Bringing from the cabin a rifle of huge calibre and a belt of long cartridges, he took his place behind the wheel and opened fire.

His fourth shot went crashing through the sloop's cabin; his sixth tore a ragged hole through her foresail. The next one struck her mast about ten feet above the deck. A gust of wind gave the timber a timely strain a minute later, and it fell to the starboard, splintered and broken. Then the sloop careened dangerously and came to a stop. The *Sally* was in safety.

THE BEND IN THE TUBE [1]

First of all, Boggs was a lunatic, which was nobody's fault. Secondly, he had a new theory concerning the redemption of silver certificates and the circulation of national banks, which was his own fault. In the third place, he was an anarchist, which was the fault of a good many people, individually and collectively.

All of his acquaintances, from those he casually addressed on the street as "How-are-you" to his blood relatives, had heard him explain his theory of certificates and circulation, and nearly all of them knew that he was a lunatic. The fact was so obvious and patent that it oozed out of every pore of his skin. It was apparent in his clothes, in his conversation, in the mixed drinks that he fancied and in many other ways. But comparatively few knew that he was an anarchist, and these, being *participes criminum,* said nothing. Swartz knew and Lowe knew, and so did Zimmerman, and Goldbloom, the Russian, and Kraus, the Austrian. But Murphy, the managing editor of the *Tribune,* was as innocent of the fact as the Grand Lama of Tibet, and equally unknowing and unsuspecting were Gaylor and Smith, who were Boggs' desk neighbors, and Hemming, who was the *Tribune's* business manager. Had these latter been wiser in their generation they might have saved themselves much trouble.

Boggs, to the outward eye, seemed an eminently harmless sort of crank. Beginning manhood as a divinity student, he had left college under a cloud of heresy, and then, dropping a step further down the scale of brute creation, he had become a reporter on the *Tribune,* a third-class morning paper in a provincial city. Ten years of hard service on the street had been rewarded

---

[1] Written in the summer of 1904. Refused by *Saturday Evening Post* and *Short Stories.* Accepted by the *Red Book,* Dec. 9, 1904. Published in the February number, 1905.

with the gift of a desk job at $1,200 a year. Now he was financial editor of the *Tribune,* and over five of its columns each morning exercised absolute control—with a reservation, that is, taking account of the superior authority of Murphy, of Murphy's boss, of Murphy's boss's boss, of the boss of Murphy's boss's boss, and finally of that awful and mysterious man, the Owner.

In theory, Hemming, the business manager, was not one of these bosses. He was not paid to regulate Boggs' doings—which was the task of Murphy and of the other bosses, in ascending scale—but as a matter of fact, the business manager of a newspaper, being the man in direct charge of the cash drawer, usually commands much respectful attention, if not affection. Consequently, when Hemming blew a blast into his speaking-tube, and the whistle at Boggs' desk shrieked shrilly, and Hemming's voice from below asked if United States Hardwood common had reached 24¾, Boggs usually answered. Hemming was in the habit of asking questions of this sort at intervals of ten minutes between the hour of noon, when Boggs usually began work in the office, and that of 3 o'clock, when the stock exchange closed. Boggs, beginning by labeling him a nuisance, ended by regarding him as the living incarnation of all that was iniquitous and depraved. But, as has been mentioned, he was business manager of the *Tribune,* and so Boggs had to answer him, and even to make a show of politeness.

Hemming had begun his career as a financier with an inheritance of $50,000 in cash, which sum, by judicious speculation, he had reduced to $20,000 in three years. Boggs, knowing this, considered him an ass, which was a just estimate. In addition, he thought him a criminal, which was scarcely logical. Boggs was seldom logical. He knew the exact difference between Sugar and sugar, his head was filled with millions of figures and he could explain the method of ratiocination whereby the promoters of the Hemp Trust evolved fabulous paper profits from gigantic factories that did not exist, but his theory of silver certificates and bank circulation bore down upon him heavily, and he believed that all speculation, whether successful or not, was as utterly pernicious as certain of the theological dogmas that he had rejected years before.

Unlike most financial reporters and editors, he had never risked a dollar on a tip, either "inside" or outside, and had never entered a broker's office, bucket-shop or pool-room except in his capacity of seeker after information for the great, uncultured public. Many a time he observed what seemed to be chances to make a safe profit, and sometimes subsequent events showed him that these chances had been good ones, but he resisted all temptations to make experiments. For his $1,200 a year he was content to edit the exchange and market reports that came to the *Tribune,* and to write his daily column of "Jottings in the Street." In his early massacre of theological principles, he had used the knife, too, upon the accepted code of ethics, but the injunction against coveting the things that are one's neighbor's he had retained.

II

Thus Boggs lived and had his being, sitting at a desk seven or eight hours a day, with a scissors and paste-pot before him, and with a growing dislike of Hemming in his soul. After his work was done in the evening, it was his custom, as it is of men whose inward strugglings are less fatiguing, to seek relaxation. The reaction that followed his days of yielding to an ascetic faith had sent him bounding into the purgatory of the unregenerate, and he had made personal tests of the flavor and virtues of many alcoholic drinks. After a while he had concluded that of all on the café card, plain draught beer was at once the most pleasing and the cheapest. Hunting about for a quiet place to drink it, he had happened upon Bauermeister's saloon, which lurked in the dark recesses of an inconspicuous side street, and in Bauermeister's, by the natural operation of the law of evolution and opportunity, he had met Schwartz, Lowe, Zimmerman and company.

It was a full year before they deigned to wish him a good evening, and after that, he had to buy many a keg of beer, glass by glass, before they invited him into the little back room to which they retired at midnight, when Bauermeister turned out the lights in his bar-room and gave his patrons their choice of slinking into dingy apartments in the rear or taking their departure. Schwartz, Lowe, Zimmerman and company had a private room of their own, for their trade was unfailing and profitable. It was in this room, which badly needed papering and scrubbing, that Boggs first hearkened unto the doctrine that whatever is shouldn't be.

At first, this rather shocked him, for he had inherited a respect for vested rights from a thousand years of eminently proper ancestors, just as he had inherited his sandy hair and the peculiar curve of his nose. But after a while he discovered that many of the things that his new friends told him coincided with his own notions. They believed, for instance, that there was something radically wrong with the American banking system, and they were opposed to laws that made a man do things he didn't want to do. Also, they talked much against the unearned increment, which Boggs soon recognized as merely another way of denouncing thieving, mortgage-owning, grave-robbing, high finance, forgery and speculation—all of which he bracketed together as subdivisions of the same crime. Thereafter Boggs began to read the works of the greater radicals, and to evolve theories of his own. Sometimes he grew sadly muddled and had to spend long hours in wakeful meditation, as, for instance, when he tried to reconcile his belief that, in the American national banking system, no rights were allowed the depositor and his theory that the acceptance of interest on money was ethically indefensible. But

Schwartz and Zimmerman showed him a way out of each of these difficulties.

"Vhatefer ain't righdt," said Zimmerman, "out to be appolished."

And so Boggs became a sort of wholesale abolitionist, with many strange theories besides that concerning the redemption of silver certificates, and by and by he found himself attacking Herbert Spencer because the Spencerian idea regarding the limitation of governmental activity had too many reservations, and criticising Darwin and Huxley because those best rewarded and protected, in human society, seemed to him to be least fitted to survive.

Meanwhile, he began work at the *Tribune* office each day at noon and pottered along until 10 or 11 each evening. After that he journeyed to Bauermeister's to discuss the lamentable state of the world with Schwartz, Kraus, Zimmerman and the others. Sometimes they palavered until dawn. At other times they went home after an hour's session, and Boggs shuffled off to his furnished room, to lie awake in the darkness and wrestle with problems that philosophers gave up as insoluble two thousand years before he was born.

One week Hemming managed, by dumb luck, to make $2,500 by a rise in Union Leather. Thereafter, dropping Copper, B. L. & N., Globe Assurance Incomes, Wire Rope and other of his old favorites he made Leather his alpha and omega. There was a ticker beside Boggs' desk—put there more for ornament and to impress visitors to the office than for any useful purpose—and Hemming, coldly perspiring in his office on the ground floor, two flights below, summoned Boggs to the speaking tube with spasmodic persistence to beg a recital of the tale its rattling told. The speaking tube system of the *Tribune* office was a relic of the old days of hand-composition and chalk plates, but Hemming preferred it to the telephone, which had strange buzzings to annoy, and waits to wait, and feminine and world-wise operators to overhear. Boggs groaned each time its shrill whistle sounded.

"How about Leather?" Hemming would ask from below.

"Eighteen and a half," Boggs would answer curtly.

"What do you think—" Hemming would begin, and Boggs would hang up the tube.

Five minutes later there would come another blast.

"Was that bid or asked?" Hemming would inquire.

"Bid," would be Boggs' reply, and then, for ten or fifteen, or even, when Hemming was enchained by callers, for twenty minutes or half an hour, Boggs would labor away at his flimsy and his market letters.

Once he conceived the idea of ruining Hemming at one stroke by giving him false quotations. He tried the scheme when there came a sudden fall in Leather preferred. Boggs told him, instead of the truth, that there was a mysterious and steady rise, and said that the stock had already reached 24, when, as a matter of fact, it was selling at 19. He took some pains with the lie, and volunteered the opinion, which he said was justified by a reliable rumor, that insiders, with straight information, were buying heavily. But either Hemming grew suspicious on account of his willingness to hold converse, or the bucket-shop man to whom the business manager's order was sent by messenger gave him warning, for apparently he didn't buy. Another time, by laying more careful plans, Boggs lured Hemming into buying wheat and had the pleasure of observing him lose $2,000 in eight minutes by the clock. But his allegation that the ticker had made a mistake was denied and disproved, and if good luck hadn't made Hemming win back the money next day by a deal in corn, he might have lost his official head.

Boggs, in time, almost grew resigned to his troubles, for he lived in constant hope that some day Hemming, as he said, would lose his hide. In three years he had dropped $30,000, and though his rate of loss had decreased with the growth of superior knowledge, and he was cautious enough to avoid such things as gold-mining schemes and 40 per cent Mexican plantation projects, there was still a possibility that some day a particularly good tip might wipe him out. Boggs believed that no merely mortal man was without his woes, and that no job, office or position was wholly pleasant. Balloonists, he used to say, had an unsurpassed view of the scenery, but there was always a possibility that it might collide with them, and millionaires, though lacking nothing else, seldom had good digestions. So he regarded Hemming as the cross that had been given him to bear, and relieved his mind by discussing the Hemming vices and iniquities with his friends, Schwartz, Zimmerman and company.

But in time there comes a straw to break every suffering camel's back, and Boggs' came when Hemming proposed that the *Tribune* subscribe to a Wall Street news service which reported the movements of certain outlawed and degenerate stocks that the ordinary reporting association did not cover. This service was designed primarily for afternoon papers, and thereon Boggs based his objections to it. The *Tribune* was a morning paper, and there was no need for it to receive Wall Street news before one or two o'clock, when the morning news associations sent out their first copy. Besides, there was the ticker, which clicked all day. But Hemming had arguments ready for all of these objections. There were thousands of readers, he said, who were interested in the outlawed stocks, and the morning news associations paid no heed to them. By subscribing to the afternoon service aforesaid, the *Tribune* would attract this large class of readers, and profit much thereby. The plan, said Hemming, commended itself to his business sense and his native intuition.

Boggs suspected that Hemming probably wanted the service for his own information and edification too, but journalistic etiquette stood in the way of saying so. Hemming, finding his arguments weak, dismissed them as of no account, and then laid his plan before Murphy, the managing editor, who, by this same etiquette, had what was ostensibly the deciding voice. Murphy flattered himself that he knew Hemming's real motive as well as Boggs, but life is a series of compromises and he observed an opportunity to make one. He had long wanted the salary allowance of the art department increased by $1,500 a year, and Hemming had long maintained that the *Tribune* could not afford it. Now Hemming diplomatically hinted that he had begun to realize the soundness of Murphy's arguments—and Murphy decided that the extra service would be a good thing. The editor-in-chief and the general manager, who do not enter into this tale, were shadowy figures in the rear, and did not concern themselves with the exchange. It was an affair of outposts.

IV

Now, in truth, began the winter of Boggs' discontent. It was a nuisance to plow through the three-score telegraph flashes that the outlaw service sent forth every day, and it was a far greater nuisance to tabulate them. When Boggs reached his desk the first day he found a huge stack of envelopes awaiting him. Soon Hemming fell into the habit of sneaking upstairs in the morning to pry into these messages. Boggs, to whom neatness and order constituted a religion, rebelled against the disarray he encountered on his arrival. So he came to the office earlier and earlier—at 11:30, at 11, and finally at 10 o'clock—cutting short his sleep and morning constitutional and disturbing the charwoman and loafing messenger boys. Besides, there was the added and tenfold nuisance of increased calls from Hemming in the afternoon. Sometimes he made three inquiries in fifteen minutes, and after a while he fell into the habit of watching the approach of the messenger boys from his office window and of calling up Boggs before they had half climbed upstairs. He had subscribed to a Jersey City financial journal devoted to booming obscure stocks for cash in hand, and had read therein that the first mortgage bonds of a certain irrigation company in Wyoming were better, as permanent investments, than British consols. Deducing from this that they were sure to soar, he bought a big block of them, and began to read the notices of auction sales of steam yachts. The *Tribune's* new Wall Street service contained frequent mention of these bonds, and Hemming discovered, by close observation, that they were usually offered just before the close of the market each day. In consequence, he fell into the habit of asking Boggs about them half an hour or so earlier and of repeating his request at intervals of from three to eight minutes.

One day, in disgust, Boggs determined to resign. The limit, he decided, had been reached. His ordinary duties, of course, were pleasant enough, and Murphy and the others, albeit they made fun of his theories and opinions, never bothered him. But the Hemming nuisance he could not bear. He was an editor, and not an office boy, and he would not consent to remain the lackey, actual or in effect, of any one. He had saved $500, and with this he proposed to make a trip to Europe. On his return there was little doubt that he could obtain a respectable position on some other paper. His worth, he thought, was known.

On a sheet of yellow copy paper Boggs wrote his resignation, and after carefully rereading it, inserted it in an envelope addressed to Murphy. Then, of a sudden, he concluded that such a mild-mannered and ladylike leave-taking would not be commensurate with the ills he had suffered. It would be too much like kissing the hand that had smitten him. So he leaned back in his chair and corrugated his brow, and in a little while he had evolved a scheme for a more spectacular departure. First of all, he would give Hemming a carefully-safeguarded bogus tip and make him lose at least $1,000. Secondly, he would walk out of the office at 5 o'clock, with the day's financial copy under his arm, and leave the *Tribune* to scramble for the news later as best it could. Thirdly, he would drop all of the office financial reference books and records of stock variations down the elevator shaft. Fourthly, he would smash the ticker. Fifthly, he would proceed to Hemming's office, downstairs, and favor that gentleman, in profane and insulting language, with his opinion of him.

V

It must be remembered (*a*) that Boggs—from his point of view, at least—had suffered much, and (*b*) that he was a lunatic. These circumstances, combined, led him to consider his plan of revenge with something akin to the pride of invention and creation. He thought so well of it, in truth, that he could not resist the temptation to unfold it to Schwartz, Zimmerman, Goldbloom and his other friends at Bauermeister's. He told them that he would soon say *au revoir* and set off for Europe, and that he proposed to depart in a blaze of red fire.

"Vhy don't you knock de tam fool's head off?" asked Kraus.

"Sure," said Zimmerman, "vhy not strike a blow?"

"How?" asked Boggs.

The others laughed in chorus.

"You know vhat Czchlytski say," said Schwartz. "You read his book? Vhat is it vhat he say?"

"Oh, that's all right," answered Boggs, "if the game is worth the sacrifice. But here, you know—well, here it's like risking your neck to kill a dog."

"Vell, vhy make a risk?" said Schwartz.

"What do you mean?" asked Boggs, rather suspiciously.

"Send heem a pomb by mail," said Schwartz.

Boggs didn't seem to take kindly to the idea.

"It's easy," said Zimmerman, an enormously fat Low German. "Kraus done it in Bremen: didn't you, Kraus?"

Kraus nodded assent.

"Did you kill a man?" asked Boggs quickly.

"No," said Kraus, "de pomb didn't go off. But dat vasn't my fault. I loaded de tam pipe all right. I put gunpowder in it *end* dynam-i-te. It didn't go off."

Boggs ran his hands though his hair and then slowly reached for his glass and wetted his lips. The others watched him narrowly and said nothing.

"I don't like to do it," he said, at length. "It might——"

"Are you afrait?" asked Schwartz insinuatingly.

"Not a bit!" exclaimed Boggs, flushing. It was tauntingly asked, this question that among companions such as he had was an insult, and Boggs resented it enough to fling it back in Schwartz's teeth.

"You get the bomb," he said, straightening up, "and I'll look after sending it."

"Done," said Schwartz, banging the table with his fist. "I haf it here tomorrow."

"Tomorrow night?" said Boggs.

"Yes, sir."

"Here?"

"Yes, sir."

Boggs' eyes suddenly lighted again.

"What kind'll it be?" he asked.

"De regular kas-pipe kind," said Schwartz. "Von inch acrost."

Boggs made a mental calculation.

"That's too big," he said. "I'll want a smaller one—say, half an inch or three-quarters thick—and two or three inches long."

Schwartz urged objections.

"It vouldn't do mooch tamage," he said.

"It'll do all I want," replied Boggs. "The way I'm going to fire it, it'd blow up a battleship."

"I make it for you," said Schwartz. "I haf it here to-morrow."

Then Boggs went home and to bed, and, what may seem remarkable, to sleep. Next morning he took a long walk into the suburbs, to think. But for some reason, his thoughts would not flow in an ordinary manner. A new development of his theory of national bank circulation occurred to him, and before long he found that it was hopelessly entangled with an idea regarding the governmental control of bucket-shops. Then he tried to remember a paragraph he had read regarding the individual's right to existence, and it grew confused with thoughts of his coming trip to Europe. He decided that he would land at Cherbourg and make a tour on foot straight across the continent, and in a southeasterly direction, toward the Balkans. Soon he caught himself wondering if the ties on the railroads there were close enough together to make walking over them possible. If they were not, he decided, he would follow the highroads.

That afternoon he worked in a sort of haze, like a drunken man, but no one seemed to notice it, for few members of the *Tribune* staff ever paid heed to him. Hemming · may have noticed that his answers to the usual questions were more willing than usual, but then Hemming was not a very observant man, and his own affairs burdened his mind.

At half-past ten o'clock that night Boggs closed his desk and left the office. He went to a rapid-fire lunch room, and after upbraiding a waiter for making him wait three minutes for a soft-boiled egg, lingered over it an hour. Then he proceeded to Bauermeister's saloon to meet Kraus and Schwartz and the rest.

Schwartz had the bomb in his pocket. At a casual glance it

appeared to be a bit of rusty iron gas pipe, sealed at both ends. It was about as long as a cigar, and slightly thicker. Boggs handled it gingerly.

"On dis ent," explained Schwartz, "iss de bercussion cap."

Boggs turned it over to see.

"You haf to trow it a goot distance," continued Schwartz, "or maybe it von't go off. Once Kraus made one like——"

"It'll get all the percussion it wants the way I'm going to throw it," said Boggs.

"Yes?" said Schwartz.

"You bet your whiskers," continued Boggs. "I'm going to give it a drop of sixty feet."

The others chuckled with professional admiration.

"I tropped one off a bridge onct," said Zimmerman. "Id fell two hundred foot—but it missed de train."

All laughed at this subtle joke, and Boggs wrapped the bomb in his handkerchief and put it into his pocket. The others affected to begin a conversation on other subjects, but it was plain that the proximity of the bomb did not add much to their comfort, and soon even Schwartz, who had made it and brought it in his pocket, grew restless. By and by they went home, and Boggs left with them.

"Good luck," said Zimmerman, as they parted at the street corner.

"Don't be skeert," cautioned Schwartz. "Rememper vhat Czchlytski says."

"So long," said Boggs. "I'll see you later."

VI

The night before he had slept soundly, but now his eyes would not close, and he lay awake until dawn, trying to reconcile the jumbled ideas that arose within him. Once he had decided to throw the bomb into the river and face his martyrdom anew, but this plan was soon cast aside. Toward morning he began to make a mental list of the clothes that he would need for his journey across the ocean, and to estimate their probable cost. This matter engaged him for several hours, and after the sun had risen he fell asleep and slept until the chorus of factory whistles awakened him to tell him that it was noon.

Boggs bounded out of bed with a start, and angry that he had slumbered so long. Ordinarily he reached the office at noon, and in all probability Hemming was already blowing loud blasts upon the speaking-tube whistle. It was a matter of a few minutes to dress and of another few minutes to hurry to the street corner. There Boggs boarded a car, and in a little while was down-town. Just as the sirens along the water-front gave notice that it was half-past twelve, he entered his office and locked the door behind him. Then he took off his coat and vest, rolled up his sleeves and vaulted to the top of a table that stood beside the tube. He drew forth the bomb from his hip pocket, and raised the flexible end of the tube, so that it stretched upward from the tin section fastened to the wall. The bomb would not go into the tube; the nickel whistle and mouthpiece blocked its way. Boggs tore off the mouthpiece and then put it loosely into its place again. Then he waited.

In a minute there was a shrill whistle. It was the signal. Hemming was at the other end of the line—far below, on the first floor, four flights below the editorial rooms.

"Hello," said Boggs, as of old. "What is it?"

"How about Eye-ex-ell Irrigation common?" asked Hemming.

"Wait a minute and I'll see," answered Boggs.

And while Hemming waited Boggs lifted the loosened mouthpiece from its place and slipped the iron cylinder into the orifice. It fitted quite snugly, though not tightly. After it had passed through the rubber section and entered the long tin cylinder that reached downstairs it would move easily enough. All that was needed was to gently urge it at the start. Boggs decided that compressed air should be the motive power and his lungs the motor. The bomb was in the tube and the end was at his lips. He blew softly at first and felt the iron cylinder slowly move through the rubber one. Then he took a long breath and blew hard, and the bomb jumped forward. In the tenth part of a second it was at the bend in the tube, where the rubber section joined the tin. There was a sharp angle there, and the bomb struck it at good speed.

Something turned Boggs upside down just then, and he forgot Hemming and the bomb. It seemed as if a huge flywheel had seized him and were whirling him around at the rate of a thousand revolutions a second. A queer blue light flashed before him, and something hard struck his head. After a while the blue light died out and it became dark and chilly.

Allen, the assistant city editor, and Oscar, the office boy, came running, for the something that struck Boggs made a loud noise. With a chair they battered down his office door and sprang in upon him. He was as bloody as a butcher, and apparently as dead as the day before yesterday.

In an ambulance they took him to a hospital, and six weeks later, when he was able to walk again, he was given a pleasant room in the State Asylum for the Insane.

VII

After all, Hemming was the chief loser, though not in the way Boggs thought he would be. By not receiving a prompt answer to his inquiry regarding Eye-ex-ell Irrigation common he lost the sum of $74.50.

Specimens of the
Untold Tales
Baltimore *Herald,* 1901

HOW Z. ANTONIUS CARAMBA INVENTED AN UN-DERGROUND RAILWAY AND LATER EARNED A COMMUTATION FOR GOOD BEHAVIOR

A politician, in many respects, is like a warrior on the battle-field, for if he would succeed in his chosen profession he must be ready for battle day and night, year in and year out. If he lays aside his side arms for one brief moment he may be set upon by a horde of his opponents and borne to the earth; if he closes his eyes for one brief second he may awake to find a bayonet piercing his spare ribs.

Even more than the professional soldier must he be vigilant, for it is only upon extraordinary occasions that the average soldier is compelled to engage more than one antagonist at a time. The politician—more's the pity!—must at all times engage at least two regiments of them—the politicians of the opposing party, and the moral and mental degenerates commonly known as reformers. Against the former he may use the ordinary weapons of his profession, but against the latter he must proceed with cau-tion and finesse, for, like the banes of civilization that they are, the reformers are crafty rascals, and in dealing with them it is necessary to keep all four eyes wide open.

In the city of Rome during the third century *anno domini* and the height of Whig supremacy, the reformers were much in evidence, just as they have been in every city and at every time since. In the spring of the year 234, rendered sore by their failure to encompass the downfall of the eminent district leader, J. Cato Oi, they conspired to ruin the business of the ward politicians in general, and after a long fight, aided by several chicken-hearted traitors in the Legislature, they succeeded in securing the enactment of a law making repeating at elections a felony and providing a penalty of 50 years in jail for the "crime"—as they denominated it—of harboring repeaters or in any manner engaging in their purchase, sale, exchange, stabling or transportation.

At first the Whig politicians laughed at this law, as they had laughed at many another "reform" measure in the past, but after M. Ippius Bichloride, the whig boss of the Tenth ward, had been convicted and sentenced for harboring 25 up-country repeaters in his cellar, and J. Catullus Vermicelli, the well known saloonist, had been sent to prison for providing a squad of professional voters with free ale, they took a tumble and saw that they were up against it for fair.

Then ensued a period of terror, for the fall election was fast approaching, and the condition of affairs made it necessary that some arrangements be made for securing at least 10,000 repeaters from out of the city. At first it was proposed to hire local talent at advanced rates, and to trust to luck, but this, it was soon seen, would be too risky. Then it was suggested that the money ordinarily spent for repeaters be devoted to the corruption of the opposition precinct workers. But this scheme also, it was decided, would not work well in practice. Then came propositions to organize a regiment of hoodlums to intimidate the opposition voters, and to establish shotgun quarantines about the polling places, and to bring repeaters to town in balloons, and to do many other things—rash, foolish and absurd. But all were weighed and found wanting.

It was Z. Antonius Caramba, the genial boss of the Third ward, that finally suggested the plan that was adopted. It was at one of the regular weekly councils of the bosses that he laid it bare.

"As you are doubtless aware," he said, "the city of Rome is honey-combed with long darksome caverns known as catacombs. They are mentioned in all of the guide books, and tourists visiting the city frequently descend into the more accessible of them and catch cold. Some of these catacombs are as secure and as safe as a bank vault. One of them begins in the suburbs, under the ruins of an old temple to Vulcan, and has ramifications extending all over the city. It is my plan that we inject repeaters from the counties into this entrance and conduct them under ground to the various polling places. From the cellar of each house in which there is a polling place we can sink a shaft downward to the nearest branch of this catacomb. Then, on election day, we can raise the needed number of repeaters to the surface, vote them, return them, and next day conduct them out to the entrance to the catacomb and dispatch them to their homes."

The assembled bosses greeted this speech with loud cheers, and next day work was begun. All of the various repeater brokers in the counties were notified by telegraph to secure at once as much stock as they could, and, two days later, 5000 men were marched to Rome, under cover of the night, and dropped into the catacombs. Two days later came 3500 more and next day 1500 more. The needed 10,000 was complete.

Two hundred precinct shepherds were sent down to look after the marshaling and manipulation of the repeaters, and 500 kegs of beer were lowered to keep them quiet. Then work was begun upon the shafts leading down from the various polling places and two days before election day all was in readiness. The precinct shepherds had their charges divided into squads, and each squad was encamped beneath the polling place to which it was assigned; the men were instructed in the manner of voting the ticket, and the more intelligent of them were taught how to vote twice and even thrice with one ballot; the judges and clerks of election were instructed in their part of the game; the police end was fixed, and arrangements were made for the return of the repeaters to their ancestral homes on the completion of their labors.

But in the plan—or rather in the execution of it—there was a flaw. Nine out of ten of the repeaters underground were peasants from the north. All their lives they had lived upon the sun-kissed and vine-embowered slopes of the Apennines and Lepontine Alps, and there they had learned to drink the juice of the grape. Beer was a new one to them. It made them bilious. They grew restive. They made loud and unseemly noises. They raised a rough-house.

Frightened and puzzled, the bosses sought to quiet them by lowering more beer to them. When they still yelled, a pipe line was laid from the largest brewery in Rome and spigots were placed at every 50 yards. But it was too late. Their unearthly shrieks had been heard. The opposition leaders were on.

An hour after they discovered the plot the opposition leaders had their plans of battle perfected. Valerianus Nero Agrippina, the big boss, personally carried it into effect.

Armed with a can of gasoline he proceeded to an alley behind the Temple to Ceres. In the middle of the alley was a ventilator manhole leading to the catacombs. Tearing off the iron top Aggripina dropped the can of gasoline into the hole. When it struck the bottom it exploded, and in a second dense clouds of black smoke were pouring out. Then he turned in a fire alarm, and in half a minute the engines were on the spot.

And then, while the Whig bosses wailed and tore their hair and gnashed their teeth, Whig firemen—their own appointees—turned streams of water into the manhole, and filled the catacombs and drove the repeaters out. Some of them were overcome by the smoke; some were drowned; some were trampled to death in the mad rush to safety, and some, the more fortunate, reached the catacomb entrance and were loaded into waiting patrol wagons and carried off to the jail.

The jig was up, and a month later Z. Antonius Caramba, the boss who had suggested the use of the catacombs, was found guilty of harboring repeaters and sentenced to 45 years in state's prison at hard labor.

The aggregate sentences of his 243 accomplices totaled 7651 years.

HOW THE REFORMERS DISPLAYED PERNICIOUS ACTIVITY AND THE ATTEMPT TO EVANGELIZE THE CELEBRATED JUNIUS O'CATO FAILED

In previous chapters of this desultory history of Roman politics, literature and life, it has been hinted more than once that the leading statesmen and politicians of Rome, during the period when the city was at the height of its splendor and power, were much bothered by the eternal and senseless attacks of the brood of he-she parasites known as reformers.

Usually, of course, the politicians, profiting by their better training and greater experience in public life, put the Carthaginian obeah upon the reformers with ease, and once or twice, as has been recorded in other places, large numbers of the latter were either driven from the city or slain. But at times, by cunning and good fortune, they managed to deal the politicians severe blows, and on several occasions—even when they were finally overcome—they gave the statesmen of the city very unpleasant quarter hours.

A case in point is remembered by those who are familiar with the history of Roman politics during the years of J. Bozzo Puritani's third term as mayor (A. D. 187–191). Puritani being a Whig, the Whigs, of course, were then in power in the city, and having held the reins for 22 years without a break, they were very naturally somewhat keen after the grafts. The division of the loot, in fact, had been reduced to a fixed system, and there was profit enough for all. This state of affairs being eminently satisfactory to all concerned—for what had the general public to do with it?—was, by the same token, a thorn in the side of the reformers and with their accustomed impertinent brashness they decided to butt in.

But before doing so they considered well the lay of the land, and the strength of their antagonists. There was to be an election in the fall. Members of the city council were to be chosen. The Whigs, having the advantage lying in the patronage, and the added advantage of a fat bar'l, might reasonably be expected to swamp the opposition by a majority of 50,000 votes in a total ballot of 64,000. They had the coin, they had the men, they had possession of the battlefield, and they had the leader—the famous Junius O'Cato. It would be a cinch for them.

Considering well all of these things, the reformers meditated long and strenuously. It would be useless to cast their lot with the opposition. In the first place, it would do no good, and in the second place, the opposition was honeycombed with corruption. Therefore, if would be necessary to wage an independent war upon the Whig machine. Referring to the works of Julius Cæsar, they found that he held that the easiest way to defeat an army was to slay the leader. On the spot O'Cato was condemned. But it would not do to kill him. That would be murder, and there would be a rope to follow. And neither would it do to assault him, or batter him, or dope him, or kidnap him. Force was impossible. They must rely upon moral suasion.

So they considered yet awhile, and then an idea dawned upon them, and they chuckled merrily and waited until three days before election day. Then, knowing that the bar'l was to be tapped next day, they hired 10 able bodied evangelists and sent them to O'Cato's home.

"The evangelists," they said, "will convert him. He will repent and resolve to lead a better life. In pursuance of this resolu-

348

tion he will refuse to permit the bar'l to be tapped, and without the bar'l the Whigs will hit the ceiling. Virtue and reform will be triumphant."

So on the night of the third day the evangelists formed in line and marched to O'Cato's palatial residence, in the Rue de Colosseum, and on ringing the bell were admitted. Then appeared O'Cato, and straightway the evangelists fell upon him and began work.

For 10 hours they labored, taking turns, and then they were relieved by a second shift, and at daybreak the members of the latter were reinforced by five picked workers from the Salvation Army. Early in the morning the afternoon papers got onto the scheme, and that afternoon they were heavy with the story. At noon the first shift of evangelists relieved the second one, and 10 singers from a leading church choir were told off to aid them. Late in the afternoon the general public began to take an interest in the thing, and by nightfall the plaza before O'Cato's house was filled with a surging, struggling mob.

To appease the demands of the latter, beginning at 6 o'clock, bulletins were posted, signed by Rev. Lycurgus Cassius, the eminent divine, and Maj. J. C. Asiaticus, of the Salvation Army, stating the effect of the evangelization.

At 8 P. M. the evangelists were relieved, and a brigade of lay workers filed in. Half and hour later two female missionaries just arrived from Ethiopia were added to the force, and a second company of salvationists, with drums and tambourines, appeared. When he saw them O'Cato grew a deathly white and seemed about to surrender. But several of his friends who were present encouraged him to be brave, and he held out manfully. At 2 A. M. a bulletin was posted, stating that O'Cato had offered the tambourinists 10,000 denarii to desist from tambourining.

At 8 o'clock next morning there arrived the celebrated Pluvius W. Nero, the foremost Græco-Roman and catch-as-catch-can evangelist of the time. The room being cleared, he attacked O'Cato singlehanded and alone, and in half an hour the latter showed perceptible signs of despair. At 1 o'clock, when Pluvius left him, he was weeping.

At noon nine slum workers from the river front appeared. At 2 P. M. they were relieved by 10 star members of the Rome Young People's Mission Band. At 2.15 the latter, easily knocked out, retired in favor of a committee from the Busy Bees. At 2.30 the latter fled and were succeeded by Company A of the Uniformed and Caparisoned Rank of the United and Benevolent Enemies of the Flowing Bowl. At 2.36 the Enemies were succeeded by Col. Brutus Bacilli, of the Salvation Army, who gave way at 2.41 to Brig. Gen. Gracchi Misisipi, who gave way at 2.53 to Maj. Gen. Virgil Nero, who gave way at 3.03 to Lieut. Gen. J. Cæsar Vermicelli, who gave way at 3.09 to Field Marshal Julius Constantine Aphophophiphrus.

At 3.30 despairing of success, the committee in charge determined upon a massed attack with horse, foot and dragons, the artillery first to shell the position and later to act as a cover for the infantry. In accordance with this plan, O'Cato was subjected to a frontal attack by two companies of salvationists, a select corps of graduate evangelists and 24 selected missionaries, experienced in field work. At the same time nine slum workers were told off to secure a position enfilading his rear.

The attack began with a heavy cannonading all along the line. Three separate shots lodged in O'Cato's bump of sinfulness; and then the infantry was rushed up, and for 15 hours the fight continued without a moment's cessation. Like a ship's crew the attacking party was divided into watches, with Field Marshal Aphophophiphrus, of the salvationists, as captain. Each watch was four hours and during their off time the workers rested.

At the end of the 15 hours the reformers began to feel alarmed.

Election day was dawning. O'Cato was yet unconverted. What should be done?

The hours passed. It was 8 A. M. The Whig workers were out in the highways and byways. The reform runners brought in reports that they were using money. O'Cato was unconcerned. He seemed to be gaining strength. He smiled.

The reform leaders on the scene of the fight grew pale. Why had he smiled? As the clock struck 12, at noon, he told them.

"Now," he said to the evangelists, "you can run along home. It has been rather tiresome, I admit, but still you have amused me. I thank you."

Bowing them out, he stopped as if he had forgotten something.

"By the way," he said, "it may interest you to know that your labor has been in vain. I knew you were coming. One of my trusty seneschals tipped me off. So I transferred the bar'l to my assistant, Mr. J. Leviticus Plato. He has divided it among the boys. By now it has been converted into beer and consumed. If there are any sporting men among you, I might venture to say that I have 1000 denarii to risk on the chance that the Whig majority will be 51,000. Are there any takers? No? Very well, then. Good day to you. Thanking you one and all, I remain, yours truly, Junius O'Cato."

And the evangelists and reformers faded into the distance.

HOW CLAUDIUS NERO IPPOLITUS ROSE TO EMINENCE AND LATER LOST HIS JOB

Lobbying, as a profession, probably reached its high water mark during the third century, A. D., when money was plentiful in the city of Rome and the Roman politicians and statesmen were willing—nay, eager—to have it adhere to their mucilaginous palms.

J. Demetrius Bacilli, the celebrated bon vivant of the time of

Aurelius Maximus—A. D., 134–192—is credited by most of the historians, including Gibbon and Macaulay, with being the originator and inventor of the art, but in the truth it attained its proudest position among the genteel occupations during the lifetime of Claudius Nero Ippolitus, who was by long odds the most distinguished of its votaries. Ippolitus, during the years between 245 and 261, was preëminent, and there was only one lobbyist in all Rome who was ever placed in the same class with him.

This fortunate one was Cyanide Africanus, son of the celebrated bunco steerer, Bichloride Africanus, and brother of the equally famous and genial saloonist, J. Iodine Africanus. To Cyanide fate awarded the honor of finally putting the curse on Ippolitus.

When the Legislature assembled, in the fall of the year A. D. 261, the two found themselves arrayed against each other in what promised to be the most bitter legislative fight in the history of Rome. Ippolitus was the agent and attorney of the Rome, Carthage and Athens Navigation Company, commonly known as the Galley Trust, which sought a franchise for the exclusive right to operate galleys upon the Tiber. Cyanide, in direct opposition, represented the Sardinian Barge and Galley Company, a powerful and independent concern, which resisted the trust's encroachments. As may be expected, the members of the Legislature hailed the fight as a windfall, for both antagonists were rich, and the bell seemed likely to ring frequently and loudly.

In truth, for a while, it was even thus, and some of the more energetic and crafty of the legislators succeeded in touching the treasurers of the two organizations for sums ranging from 1000 denarii to as much as 10,000. But after a time it became evident that the legislative chasm was so deep that neither could hope to fill it with money, and the two, under a flag of truce, held a conference, and decided to dispense with bribery. An agreement was signed whereby each contracted to forfeit to the other 10 times the amount of any sums it might be detected in offering to members of the Senate and House, and it was mutually agreed that only the more refined methods of molding legislative opinion should be employed during the remainder of the contest.

This, beside exciting the ire of every member of the Legislature, doubled the difficulty of the task set before Ippolitus and Cyanide, for while open bribery is a job which even a novice may undertake with fair hopes of success, the finer points of lobbying demand a degree of skill and natural talent possessed only by the masters of the art.

Ippolitus, during the week succeeding the signing of the protocol, spent his time endeavoring to hit upon a scheme which should insure victory without necessitating a violation of the agreement. Shut up in his palatial apartments at the Jupiter Hotel, he thought and thought and thought. Ever and anon he rang the bell and ordered a Mamie Taylor, and as its glittering drops trickled down his throat in a pellucid stream, his brain spun ideas like a loom. But one after the other seemed lacking in practicability, and finally he determined that he must put originality aside and fall back upon some old and time-worn plan that had been tried and found adequate in practice.

Then he thought again, and finally there ran through his mind a catalogue of the average Roman's weak points.

"First of all," he said to himself, "the typical legislator is a grafter. He craves coin. But the agreement forbids. In the second place, he is fond of fast horses. He likes to own them. But they are too expensive as presents. In the third place he is a flashy dresser. He adores diamonds. But diamonds cost even more than horses. In the fourth place he has a sneaking admiration for the little brown jug. He loves—but hold! Why not? I will give a dinner. Every self-respecting Roman is an epicure. Gormandizing is the national vice. I will give a dinner with champagne *ad lib.,* with turtle soup and canvasback ducks, and clam chowder and nine kinds of wine. I have it!"

And then Ippolitus fell to meditating upon the details of the feast. There were 250 members of the Legislature. Of these he owned 69 absolutely. The opposition owned 62 more. The latter, he knew, he couldn't hope to buy. This left 119 in the open market. He would invite the 119. A hundred and twenty-five plates—allowing for himself and a few extras—at 100 denarii a plate would be 12,500 denarii. He would ask for 25,000. This would leave him a personal profit of 100 per cent.

Ippolitus' clients—the trust magnates—gladly allowed him the sum he demanded, and he at once issued invitations to the 119 and set about making preparations for the feast. In the hands of the boss chef of the Jupiter Hotel he placed 12,500 glinting denarii.

"Cut loose," he said, "and do yourself proud."

With tears of professional joy the chef cut loose, and for 10 days he labored day and night. And then the night of the banquet came and——

But why describe it in detail? It was the most elaborate feast in the history of Rome. Nero's feasts were shoved back in the ten-twent-thirt class. Epicurus' philosophy was put on the bum. Belshazzar's choicest efforts were made to resemble a trio of counterfeit 10 denarii notes.

At 11 P.M. the 119 were mellow. At midnight they were orey eyed. Ippolitus arose to make a speech, and with their goblets in their hands and geniality and good fellowship and loving kindness in their hearts, the 119 hearkened unto him. He was never more eloquent and he never had a more sympathetic audience. In a moment they were cheering him; in another moment they were giving loud hurrahs for his clients, the trust magnates, in another moment they were weeping softly at the iniquity of the trust's rival.

Suddenly someone at the far end of the table set up the cry: "To the council chamber!"

It was taken up, and soon the 119 were staggering, galloping and rolling down the street to the Forum.

"We will pass the bill!" they shouted. "Vive le trust! A bas le Sardinian Barge and Galley Company! Hoch Ippolitus! Conspuez Africanus!"

They rushed to the Forum and up the broad marble steps and through the big front door and so into the council chamber. Ippolitus smiled broadly.

But the 69 legislators who were owned by the trust and the 62 who were owned by the opposition were before them. The latter were sore because they had not been invited to the banquet and given an opportunity to sell out. The former were sore because they had not been invited to the banquet and given an opportunity to sample the champagne. They had combined!

As Ippolitus, at the head of the trusty 119, rushed into the chamber the sore ones were taking a final vote upon the bill giving the trust the monopoly it desired. The roll call was nearly ended. There had been 128 "nays."

The clerk did not stop.

"Mr. Ysippi," he called.

"Nay!" shouted the genial representative of Caligulas county. He was a trust minion—or had been.

"Mr. Zimpano," called the clerk.

"Nay!" bellowed Zimpano.

"Mr. Zuzziguzzigus," called the clerk.

"Nay," shrieked Zuzziguzzigus.

"The clerk will please count the vote," said the president pro tem.

There was a pause. Ippolitus fell in a swoon.

"A hundred and thirty-one 'nays,'" said the clerk, "and no 'ayes.'"

"This being a constitutional majority," said the president pro tem, "the bill is defeated."

Ippolitus, regaining consciousness, stabbed himself with his pocket knife. The 119 faded into the night. Cyanide Africanus laughed.

HOW THE MERIT SYSTEM WORKED BACKWARD AND FORWARD AND THE MARCH TO THE SCAFFOLD WAS BEGUN

When the merit system was introduced into the Rome police department, in the year A. D. 157, all of the prophets predicted that it would lead to the downfall of the politicians who had made a living by selling places on the force, for since the earliest times it had been an axiom that politics and civil service reform were utterly unmixable.

This forecast, unfortunately, was partly a true one, for it was not long before trouble arose. When the civil service examining board submitted the first list of eligibles, it was found that the 10 men at the top of the list were rank outsiders with no more political backing than a Phœnician galley slave. The 10 men at the bottom, contrariwise, were stalwart precinct workers who had labored long and faithfully in the service of the machine, and who, not without reason, might expect the party to do something for them.

But the police commissioners, in view of the law requiring all appointments to be made "from the top of the list"—these were the very words of the statute—were compelled to name the 10 unknowns. A score or more of times they found it necessary to repeat this unpleasant act, and by and by the politicians, becoming more and more disgruntled, determined to plunge into their sea of troubles, and, by opposing, end them.

So they took up a collection of 500 denarii and employed R. Ippus Ophphro, a noted magician, to devise a scheme for circumventing the law. After taking their money and biting each coin, to make certain that it was genuine, Ophphro retired to his cave in the outskirts of the city and lay doggo for nine days and nine nights. Then he resurrected himself and announced the result of his meditation.

"The law," he says, "provides that the appointments must be made from 'the top of the list.' This is mandatory. If you violate it there will be striped togas and the lockstep to follow. So far, so good.

"But the law says nothing regarding the manner in which the list is to be pasted on the wall. I propose, therefore, that the eligibles be entered in the usual order, and then, that the list be turned upside down."

The scheme was so cunning and so simple that the politicians, after kicking themselves for not having thought of it themselves, thanked Ophphro profusely and proceeded to put it into practice.

Next day 10 of the previous appointees were fired "for cause" and 10 earnest, hard working precinct shepherds were given places on the force. During the week following 54 other unknowns were given the car-spring start and 54 workers of known fidelity were measured for their uniforms and clubs. The scheme worked like a charm. For two months all went well, and the ancient Roman equivalent of the goose hung high.

But then there appeared upon the scene a brace of prying, prowling ghouls of the breed known as reformers. They were the same who had brought about the enactment of the merit law, and when they learned how it was being systematically put to the bad they were furious. Two of the Roman newspapers, with the usual evil yellowness of the daily press, rushed to the aid of the rascals, and soon there was a wild and tumultuous cry for an investigation.

For several days the storm raged, increasing in violence each

357

day, and finally the powers were driven to the necessity of appointing a committee of investigation. This committee was made up of aldermen and was constituted as follows, to wit:

Ald. Horatius Ossius Cruso, boss of the Seventeenth ward and leading saloon-keeper of the locality known as "the Sty."

Ald. Octavius Nero, boss of the Ninth ward and custodian of the garment workers' vote.

Ald. J. Cæsar Thyrzuruzigus, acting boss of the Twelfth ward and leader of the Gaelo-Roman Whigs.

It was an excellent committee—from the standpoint of the politicians—and when it settled down to work their hopes ran high. Its report, they thought, was foreordained. There could be no mistake.

But then there arose another clamor from the so-called reformers and the prejudiced press for a report counseling the dismissal and imprisonment of the police commissioners. This clamor broke like a fierce storm, and to counteract it the politicians raised a clamor for a report of the kind that they confidently expected. As a result the people of Rome became divided into two great factions—the one favorable to the commissioners and the other unfavorable. The investigating committee, like grist in a mill, was ground between the two forces.

For a while the committeemen remained under cover and attempted to temporize. But it was soon seen that this would not avail, and before long the examination of witnesses was begun. Half of the witnesses—those selected by the reformers—gave evidence damaging to the commissioners. The other half—chosen and trained by the politicians—gave evidence in rebuttal. If they reached a verdict favorable to the police commissioners they knew the reformers and newspapers would drive them out of town. If, on the other hand, they reached a verdict favorable to the reformers, the politicians and bosses would give them one way tickets on the Salt Creek stern-wheel steamer to the murky swamp of Political Oblivion. Therefore, it came about that they were on the hooks, and all day and all night they sought means of postponing the crash long enough to give them time to seek a means of saving their skins.

But after the days had become weeks and the weeks months it became apparent that both sides would wait no longer. In great headlines and heavy black 50-point type and in strident tones and loud yells the press and the reformers demanded a report. Similarly, albeit quietly, the bosses gave the word that a report must be forthcoming.

"The police commissioners are corrupt!" bellowed the reformers *et al.* "Drive them out!"

"The public be boiled in oil!" said the bosses. "The police commissioners are blameless! Exonerate them!"

So the committeemen groaned between the millstones and their woes were heavy upon them. Apparently, it was all up. They were doomed—no matter what the character of their findings.

It was Thyrzuruzigus that suggested the means of his and his colleagues' salvation.

"Let us make a report," he said, "announcing that we have been unable to come to a decision. Let us disagree!"

"Eureka!" exclaimed Nero.

"Eureka!" exclaimed Cruso.

And so they announced that the evidence was so evenly divided that they were unable to sift the fact from the fiction, and with calm smiles they waited for their respective assailants to subside. But herein they miscalculated, for instead of merely antagonizing one faction, they thus antagonized both, and during the night following the day upon which their report was published a mob, composed partly of politicians and partly of reformers, visited them at their homes, and dragging them forth in their pajamas, hanged them to telegraph poles in full view of their weeping families.

HOW J. SOCRATES LITHIUM ELEVATED THE STAGE AND LATER WAS ELEVATED HIMSELF

J. Socrates Lithium first came into view as a king of the roped arena in the year 137 A. D., when he won the middleweight championship of Carthage from the famous Gazazzus Illii, who will be remembered by all students of the manly art as the originator of the celebrated gizzard blow. Socrates, after vanquishing Gazazzus, issued a defi to the massed Carthaginian pugilists of all classes, and two months later, by defeating, with great slaughter, the justly noted Ifius Cato Gazabo, the heavyweight champeen, he forced himself into the heavyweight class and looked about him for new worlds to conquer.

Just at this time the well known pugilistic impresario, Col. Alchimeded Cohnli, struck by his promising talents, offered to manage him, and Socrates, well aware of Alchi's cunning and influence, eagerly accepted. Thereupon Alchi took him to Rome and posted a forfeit of 10,000 denarii with the sporting editor of the Rome *Argus* to guarantee Socrates' presence in the ring, three paces in front of any knockout distributor who cared to meet him.

Five minor lights at once challenged him, and on five successive days he fought them at the Colosseum. The first was Gashouse Julius, the Athenian champion. Eighteen thousand sports, at 25 denarii each, witnessed the battle. In the ninth round Socrates went down, and the referee counted seven on him. But before the fatal 10 was uttered he was up again and at his antagonist, and in the 16th round a straight blow on the angle of the peritonium settled Julius' business.

Next day Socrates met the famous Alexandrian Coffee Cooler. Nine seconds after the gong sounded the Cooler was being hurried to the Rome City Hospital in a high speed ambulance.

Next day Socrates met Cicero Oi, who was regarded as the

hardest hitter in the then known world. Before he could deliver a single blow Socrates had put him to the bad with a gentle tap on the epicycloid curve of the nose, and his seconds threw up the sponge.

The day following Socrates defeated Young Brutus in seven rounds, and on the next day fought the last fight of the series with the renowned Prof. Cassius Casabianeau. At the end of the 56th round both contestants seemed as fresh as daisies, and the spectators settled down for an all night battle. But suddenly, early in the 57th round, Socrates handed out a hot one athwart the medulla oblongata and Cassius fell backward over the ropes. He was unconscious for three days, and when he finally awoke he anxiously inquired of his physicians if the train which ran over him had killed anyone else.

Then Socrates set out on a hunt for a go with the champion of the then known world, Leonidas Graccus. Leon, very naturally, was not very desirous of meeting him, and for seven years the two exchanged heated repartee, and issued proclamations denominating each other fakers and bluffs. Finally, however, Socrates posted a forfeit of 50,000 denarii and the sporting papers of the day, taking this as evidence that he was in earnest, began to roast Leonidas for refusing to meet him. In the end, therefore, Leonidas was forced into a fight, and Socrates in the 257th round, before an audience of 345,000 sports, struck him full in the neck, broke five of his ribs, knocked out nine of his teeth, fractured his collar bone and his left ankle, dislocated his skull, and put him out. Then Socrates was awarded the diamond studded belt of the *Revue de Police,* and the sports of the day hailed him as the champeen of the then known world.

After a triumphal tour of the country, during which he received the homage of the provincial connoisseurs, he returned to Rome, and in January, A. D. 145, opened a palatial beer-shop in the Via Pluvia. The place at once became the Mecca of the sporting élite, and nightly Socrates stood behind the bar and graciously shook hands with his battalions of patrons. Ten expert bartenders were kept busy mixing the famous Soc. cocktails, and Soc. brandy smashes, and Soc. highballs, and in handing out the famous Soc. pale and dark beers, the Soc. mixed ales, and the Soc. long Havana filler, Cuban handmade cigars. Soc. was prospering like a bloated bondholder, and like all prosperous people it became a disease with him, and he came to harbor a desire to prosper even more.

Therefore, when the famous theatrical manager, Asinine Bozzo, proposed that he go on the stage, he jumped at the proposition with extreme delight. Bozzo pointed out to him that things dramatic were at a low ebb in Rome, that the leading actors of the day were hams, and the leading vaudevillians cobblestone pavers, and that the stage, if it was to be saved at all, needed immediate and energetic elevating.

"There is one man," said Bozzo, "peculiarly fitted to do the elevating. There is one man designed by the gods for the job. There is one man possessing the beauty and the intelligence and the art. And you're him."

Socrates was much pleased by this flattering tribute and at once signed a contract to appear upon the boards as the hero of a play. Next day he and Bozzo talked over the matter and come to the conclusion that the play had best be a realistic melodrama, affording Socrates a chance to perform heroic deeds. In the last act, they decided, he must fight the villain and overthrow him, and at the fall of the curtain he must clasp the heroine to his bosom.

Having fixed these details, Bozzo summoned Bichloride Cato, his staff dramatist, and two days later, by laboring day and night, Cato had the play finished. A week later it was in rehearsal and three days after that it was produced for the first time at the Rome Opera House.

It was a hit from the start and the critics of the day were

enthusiastic regarding Socrates' realistic acting. After a three months' run, during which the opera house was crowded at every performance and thousands of would-be patrons were turned away, the company took the road and began touring the Roman provinces.

And then began trouble. Socrates, it will be remembered, was required to fight and overthrow the villain in the last act. The first night of the engagement at Pompeii, he was feeling unusually vigorous. As a consequence, he struck the villain so hard that the actor who was playing the part—Bacchus Arithmaticus was his name—was killed. Next night another villain was engaged. He lasted three weeks. Then Socrates employed a heavy, brutish actor named Virgil O'Bingii. Bingii was killed by a chance blow on the night of his first appearance.

During the balance of the tour 17 villains were killed, and it became almost impossible to secure actors to take the part. Finally, on the night the company set sail from Naples to fill its dates at the various oases in the Sahara Desert, Socrates engaged three large and vigorous stevedores, who knew nothing of acting but were able to catch cannon balls with their naked hands. It was an up-hill job teaching them their parts, and they cut but sorry figures on the stage, but by the time the African coast was reached one of them was letter perfect and he went on the first night at Tripoli. Next morning his remains were interred in the Protestant Episcopal Cemetery. That night stevedore No. 2 appeared in the cast, and Socrates was delighted to find him strong and solid. For three weeks he acted the part without mishap and Soc. began to grow careless. As a result Stevedore No. 3 found his services required and the staff undertaker of the company was busy again. No. 3 lasted just seven days. It was at an oasis called El Behib that he met his fate. At the end of the last act Socrates closed in upon him and the nightly fight began. In striking what was to be the final blow, Socrates slipped, and the full force of his mammoth muscle reached the villain's jaw. The latter, in consequence, was thrown backward with such force that he sailed clear through the side wall of the town hall and the coroner had a hard time next morning finding him.

Then Socrates was up against it for fair. Rome was 3500 miles away, and he was booked ahead for three months. But he had no villain, and the show without a villain would be like a stein of beer without foam. What was he to do? At first he thought of playing both parts himself. But this would be manifestly absurd, because he couldn't well fight himself, and if he did he might kill himself. Then he bethought him of employing local pugilists at each town. But his fame had preceded him, and no candidates for the job would be likely to appear.

Finally, while meditating the matter, he thought of a plan which might be used as a last resort. He would assign the property man of the show to play the part and permit him to pad himself with boiler iron and car springs. The property man, upon being approached, refused absolutely to consider the proposition, but later, when he was threatened with discharge and in consequence confronted with the possibility of being compelled to walk all the way back to Rome across the desert and the Mediterranean Sea, he thought better of it, and at last agreed to accept the rôle, if he were permitted to design his own padding.

This concession Socrates readily granted, and the property man worked all the afternoon upon his armor. The base of it was a German comedian's costume designed to accommodate a generous corporation or overhang. In this space the property man securely fastened a mattress, two pillows, three heavy planks of oak and a sheet of galvanized roofing. Then from a local newspaper he borrowed the plate from which was printed the first page of that morning's edition, and, after fastening it in place, filled in the intervening space with the heavy iron balls used to produce thunder behind the scenes.

Thus accoutered and caparisoned, he set out to play the part, and though his appearance was grotesque and he could scarcely walk unassisted, he made a hit in the first act and a bigger hit in the second act, and when the curtain rose upon the last act all seemed well.

At the climax, when it was Socrates' business to fight the villain, the property man sailed in unafraid, for he knew that nothing short of a ball from a 10-inch cannon could penetrate his armor. Socrates, with the same knowledge in mind, sailed in also, and at the grand finale he let loose.

The resultant blow was heard for miles, and the property man, though uninjured, dropped as if he were shot. In addition, the force of it was so great that the canvas inclosing the iron and steel burst like a squashed egg, and printing plate, galvanized iron and iron balls went bounding out into the auditorium with the force of rifle shots. One of the balls struck the mayor of the town— who was seated in a box—in the face and killed him instantly. The sheet of galvanized iron decapitated nine people, and the printing plate printed the first page of the local paper upon the features of its dramatic critic.

As a result there was a lynching bee, and the angry populace hanged Socrates to a telegraph pole in front of the town hall.

HOW J. CATULLUS BRAGGADOCIA WENT THE LIMIT AND, BY PUTTING HIS STAKE ON THE RED, WON OUT

Love, in the opinion of Cato J. Bozzo, was a thing sacred and sublime. In the opinion of J. Catullus Braggadocia it was a matter of dollars and cents. Cato was young and sentimental and an earnest believer in the pure, the good and the beautiful. Braggadocia held that the purest thing on earth was 10-year old rye whisky; that the best thing was a good graft, and that the most

beautiful was a 1000 denarii greenback. Cato represented Faith;
Braggadocia was the mouthpiece of Wisdom.

Cato was a son of the celebrated statesman and politician,
Claudius Ippius Bozzo, whose management of the gubernatorial
campaign of A. D. 307 anchored Rome in the Whig column and
secured for him personally a niche in the Hall of Fame and a vast
bar'l of minted coin. Braggadocia was the son of the eminent
galley owner, Jupiter Pluvius Braggadocia, Jr., who was hanged
in the year 301 A. D. for sinking a galley load of Sicilian slaves off
the Greek coast, in order to secure the insurance. As the humor-
ists of the time were wont to remark, he got it in the neck, but
history also records that he got it—or, at least, his heirs did—in
cold, glinting denarii—347,000 of them, and Catullus, his son, on
reaching the age of 21 came into a fortune estimated at 5,000,000
denarii.

Braggadocia the younger had been educated at great expense
at the University of Athens, and was a young man of distinct
culture and refinement. At 18 he was already expert in distinguishing between genuine Rhine wine and the Ligurian article,
and when he reached his majority he was looked upon as the
greatest living authority upon games of chance.

In the year 311 A. D. he invented a system which bust the keno
bank operated by Lysander Caramba, the eminent Roman politician, and a year later he secured the three card monte and shell
game privileges of the Forum, and in two months raked in profits
aggregating 2,000,000 denarii. So many senators went dead
broke in bucking his games, in fact, that the Senate was forced
to adjourn three weeks before the legal time, because nine-tenths
of the senators were busted and the boarding house keepers of
Rome refused to trust them any longer for their board and lodging.

In the year 315 A. D. Braggadocia attracted fresh attention by
managing the most notable fistic carnival in the history of Rome.
It being unlawful at that time to pull off fights within the bound-

aries of the empire, Braggadocia hired a seagoing scow, with a capacity of 5000 passengers, and the fight took place upon its deck while it was moored in the Mediterranean 10 miles off the coast. It was in this fight that young Pharaoh, the Alexandrian Coffee Cooler, wrested the championship of the then known world from Cyanide, the Carthagenian champion. Braggadocia made a profit of 457,000 denarii on the fight, and with the money bought a race horse and set up shop as a charioteer.

At the fall meeting at the Colosseum, in the year A. D. 321, he won the championship behind a double team of wild Arabian horses. The purse was 200,000 denarii, and as the winning of it made his total assets a round 4,000,000, he determined to settle down and lead a quiet, retired life. In accordance with this idea he built a magnificent palace a short distance from Rome and laid in a stock of wines and cigars estimated to be worth a cool million. In addition, he erected a private theater for his own amusement and employed a special musical comedy company to entertain him and his friends exclusively. The chorus was the largest and the most beautiful in Rome. Having a fondness for mixed ale, he erected a brewery on his estate and laid a pipe line from it to his boudoir.

Here he lived for two years, gradually acquiring the reputation of being the best fellow in the then known world. In the year 323 A. D. he was elected an honorary member of the Society for the Prevention of the Adulteration of Malt Liquors, and president emeritus of the Merry-Merry, an organization of stage favorites. A year later he attracted attention by driving a team of mules into the Temple of Venius during the ordination of a priest, and was accorded membership in the Hooligan Club.

Then he attracted fresh attention by making the members of the House of Representatives intoxicated at a big banquet, and afterward turning them astray half naked, with green rings painted all over them. For this exploit he was fined 1000 denarii and costs and elected president of the Society of Rough-Housers. Then he came once more into the public eye by taking a daily bath in a tub-full of crême de menthe, and soon after came his crowning honor, his election to the honorary presidency of the Moral Lepers' Association.

This, in fact, seemed to mark the turning point in his career. Thenceforth his fortunes began to wane. Early in the year 326 A. D. he lost 50,000 denarii on the races, and soon after he lost a million in a crooked faro game operated by the famous J. Cassius Oscuro. In a rage he seized Oscuro by the scruff of the neck and drowned him in a keg of brown stout. For this he was arrested and charged with disorderly conduct, and it cost him another million to bribe the J. P. before whom he was arraigned and secure his liberty. Then his château near Rome burned down two days after the insurance upon it had expired, and a barrel of chemicals in his brewery exploded and wrecked the building, killing the brewmaster. Then he lost 400,000 denarii on the stock market, and was compelled to pay 300,000 denarii damages to a policeman whom he knocked down, in a spirit of harmless levity, and rolled into a manhole leading to the catacombs. Next he was arrested and sentenced to three months in jail for attempting to swindle his aunt, and when he was set free again he found that his total assets were 9 denarii in cash, two suits of clothes, a gold watch (in hock) and a free pass to the annual ball of the Chorus Girls' Protective Association. He was dead broke, and like a wise guy, he realized it.

Without delay, therefore, he set about a hunt for a means of relief. After two days' cogitation he decided that three avenues were open to him. First of all, he could graft; secondly, he could marry a girl with money, and in the third place, he could go to work. By a process of elimination he came to the conclusion that the second alternative was the only reasonable one. So he at once decided to choose it, and next day he employed a prominent mercantile agency to prepare for him a list of eligible girls.

When he received it he scanned it closely. Upon it there were 34 names. Twenty-seven of them he discarded because their bearers were merely heiresses and not wealthy in their own right. He wanted the money, in cash. Three more he discarded because they were too old, and one more because she had been married before. This left two candidates, and he at once selected one of them—Miss Juliana Vulcan Brutus, daughter of the late Colorado Maduro Brutus, the oil king.

Miss Brutus was worth 9,000,000 denarii. In addition she was affianced to Cato J. Bozzo, the young man mentioned at the beginning of this chapter. Cato didn't want her money. He loved her. He believed that love was a thing sacred and sublime. Braggadocia didn't. He thought that it was a matter of dollars and cents, and as has been stated, he needed the money. So he immediately called upon Miss Brutus, proposed for her hand and was ejected by the butler.

"I am engaged to Mr. Bozzo," said the enraged girl. "We are to be married in a month. How dare you!"

Braggadocia smiled and departed, and that night he forwarded to Miss Brutus a bundle of newspaper clippings recounting the story of his life. One of the clippings set forth the reasons for his election to the presidency of the Moral Lepers' Association. Another, from the *Revue de Police,* was illustrated by a wood cut showing him driving the team of mules into the Temple of Venius. Another clipping told of his gambling exploits, and a fourth stated that he was the blackest sheep that ever pastured in the fields of Rome.

Then he engaged a friend, Zero Gazzamanii, to call upon Miss Brutus and confide to her that he (Braggadocia) was past redemption.

Next day Miss Brutus sent for him and pleaded with him to reform. He was much affected by her words and wept profusely, and on leaving kissed her hand.

A week later he had a report circulated to the effect that he had taken to drink and Miss Brutus sent for him again. He arrived, smelling strongly of Scotch whiskey—he had taken the precaution to empty a bottle into his overcoat pocket—and Miss Brutus begged him, for her sake, to reform.

He promised, but next day he had himself arrested on a charge of assaulting a policeman, and the day after he hired a man to mention him as co-respondent in a divorce case.

That afternoon—but what's the use?

Two weeks later, upon an appointed day, Cato J. Bozzo and his best man appeared at the Brutus residence. They found the household in a turmoil. The bride-to-be had disappeared. Two hours later, at the moment Cato fell in a dead faint, she and Braggadocia were quietly united by a justice of the peace.

Mencken and Harrison Hale Schaff

The following letter from Mr. Schaff, who is still in possession of the complete correspondence received from Mr. Mencken twenty-five years ago, is important enough to be made public.

Broadlands, Southborough, Mass.

My dear Dr. Goldberg:—

In the spring of 1905 the firm of John W. Luce and Company, with which I was then and am still associated, received a letter calling their attention to the possibility of an increased interest in the plays of George Bernard Shaw. Our correspondent pointed out that *Candida* had been produced the previous season with some success and that in the fall Arnold Daly would inaugurate another season of Shaw plays. Up to that time Shaw's representation in American publication lists was limited to 'Plays Pleasant and Unpleasant,' brought out by Herbert Stone of Chicago, without attracting special attention, and a slender little volume on our list, Shaw's brilliant essay, "On Going to Church." Probably, as our firm was one of the few which at that time thought Shaw good enough to print, the writer, who signed himself Henry L. Mencken, ventured to approach us with a proposal to write a volume of twenty to thirty thousand words of descriptive and critical comment on the then published plays of Mr. Shaw and offered to prepare and submit a portion of the manuscript if we approved the plan and would entrust the work to him.

Mencken at that time had some newspaper experience and had contributed to several magazines. He assured us that we had never heard of him, which was the fact, and gave us as a reference

Ellery Sedgwick, at present editor of the *Atlantic Monthly,* who was known to us. We did not, however, trouble Mr. Sedgwick for his opinion. I mention the reference in justice to both gentlemen as significant that at the outset of their careers, both of which became distinguished, each recognized in the other capacities of accomplishment and judgment now fully realized.

We wrote Mencken at once that his proposal interested us and if his manuscript came up to his expectations and our hopes we would undertake the publication.

Then followed the exchange of a number of long letters in which Mencken outlined more fully the plan of his book which was in the main to follow Shaw's own essay on the *Quintessence of Ibsenism,* and we, our suggestions on various points. In due course a portion of the manuscript was submitted and returned for revision. The introduction was entirely re-written. Both Mencken and ourselves were anxious that the book should be creditable and he spared no pains nor labor in his work. If a criticism, or a suggestion of omission or addition was made and met his approval, he at once went to work and incorporated it in his manuscript. On the other hand, if he questioned the advisability of doing so he stated his reasons fully, interestingly and with the warmth characteristic of his personality. Along in the fall of that year the book was published and at once attracted favorable and extended criticism from the literary editors and enjoyed a very fair and steady sale.

Mencken was gratified by the reception accorded his book and was anxious to follow it up with another volume. His suggestion was a book for playgoers in which he proposed to embody a digest and criticism of the current drama. In his capacity as dramatic critic he had accumulated a large amount of material for such a book and had to a certain extent tabulated it. We, however, were not very enthusiastic over the proposal and suggested that he now undertake the work of presenting to the English reading public the philosophy of Frederich Nietzsche. It happened that, in replying to Mencken's first letter proposing the Shaw book, I mentioned our plan to have such a volume prepared as it was apparent that the Nietzschean philosophy had exerted a strong influence on the English and Continental dramatists including Mr. Shaw on whom he was proposing to write. In replying at that time he said: 'Truly there must be something in mental telepathy for just as your note of the 14th reached me I was thinking of an article showing how Nietzsche has influenced, not only Sudermann, Hauptmann and Company, but also Kipling and Roosevelt, and how Nietzsche himself was merely the successor of Spencer.— But though I am tolerably familiar with Nietzsche and know Maeterlinck, Sudermann and Hauptmann pretty well and Ibsen and Pinero better, I scarcely feel that I could undertake the book you suggest. That is because I think the writing of it would involve a close study of a good many lesser men—philosophers and playwrights—of Germany and Scandinavia. Of these I know little and my German is so bad that I would encounter enormous difficulties in trying to learn more. Besides, the task is one for a man of ample leisure and thorough scholarship. I have little of the former and make no pretense to the latter. Nevertheless, it was my purpose to work in part along those lines in the proposed book on Shaw.'

With increased confidence in himself as the result of the success of his Shaw book Mencken re-considered his qualifications as a German scholar and proceeded to read the endless volumes of Nietzsche's æsthetic and philosophic works in the original and as in the case of the Shaw book outlined very fully his plan of the work. Taking this with me I went to Baltimore and discussed the matter with him at some length. As in the case of the Shaw book the various instalments of manuscript gave rise to no little criticism, suggestion and changes to which Mencken responded as before with arguments, acquiescence, rejection, infinite good temper and a willingness to contribute unending industry.

To those familiar with his style it will be no surprise when I say that among the bones of contention were some of the bizarre and extravagant expressions with which the manuscript was garnished. Stoutly he contended for the retention of many of them,—and some survived. Others in the spirit of compromise were modified or eliminated.

Clarity, force in expression and something of the element of surprise were what Mencken wanted, and very rightly. He was one of the early ones to discover that words are not invariably to be used as the exact dimensional factors in a problem of ideas but at times as symbols by which the creative literary artist suggests the vibrant, colorful, tonic panorama of his thoughts.

On publication, *The Philosophy of Friedrich Nietzsche* was an immediate success and gave the author a firm position in the field of letters and seriously threatened to establish him as a philosopher of truly academic pretentions. This latter prospect frightened him nearly to death. On the other hand our firm would have been glad to have had him plant himself on that firm ground and devote his efforts to the serious and somewhat formal exposition of the varying currents of modern philosophy and social psychology. But to be branded as academic was the last thing in the world that Mencken desired and with a naturally philosophic and scholarly turn of mind he went to every length to record an antagonism to all the formalities that make up the traditions of that cult.

Following the work on Nietzsche we undertook with Mencken a new translation of the Ibsen plays under his editorship, but only two volumes were issued, "The Doll's House" and "Little Eyolf." A variety of reasons contributed to the dropping of the undertaking, not the least of which was the increased demand on Mencken's time incident to his growing responsibilities on the *Smart Set*.

Following the Ibsen adventure, a preface or two, and that amazing little play, "The Artist," which stands out as one of the very finest of modern satires in any language, complete the list of Mencken's work published through our firm.

While it is true that the years in which he was in close touch with John W. Luce and Company were at the outset of his career and on the whole a formative period for him, it should not be forgotten that Mencken came to us with a by no means indifferent equipment. He had to his credit several years of active and varied newspaper work under editors who took pains to train their young men in the best traditions of journalism. He had published privately a book of poems and contributed a number of stories and articles to different magazines. To this must be added a wide reading in the fields of literature which reflected the highest type of intellectual development of that day, philosophy and drama. The novel then, as now, with rare exception, had nothing to offer; intellectual literary progress was and had been for some time in the hands of the European dramatists who translated into a popular form of presentation the work of the philosophers.

Mencken's judgment in general and particularly of what he read was surprisingly mature. He had acquired the foundation of a style and had definite ideas as to how he hoped to develop it. Already he was orienting himself to the viewpoint he has maintained in recent years and if his philosophic foundations were somewhat nebulous, gathered as they had been largely through the presentation of the dramatists, he was thoroughly impregnated with them. His work on the Shaw volume and the Nietzsche clarified and crystallized these ideas. The influence of those two books has been wide but to none so intense as to the author himself; the Shaw, in matters of personality and temperament, the Nietzsche, as to fundamental ideas. To them I wish we might have added a volume of æsthetics, but then of course was not the time for Mencken to even consider such a work. And to all this

should be joined the dynamic energy of ambition and industry cou-
pled with good temper and a boundless reserve of pure fun.

Philosophically Mencken is an aristocrat, jealously guarding
personal dignity by the suppression of any vulgar display of his
emotional reactions, which are many, highly sensitive and inclined
to be sentimental. Temperamentally, he is the mediæval Latin
student of John Addington Symonds' "Wine, Women and Song"
—a counter balance in nice adjustment, which limits the complete
realization of either his philosophic or temperamental tendencies.

If the creative artist is interesting in retrospect he is doubly so
in the potentialities of the future and though speculation as to the
trend of future events and accomplishment is always hazardous,
there is a world-old urge to venture into that doubtful field. In
the last twenty years Mencken has not changed fundamentally.
A wider experience and increased activities have simply given to
him a greater facility and smoothness in operation. It still amuses
him that a president of the United States should have been vapid
enough to qualify as a good Elk and his successor so crude as to
make a doubtful addition to the Rotarians. Methodists still serve
him as a symbol of social and cultural development, while the
inherent ignorance and vulgarity of the masses (which is an obvious and accepted fact that long since ceased to occasion the
slightest wonder or resentment on the part of those capable of
sensing conditions), still serve him as a phenomenon on which to
expatiate with a vocabulary of ascending invective that becomes
more and more difficult to make effective as its intensity increases,
and which if persisted in must become as toneless as a tuning fork
vibrating in those high ranges that the ear fails to record. On
the other hand Mencken's field of vision has broadened notably
and with it has come an interest in major social and political problems. His mind, if anything, is more alert, his reactions quicker,
his powers of penetration greater. There is even a suggestion of
a slowly dawning moderation, not by any means a re-valuation of

values, but a more constructive taste in the selection of material for valuation, and with it will come, I suspect, a realization that tolerance rather than prejudice is the aristocratic gesture of disdain; then we shall see a period of brilliant creative accomplishment that Mencken's fine capacity for sound scholarship so well qualifies him to achieve.

HARRISON HALE SCHAFF

Boston,
  August, 1925

Henry L. Mencken and Myself

It was sometime during the Spring or Summer of 1908, and my second year of editorial control of the Butterick Publications, that there came to me a doctor by the name of Leonard K. Hirshberg who explained that besides being a physician of some practice in Baltimore he was a graduate of Johns Hopkins and interested in interpreting to the lay public if possible the more recent advances in medical knowledge. There had been various recent developments, as there always are. Some phases of these he proposed to describe in articles of various lengths. And then it was that he announced that, being a medical man and better equipped technically in that line than as a writer, he had joined with a newspaper-man or editorial writer then connected with the Baltimore *Sun,* Henry L. Mencken. The name being entirely unfamiliar to me at the time, he proceeded to describe him as a young, refreshing and delightful fellow of a very vigorous and untechnical literary skill, who, in combination with himself, would most certainly be able to furnish me with articles of exceptional luminosity and vigor. Liking two or three of the subjects discussed, I suggested that between them they prepare one and submit it. In case it proved satisfactory, I would buy it and possibly some of the others.

In less than three weeks thereafter I received a discussion of some current medical development which seemed to me as refreshing and colorful a bit of semi-scientific exposition as I had read in years. While setting forth all the developments which had been indicated to me, it bristled with gay phraseology and a largely suppressed though still peeping mirth. I was so pleased that I immediately wrote Hirshberg that the material was satisfactory and that I would be willing to contract with him and his friend for one of the other subjects he had mentioned.

And then some weeks later in connection with that or some other matter, whether to discuss it more fully or merely to deliver it or to make the acquaintance of the man who was interested in this new literary combination, there appeared in my office a taut, ruddy, blue-eyed, snub-nosed youth of twenty eight or nine whose brisk gait and ingratiating smile proved to me at once enormously intriguing and amusing. I had, for some reason not connected with his basic mentality you may be sure, the sense of a small town roisterer or a college sophomore of the crudest and yet most disturbing charm and impishness, who, for some reason, had strayed into the field of letters. More than anything else he reminded me of a spoiled and petted and possibly over-financed brewer's or wholesale grocer's son who was out for a lark. With the sang-froid of a Cæsar or a Napoleon he made himself comfortable in a large and impressive chair which was designed primarily to reduce the over-confidence of the average beginner. And from that particular and unintended vantage point he beamed on me with the confidence of a smirking fox about to devour a chicken. So I was the editor of the Butterick Publications. He had been told about me. However, in spite of *Sister Carrie,* I doubt if he had ever heard of me before this. After studying him in that almost arch-episcopal setting which the chair provided, I began to laugh. "Well, well," I said, "if it isn't Anheuser's own brightest boy out to see the town." And with that unfailing readiness for any nonsensical flight that has always characterized him, he proceeded to insist that this was true. "Certainly he *was* Baltimore's richest brewer's son and the yellow shoes and bright tie he was wearing were characteristic of the jack-dandies and rowdy-dows of his native town. Why not. What else did I expect? His father brewed the best beer

in the world." All thought of the original purpose of the conference was at once dismissed and instead we proceeded to palaver
and yoo-hoo anent the more general phases and ridiculosities of
life, with the result that an understanding based on a mutual liking
was established, and from then on I counted him among those
whom I most prized—temperamentally as well as intellectually.
And to this day, despite various disagreements, that mood has
never varied.

Subsequent to this there were additional contacts based on this
instantaneous friendship. He visited me at my apartment in New
York and I in turn repaired to Baltimore. We multiplied noisy
and roistering parties. Sometime during 1908 or 9—or whenever
it was that the old Col. Mann's *Smart Set,* owing to various
scandals in connection with its management, was reorganized and
a new editor sought, a managing editor of mine came to me with
the news of this thing. He was a capable fellow but not as I
saw it suited to the particular work he was doing for me—nor to
the editorship of the *Smart Set* for that matter. Yet, because I
had been pondering how to replace him without injury to himself,
I now encouraged him in the thought with which he had come
to me—i. e.—that with my approbation and aid he would apply
for the editorship of the same. And why not he as well as another? If they did not like him, they could soon get rid of him,
could they not—said I. So I stirred him with the plausibility
of the idea and he immediately proceeded to apply for the place,
and, to my satisfaction, as well as astonishment, secured it.

But as was the custom of some others whom I had advised in
this fashion in times past, he soon returned to me with the request that I aid him in outlining a policy and a suitable staff or
list of contributors for his magazine. And, in discussing what
regular and permanent features might be introduced and who
would be most likely to lend lustre to the magazine by their work,
I suggested that as intriguing as anything would be a Book Depart-

ment with a really brilliant and illuminating reviewer. Instantly the one name that appealed to me as ideal for this work was that of Mencken. I insisted that he could not do better than get this man and that he should engage him at once. This he did. And this was the beginning of Mencken's connection with the *Smart Set*, which subsequently led to its control by himself and George Jean Nathan who was already doing dramatics for the magazine, if I am not mistaken, when my youthful aspirant and assistant moved in.

THEODORE DREISER

New York,
    August 24, 1925

THE FREE LANCE

PROPOSED design for a button to be worn by the salacious old deacons of the Anti-Saloon Leg:

EXTRACTS from the estimable *Sunpaper* of February 2, 1916:

Mayor Jacobus Hook yesterday made City Collector J. Harry Preston a present of a box of Gorgonzola cigars in appreciation of his unprecedented tax collections during January.

MEANWHILE, will some sapient moralist kindly step up and tell the Police Board just *how* it is going to put down the handbooks. The Soper-Niles-Ammidon board was full of faults, true enough, but certainly no one will allege that its members lacked moral ardor or that they were secretly in favor of racetrack gambling, and so disposed to protect it. And yet racetrack gambling went on under their very noses. The corridors outside their uplifting atelier were thronged with handbooks all day, and now one even hears charges that their very telephones were used by the fraternity.

THE fact is, of course, that gambling is one of the vices that are practically ineradicable. The law may proceed against certain forms of it, but the net effect of the crusade is merely the promotion of other forms. Baltimore has closed up the old-time, so-called first-class gambling houses of the sort kept by the Hon. Doc Slater, but certainly no man who knows the town would say that gambling itself has been stopped, or even

THE FREE LANCE

SECOND reading of the Kicking Leg in the moral columns of the *American Issue*, Maryland Edition:

TEN thousand dollars cash to Hon. Tom Hare, D. D., for a frank answer to the following question: If this levantine ikon is nothing but a harmless stocking advertisement; if it conceals no aim to delight the rabelaisian old deacons; then why the *caleçon*, the *pantalets*, the *unterhosen*, the *sottocalzoni*, the *calzoncillos*—in plain English, the frills to nor'east? Again and furthermore Ten thousand dollars cash to Dr Hare if he will throw an enlargement of this wood cut upon the screen the next time he lectures on the Booze habit before any reputable baraca class. Yet again: Ten thousand dollars cash to Dr Hare if he will present a bromide enlargement of it, four by six feet in size, to the Central Young Men's Christian Association

IF you missed a correspondence between Dr Howard A Kelly and former Magistrate James T O'Neill in the *Star* of Saturday last you missed some curious facts about the boons and usufructs of the uplift. This correspondence was provoked by a speech delivered by Dr Kelly in a Baptist church at Germantown, Pa telling of the labors of the vice crusaders in the Eastern police district, the Hon. Mr O'Neill's old bailiwick. Thus the press report

They butted in, according to Dr Kelly, and diagnosed the cancer in the city's heart Then, with Governor Goldsborough behind them he said they accomplished the reduction of the number of saloons and brothels, *had some policemen discharged and others transferred*, and took other measures, until today Captain House reports that the arrests are less than 80 per cent of what they were before this work of personal service was attempted

FACSIMILE REPRODUCTIONS OF PORTIONS OF THE FREE LANCE, MENCKEN'S COLUMN IN THE BALTIMORE *SUN*

Index

Abell, Walter W., 117, 122
Abhau, Anna Margaret, 56
Abhau, Carl Heinrich, 56
Abhau, Grandfather, 73, 74
Adams, J. H., 122
Addison, 90
Adler, Alfred, 159
Adler, Elmer, 203
Anderson, Sherwood, 195
Anderson, William H., 124
Archer, William, 241
Aristotle, 91, 231
Arnold, 148
Arvin, 275
Austen, Jane, 90

Bach, J. S. B., 48, 178, 179
Bakounin, 154
Bal, 37
Barclay, 6
Barnum, 210
Baroja, 217
Baudelaire, 272, 278, 279
Beethoven, 5, 11, 91, 150, 178, 179,
    182, 183, 263
Bellamy, 74
Belz, 52
Bentley, 38
Berger, 44
Berlichius, Burchard, 37
Berlichius, Magdalena Sybilla, 37
Berlioz, 183
Bernard, 36
Beyle, 38
Bismarck, K. W. F., 47
Bismarck, Karl Otto Edward Leo-
    pold, 32, 47, 234

Biggs, 266
Bizet, 182
Black, H. Crawford, 122
Black, Harry C., 122
Blanco-Fombona, R., 3
Bonaparte, 151, 163, 234
Bone, Scott C., 110, 111
Boyd, Ernest A., 11, 195
Boyer, N., 119, 120
Boyle, Robert, 37
Boynton, 71
Boynton, P. W., 263
Brahms, 91, 148, 179, 180, 185, 186,
    238
Brentano, 117
Brontë, Charlotte, 90
Brooks, Van Wyck, 104, 282
Brownell, 232
Buckle, 92
Bunyan, 154
Burnam, 38
Butler, 281
Byron, 90

Cabell, J. B., 3, 263
Calverton, 268, 270
Carleton, 74
Carlyle, 11, 38, 90, 148, 276, 283
Carter, R. I., 97, 108, 109, 116, 177
Cave, 38
Cellini, 3
Cézanne, 65
Chambers, 74
Chase, A. M., 93, 94
Chaucer, 90
Chekhov, 30, 31
Cheops, 22

INDEX

INDEX